The Poetry and Politics of Allen Ginsberg

By

Eliot Katz

Published by Beatdom Books

Published by Beatdom Books

Copyright © 2016 by Eliot Katz
Cover photograph © Steve Groer
(www.groerphoto.com)

All rights reserved. No part of this book may be reproduced in any form or by any electronic or mechanical means including information storage and retrieval systems, without permission in writing from the author. The only exception is by a reviewer, who may quote short excerpts in a review.

View the publisher's website:
www.books.beatdom.com

Printed in the United Kingdom

First Print Edition
ISBN 978-0-9934099-0-5

Permissions:

Excerpts from 53 poems from *Collected Poems 1947-1997* by ALLEN GINSBERG. Copyright © 2006 by the Allen Ginsberg Trust. Reprinted by permission of HarperCollins Publishers.

Excerpts from *Deliberate Prose: Selected Essays 1952-1995* by Allen Ginsberg. Copyright © 1999 by The Allen Ginsberg Trust. By permission of HarperCollins Publishers.

Excerpts from *Spontaneous Mind: Selected Interviews 1958-1996* by Allen Ginsberg. Copyright © 2000 by The Allen Ginsberg Trust. By permission of HarperCollins Publishers.

Various poems by Allen Ginsberg Copyright © 2007; The Estate of Allen Ginsberg, used by permission of The Wylie Agency (UK) Limited.

Acknowledgements

This book is a thoroughly revised and updated version of a dissertation that I wrote at Rutgers University in the late 1990s, and I am grateful to my partner, eco-poet and novelist Vivian Demuth, and to my longtime friend, one of America's most insightful political philosophers, Stephen Eric Bronner, for suggesting that I finally turn it into a book. During the initial writing of my dissertation, Stephen Bronner also offered crucial advice on questions of political and aesthetic theory. I am especially indebted for this book to Alicia Ostriker—an extraordinary poet and literary scholar—who served as my original dissertation adviser at Rutgers and did more than anyone else to help me think through many of the ideas that appear in this work. Thanks also to my other dissertation advisers from the Rutgers English Department, Harriet Davidson and Michael McKeon. And thanks to David Wills at Beatdom Books for taking this book on, for thoughtful editing suggestions, and for creating an exciting press to publish new works in the field of Beat Generation-related writings.

Thanks also to longtime poet-friends and poetry collaborators who are, like me, part of next generations of Beat-inspired literary circles and who have offered decades of inspiration and motivation for my writings—including Danny Shot, Andy Clausen, Jim Cohn, Dave Cope, Anne Waldman, Antler, Nancy Mercado, and the late Jeff Poniewaz; my friends Bob Rosenthal, Peter Hale, and Bill Morgan at the Allen Ginsberg estate; Michael Thompson, editor of the online journal of progressive political culture, *Logos*; the late poet-activists Adrienne Rich and Amiri Baraka for their longtime friendship and artistic inspiration; and Johanna Lawrenson and the late Abbie Hoffman for their friendship and activist teachings. Of course, most of all, I thank Allen Ginsberg, who was a generous teacher and a longtime friend. As a poet, my work has been influenced by a wide range of international and American political poets from Pablo Neruda, William Blake, and Vladimir Mayakovsky; to Muriel Rukeyser, Walt Whitman and Langston Hughes; but Allen Ginsberg is certainly the poet who has inspired my own literary work more than any other writer.

An earlier version of my chapter on "Howl" appeared in *The Poem that Changed America: "Howl" Fifty Years Later*, edited by Jason Shinder and published by Farrar, Straus and Giroux. Thanks to HarperCollins and the Allen Ginsberg Estate for permission to quote extensively from Ginsberg's work.

I would like to add one more unusual category of thanks. For the last seven years, I have been struggling with and trying my best to keep in check Lyme disease, which can be far more debilitating and far more difficult to diagnose and treat than most people realize, when it is not caught early because one does not see a tick or bulls-eye rash. It is a subject that I hope to write more about in a future book. Then, when the manuscript was about 90% complete and I was also thinking that I was 90% recovered back to my old healthier self, I started having neck pain, and, after getting a scary MRI, ended up needing a difficult cervical laminoplasty operation on my cervical spine to prevent the possibility of paralysis. For helping to keep my health well enough to write and complete this book in recent years, I would like to thank a range of health care practitioners: Dr. Jeffrey Morrison, Physician's Assistant Jerry Simons, Denise Antoine Greenidge, and the rest of the staff at the Morrison Center; Dr. David Langer (the neurosurgeon who literally saved my neck) and his staff, including Andrea and Catie; Dr. Benjamin Asher, Dr. Ingebord Dziedzic, Dr. John Vilkelis, Dr. Dominic Frio, Dr. Sudhir Gupta, Tracy

Hans, Dr. Robert Strell, Dr. Anthony Orlando, and Marcia Wholf. And, lastly, a very special thanks to Roger Sverdlik, an old table tennis friend from my teen years, who was once among the top five table tennis players in the U.S.—after we renewed our friendship and our table tennis that had lapsed almost four decades, when my neck went bad, Roger spent an extraordinary amount of time helping me and helping me navigate the medical system up to and after my surgery. This book certainly would not have been finished if not for the help of Roger and the health care practitioners mentioned in this paragraph.

Table of Contents

p. i	Preface
p. 1	Chapter 1. Introduction: Challenging the Boundaries of Poetry and Politics
p. 35	Chapter 2. "Howl": The Work Heard Round the World
p. 101	Chapter 3. Politics and Family History: Kaddish and other Poems
p. 134	Chapter 4. "Wichita Vortex Sutra" and the Anti-Vietnam War Years
p. 172	Chapter 5. "Plutonian Ode" and Continuing Lifelong Activism
p. 224	Chapter 6. "To Breathe Freely": A Progressive Political Poetics
p. 283	Afterword: "Elegy for Allen" (poem)
p. 288	Notes
p. 298	Works Cited
p. 313	Index
p. 328	Author Bio

Preface

In both his poetry and his life, Allen Ginsberg was one of the most politically engaged writers of his era. Influenced by such key literary predecessors as William Blake and Walt Whitman, and raised by a communist mother Naomi, and a Debsian democratic-socialist-poet father Louis, Allen Ginsberg learned how to turn his political ideas and observations into some of the most memorable and widely read poetry of the 20th century. In his personal life, he actively supported and participated in a wide range of organized political movements, beginning with the movement to end the Vietnam War and, in ensuing years, movements for such progressive causes as gay rights, civil rights, environmental protection, nuclear disarmament, and avoidance of the 1991 Gulf War. He was an active member of the PEN Freedom to Write Committee, opposing censorship East and West, and served on the advisory board of numerous progressive organizations, including the media watch group, Fairness & Accuracy in Reporting (FAIR), and a national student activist group that I worked with during the late 1980s and early 1990s, Student Action Union. From 1980 until his death in 1997, during the years that I knew Allen Ginsberg as a one-time student (at Naropa Institute in Boulder, Colorado) and a longtime friend, he was constantly writing or calling government offices to advocate for improved social policies and urging younger poets like myself to do the same. In addition, many of the next-generation poets whose work Ginsberg praised, mostly writers whose work was not well-known in larger or more mainstream literary circles, were progressive poets deeply concerned with social and political issues.

This book attempts to begin to fill what seems an

important gap in Ginsberg scholarship. Although many of Allen Ginsberg's best poems explore political themes in deeply interesting ways, there has not yet been a serious, book-length attempt to take a deep look at Ginsberg's politics or at his poetry as political poetry. In his otherwise excellent introduction to an early scholarly collection of essays on Ginsberg, editor Lewis Hyde pointed to a scarcity of critical attention to Ginsberg as a political poet, and offered this unfulfilling explanation: "We have as yet, no full account of Ginsberg as a political poet, these essays notwithstanding, and if our response to this portion of his work has been spotty it is probably because his politics takes its shape from his spiritual concerns, and it is in this last that we shall find its meaning."[1] Hyde's remarks echo those of Paul Carroll, who earlier had written: "Allen Ginsberg's real accomplishments as a poet do not come from his public image or his political and social poems. The great Ginsberg poems are private. ('Howl'—that labyrinth of personal sorrow—is a very private poem.)" (94)

Since the creation of the Beat Studies Association in late 2004, there has been some additional critical attention paid to the public aspirations of Ginsberg's work, as well as to more general questions about the political reverberations of Beat Generation literature. A wide range of scholars associated with the Beat Studies Association—including Ronna C. Johnson, Nancy M. Grace, Jennie Skerl, A. Robert Lee, Tony Trigilio, Maria Damon, Kurt Hemmer, and Clinton Starr—have shed much-needed light on such crucial and previously neglected issues as women writers of the Beat Generation, African-American Beat Generation poets who had in the past been excluded from too many studies of countercultural art, and some of the various ways in which the informal community groups that coalesced in Beat literary spaces in the mid- to late-1950s helped pave the way for the larger social movements of the 1960s.[2] And several short essays have focused on certain political aspects of a few of Ginsberg's poems.[3] But it is still the case that, until now, no in-depth attempt has been made to look at the ways in which Allen Ginsberg's writing

Preface

works as political poetry and at the ways in which his poetry and activism have influenced American politics and political culture in the ensuing decades.

To say that someone is a political poet does not, of course, mean that politics is the only thing the person writes about. In addition to social concerns, Ginsberg's work also contains powerfully expressed psychological, spiritual, autobiographical, familial, sexual, and literary themes, as well as poems of daily life and observations. Often, what is most striking about his poems is their lively exploration of the ways in which these varied concerns interrelate. But, at least from my own personal view, I think it is fair to say that what has resonated most in the minds and imaginations of readers across the planet for over half a century has been the keen sense that here is a poet devoting considerable literary skills and energies to help envision and create a more just, peaceful, and egalitarian world.

Prevailing mythology says that 1960s radicals became more conservative as they got older. Along with thousands of known and unknown organizers from that era who continued to display long-term progressive commitment, whether by public activism or private lives spent in professions like social work, public interest law, or education, Allen Ginsberg's life and work help put the lie to that myth. As he got older, Ginsberg got sharper, more committed to building a compassionate world, and better able in interviews to explain his ideas in clear, concise language that was usually difficult for open-minded, reasonable people to refute. Throughout his life, his progressive social commitment never wavered. From his outspokenness against Eisenhower-era political and sexual repression to his protests against the Vietnam War, from his willingness to sit on the railroad tracks in Rocky Flats, Colorado, to stop the shipment of plutonium to his opposition to the 1991 Gulf War, Allen Ginsberg consistently put his body and his poetry on the line.

Furthermore, Ginsberg refused to be conned into accepting dominant Cold War dualities. He was consistent in his criticisms of U.S. and other Western capitalist exploitation while also vocally opposing authoritarian Soviet-style alternatives. Throughout his life, Ginsberg kept neatly organized file cabinets filled with little-known political and literary information, and a comprehensive rolodex of writers, political organizers, and journalists working for both the mainstream and the alternative press. This rolodex was incredibly helpful in the pre-Internet days to those of us who needed difficult-to-find phone numbers or addresses in order to help organize or publicize upcoming meetings, events, and rallies. Along Shelleyan lines, I think it would be fair to say that Allen Ginsberg was a democratic conscience of Cold War America—often unacknowledged by the political pundit class, but probably better known during his lifetime than any other poet who had come before him.

Allen Ginsberg had a rare ability, through both his poetry and activism, to radicalize young people—to open up their radical eyes—and to help prop open a wide range of difficult-to-find doors to worlds of progressive politics and culture, enabling his work to achieve an enormous influence on six decades of American dissent. Ever since 9/11, we have moved back toward a time somewhat like the era Ginsberg described in "Wichita Vortex Sutra" when "almost all our language has been taxed by war." In an era filled with too much military conflict, regressive economic policies, and the backsliding of civil liberties, the legacy of Allen Ginsberg remains as important as ever.

Chapter 1:
Introduction:
Challenging the Boundaries of Poetry and Politics

Allen Ginsberg's impact on the wider culture was rare for a poet during his or her lifetime, and "Howl" was easily the most influential American poem of the second half of the 20th century. In American literature of the last hundred years, only T.S. Eliot's "The Wasteland" was comparable in its effect on the way that poetry would be written and read in future decades. But "Howl" did far more than "The Wasteland" to change the way that large numbers of Americans, especially young people, would think about their place in the world, the music they would create and admire, the clothes they would wear, and the new ways in which they would learn to view sexuality, religion, spirituality, and social policies during and after the Cold War.

In the realm of music, the most influential rock and roll band of the 1960s and the era's most important singer-songwriter were inspired by Ginsberg and the Beat Generation. The Beatles chose their name in part because John Lennon wanted to include "Beat" within the name of the band, and Ginsberg would later become personal friends with members of the group. An old friend of John Lennon's, Bill Harry, has described the way that he and Lennon and a small group of friends from the Liverpool College of Art used to sit at a local pub reading Ginsberg's poems to each other. According to Harry, their favorite was "Howl."[1] Bob Dylan has long credited Ginsberg as being one of his major literary influences, calling him "a lyrical genius" and "the single greatest influence on American poetical voice since Whitman."[2] In his *Chronicles: Volume One*, Dylan writes that "Howl," along with Jack Kerouac's *On the Road* and Gregory Corso's *Gasoline*, "were signaling a new type of human existence," (34) and that when he moved in his teens from the small town of Hibbing, Minnesota to the city of Minneapolis, he was "looking for what Allen Ginsberg had called the 'hydrogen jukebox world'." (235) It is difficult to imagine what American culture, in the sixties and in subsequent decades, would have looked like without the impact of Bob Dylan and The Beatles, and, by extension, it is therefore difficult to conceive what it would have looked like without Allen Ginsberg and the Beat Generation.

Ginsberg's poetry and activism also provided inspiration to some of the most important leaders of the 1960s counterculture and youth-led New Left. Activists like Students for a Democratic Society (SDS) cofounder Al Haber, SDS activist and Port Huron Statement author Tom Hayden, Redstockings cofounder Roz Baxandall, and Yippie cofounder Abbie Hoffman have all cited the influence of Beat literature in general, or Ginsberg's poetry in particular, on their politically formative years. In his autobiography, originally published as *Soon to Be a Major Motion Picture* and posthumously re-issued as *The Autobiography of Abbie Hoffman*, Hoffman described his 1967 move to New York's Lower East Side, where he would soon become one of the most well-known organizers of the local and national antiwar movement: "We had no way of knowing that we had just taken a $101-a-month front-row seat to the cultural revolution. The local countercultural institutions were all in a ten-block radius: Paul Krassner's *The Realist*, Ed Sanders and his Peace Eye Bookstore, resident poet Allen Ginsberg." (92) Later in the book, Hoffman wrote of Ginsberg's poem "Howl": "It was inspired by the Gods. Just as they had spoken to Isaiah and Jeremiah, they talked to Ginsberg and Ginsberg took his poetry into the streets. Jews don't have saints, they just

Introduction

have Ginsbergs every once in a while." (123) In *Best Minds*, Paul Krassner recalled Abbie Hoffman's words on a panel at Naropa Institute in 1982—a panel which I also recall, having been in the audience—with Hoffman describing how he had memorized "Howl" for two years and offering the following credit to the Beat Generation: "If we were the warriors of a social revolution, then the Beats were the prophets who predicted and guided that social revolution." (155)

Al Haber was the major founder of SDS, generally considered the most significant activist group of the 1960s New Left. In a key essay of the early sixties student movement, "From Protest to Radicalism: An Appraisal of the Student Movement 1960," Haber wrote: "The term 'beat'.... has come to characterize all those who have deviated from the traditional college patterns. They are variously professional students, bohemians, political types, and non-students who still seem to be around....This group in time of dissension and irresolution, acts, and in so doing, takes the first step toward radicalism; the participation crystallizes commitment."[3]

A fellow early organizer of SDS, Tom Hayden was the main author of the Port Huron Statement, the well-circulated manifesto announcing SDS's organizing principles and world-view. (I will look at this document in more detail in my next chapter in conjunction with "Howl.") It was in the Port Huron Statement that SDS announced its commitment to "participatory democracy," a compelling notion that would soon help motivate a new generation of young people to think in more radical terms about the possibilities of doing meaningful politics in America. In his book, *Rebel: A Personal History of the 1960s,* Hayden wrote about the impact of Kerouac's novels on his development, noting that Kerouac offered one of "several alternative cultural models beckoning to those of us who, in a few years, were to become activists."(16) About Allen Ginsberg, Hayden has written: "He led an exemplary public life, blending Old Testament prophecy with Buddhist centering, creating a monumental body of creative work while still finding time to teach the next generation (like my kid Vanessa, a writing student of his)."[4]

One of the early SDS organizers, Bob Ross, was known as a fan of the Beat poets. In a phone conversation, Ross told me that he had read Ginsberg in high school and Ginsberg's poems provided a "certain dissonant, dissident mindset" that carried forward and helped prepare him for being an activist. Ross also recalled that the Beat subculture at the University of Michigan in the late 1950s and early 1960s was the only racially integrated subculture on campus.[5] A similar sense of the way that Beat poetry provided activist inspiration is described by another early 1960s student organizer, Betty Denitch, in Maurice Isserman's *If I Had a Hammer*: "We knew the Beat poets....There was a sense that something was really wrong, something inhuman about the way of life that people were encouraged to live in our society."(60)

Given the impact that Ginsberg and other Beat Generation writers had on some of the era's key student organizers, it is not surprising that, in their book on the 1960s, *America Divided*, historians Maurice Isserman and Michael Kazin begin their chapter on "The Making of a Youth Culture" by describing the October 1955 evening when Allen Ginsberg first read "Howl" in San Francisco's Six Gallery. According to Isserman and Kazin, that evening "was a declaration of independence from the rigid, authoritarian order the Beats believed was throttling the nation."(149) The new "declaration of independence" that "Howl" came to symbolize would soon gain national publicity through articles about the Beat Generation in such mainstream publications as *Life Magazine* and *The New York Post*, and through the widespread public attention that City Lights Publishers received after its victory in a precedent-setting, anti-censorship trial following the publication of *Howl and Other Poems*. That trial received renewed attention in recent years as a result of a widely reviewed 2010 Hollywood film, *Howl: The Movie*, which starred James Franco as Allen Ginsberg and which included a re-enactment of portions of the *Howl* trial.

Introduction

Ginsberg's influence on 1960s youth culture did not derive solely from his writings. He was also a participant in many of the era's most well-known rallies and marches, including the 1967 march on the Pentagon and the protests in Chicago outside the 1968 Democratic Party convention. He was even a movement strategist at critical moments. One of the co-founders of the Yippies, Jerry Rubin, met Allen Ginsberg in 1965 when Rubin was co-chair of a committee organizing against the Vietnam War. Rubin relates the way Ginsberg influenced the antiwar movement with tactical suggestions for non-violent, theatrical protests: "He suggested we march to Beatles' music....He suggested there be huge floats. So instead of its being a march of 10,000 angry people who wanted to stop the war, it would be a parade....I think it was the first time I ever thought of politics being theatrical. Allen's ideas opened my mind to the possibility of what you might call, psychedelic politics, a politics that's inspired by imagination."[6]

The influence of Ginsberg and other Beat Generation writers on young people has not yet ceased, nor even slowed down very much. One can see this influence in contemporary activism by taking even a cursory look at the theatricality—the huge puppets, the creative signs, the dancing and drumming—of the global justice protests beginning with Seattle 1999, of the international protests before and during the early stages of the Iraq war in 2003, and of the Occupy Wall Street protests that took place all throughout the U.S., beginning with Zuccotti Park in New York City in 2011, where an OWS-created "People's Library" included a special shelf of Allen Ginsberg's books. Titles by Ginsberg, Kerouac, Burroughs, and other Beat Generation writers continue to sell; films about their lives continue to get made, with well-known actors (most recently, Daniel Radcliffe of Harry Potter fame) enthusiastically agreeing to portray Allen Ginsberg; and university courses in Beat Studies are becoming more prevalent on campuses throughout the country, spurred by the creation of the Beat Studies Association a decade ago. Sixty years after "Howl," one still sees a wide range of writers, musicians, and activists describing the first time they read Ginsberg's signal poem, noting how meaningful it was to meet Ginsberg in person after a reading, or crediting Ginsberg as a key inspiration for the flowering of literary or political creativity.

In 1998, about a year after Allen Ginsberg's death, I worked with his longtime assistant Bob Rosenthal, the writer Ed Sanders, and others to organize a big tribute to Ginsberg at the Cathedral of St. John the Divine, featuring musical performances by Patti Smith, Philip Glass, The Fugs, Stephan Smith, Natalie Merchant, and David Greenberg; as well as readings and talks by Anne Waldman, Ed Sanders, Jayne Cortez, Bob Rosenthal, Eileen Myles, Dave Dellinger, Andy Clausen, and myself. The theme of the evening centered on honoring Ginsberg's activist contributions, as evidenced by both his poetry and his organizing life. A multi-generational, overflow audience of more than 2,500 people came out to pay tribute to his work, helping to prove that the widespread appeal of his legacy remained alive and well.

In May 2000, as part of the global justice movement, I participated in demonstrations in Washington, D.C. against the exploitative policies of the World Bank and International Monetary Fund, which too often when lending money to developing countries require those countries to institute economic austerity programs that harm the environment and exacerbate problems of poverty by cutting social safety nets. The demonstrations were following up on the more widely publicized 1999 protests in Seattle that successfully shut down meetings of the World Trade Organization. At one tense moment during the D.C. demonstrations, a guy who appeared to be a World Bank delegate began bouncing himself hard like a battering ram against a line of young people who had formed a blockade in front of a particular sidewalk that led to one of the buildings in which the bank meetings were taking place. As the delegate became angrier and angrier at his inability to break through the blockade and reach his meeting,

Introduction

and as he grew more violent in his thrusts against the line of youth, another group of young people moved in behind the guy and started chanting: "Om....Om....Om." This was the Buddhist chant that Allen Ginsberg had used in trying to calm emotions at the 1968 Democratic Convention protests in Chicago. The chant successfully deflated the tension in Washington, D.C. 2000, and I smiled thinking about how Ginsberg, in small ways as well as large, has continued to inspire new generations.

The fact that Ginsberg's work has resonated with young writers and activists long after its initial impact in the mid-1950s has certainly been noticed and nervously acknowledged by conservative commentators. Here is Norman Podhoretz writing about Ginsberg's appeal in more contemporary times: "There is enough resemblance between the current situation and the cultural climate of the 50s to fear that his siren song may yet find its insidious way into the ears of yet another generation of restless kids."(40) What Podhoretz seemed to fear is what many of us have grown to appreciate: that young people who read Ginsberg's work quite often come away with a strengthened belief that it is possible to create a far better world, one with considerably less poverty and war, with much cleaner air and water, and with a stronger commitment to civil liberties, civic participation, and democratically accountable social institutions.

And, of course, it is not only within the United States that Ginsberg's poems have inspired poets and activists. If one reads through the 1984 festschrift, *Best Minds*, one sees moving tributes from translators and writers in Poland, Greece, Japan, Russia, England, France, Hungary, Italy, Czechoslovakia, and Romania. The international influence of Ginsberg and other Beat Generation writers can also be seen in the recent collection, *The Transnational Beat Generation*. How is it that a poet can inspire so many people in so many places for six decades and counting? To begin with, it helps to have powerful poems and a compelling social vision.

The Poetry and Politics of Allen Ginsberg

* * *

In writing about Ginsberg's influence on politics and culture, as well as in writing about more general issues of socially concerned poetry, I believe it is both helpful and honest to state up front one's own political preferences and one's own theories about the relationship between poetry and politics, since too often literary reviews are used as cover or camouflage to express political disagreements. In politics, I consider myself a democratic leftist, or a democratic socialist. I believe that people ought to have a far greater say in the political and economic decisions that affect their lives, and that the original socialist ideals—contrary to the way that "actually existing socialism" developed in the Soviet Union and other countries of the Soviet bloc—included bringing more democracy, not less, to people's lives by making our social and economic institutions more publicly accountable. I believe that our current social climate is in dire need of far more economic fairness; ecological protection; affordable housing and healthcare; energetic safeguarding of civil liberties, including freedom of expression; and protection against discrimination based on gender, race, sexual orientation, or disability. Almost every country today uses some version of a mixed economy—for me, a healthy recipe would allow the market to nurture such things as small-business job creation and technological innovation, while the government would have a responsibility to ensure basic human rights and needs like housing, health care, free speech, food, and education. I call myself a democratic leftist or democratic socialist with the understanding that, because of the sordid history of too many authoritarian national leaders calling themselves socialist in the 20th century, different labels will undoubtedly be needed in different countries and different contexts to describe progressive ideas about expanding human rights and liberties. The language that works for progressives in Bolivia or Brazil may not work for progressives in Poland, the Czech Republic, or Uzbekistan. Similarly, what language works in New York City or San Francisco may not work in

Introduction

more conservative parts of the American south or rural midwest.[7] I will therefore try to avoid being too dogmatic about ideological labels—and, indeed, I will show how this notion of avoiding ideological dogmatism marked Ginsberg's own politics.

In my explorations of political poetry, I will also try to avoid being dogmatic about some key aesthetic issues. The 20th century saw a wide range of theories developed and debated regarding the relationship between politics and art.

In aesthetic debates in the early part of the 20th century, some on both the left and the right proposed viewing politics and art as ideally partitioned into completely separate spheres. On the left, the influential Frankfurt School theorist Theodor Adorno championed a high-modernist style that in his view was best able to resist political appropriation by a capitalist culture industry that habitually attempted to co-opt the works and energies of well-meaning writers and artists. On the right, in America, notions of viewing art and politics as best kept apart were most famously fostered by the generally conservative group known as the New Critics, whose influence was peaking just around the time that Allen Ginsberg was typing "Howl." The New Critics believed that, in poetry, as John Crowe Ransom put it, "the rewards of many a historical labor will have to be disproportionately slight."(235) Rather than advocating explicit social visions, according to the New Critic, Cleanth Brooks, "paradox is the language appropriate and inevitable to poetry."(292)

This arbitrary idealization of a poetic sphere left largely uncontaminated by political discourse—possibly with the exception of a few flickers—is a view that has continued through the decades to hold some sway in large segments of the academy and in some influential literary-institutional venues. For example, in a 1990s piece in the *New York Times Book Review*, the influential poet and critic J. D. McClatchy praised the work of Irish poet Seamus Heaney because, despite writing from the center of a long-running and stormy political conflict, Heany "has concerned himself less with any commentary on social conditions than with an analysis of the heart—its longing, its hollows and, yes, its violence."[8] McClatchy complimented Heaney's essays for, in his words, dismissing "Marxists, feminists, anyone who prefers to read a poem as a set of discourses."[9] According to McClatchy, the best poems are more likely to display "psychological realism," while a "poet's political views will more likely turn up in his prose."[10]

In a *New York Times Book Review* piece in October 2010, the literary critic Lee Siegel wrote an article specifically about Allen Ginsberg and the Beat Generation that included similar assumptions. In his article, Siegel declared that Ginsberg and his fellow Beat Generation writers were interested only in individual freedoms, not larger social issues, and he went on to compare Ginsberg and his colleagues to the right-wing Tea Party movement—an outrageous comparison that was only possible by Siegel ignoring Ginsberg's deep interest in progressive political activism, and by ignoring Ginsberg's decades of hands-on work to improve government policies by making them more peaceful, more egalitarian, and more ecologically sustainable. Of course, it is important to note that the major writers who came, as a group, to be known as the Beat Generation, did not all share the same political philosophies, and some, especially Kerouac, occasionally veered toward right-wing politics—but most of the Beat writers were politically progressive, believing in causes like peace, racial justice, economic fairness, and ecological sustainability that could fairly be seen as the antithesis of the Tea Party's social program.

One of America's most influential contemporary literary critics, Harold Bloom, has displayed a similar antipathy toward political poetry. Writing in overarching rejectionist fashion in his introduction to *Contemporary Poets,* Bloom asserts: "I myself am not much moved by the work of Allen Ginsberg or of Amiri Baraka, or of the recent phase of Adrienne Rich" (ix)—the "recent phase" of Rich being a less-than-subtle way of referring to her more explicitly political verse.

Introduction

In the 1990s, with the ascendancy of postmodern theory within academia and the mass popularity of a hip-hop-influenced "spoken word" poetry that was more than willing to address urgent social needs, the view that poetry and politics ought to be compartmentalized into separate rooms seemed to be losing some of its cultural clout, but it later reared its head again in America's post-9/11 popular culture, as artists from Whoopi Goldberg to The Dixie Chicks were excoriated by right-wing talk radio and mainstream television for having the audacity to express anti-Bush and anti-war opinions during public cultural performances.

Conversely, during the 20th century, we also saw many cultural critics who advocated conflating art and politics into one large arena. In its crudest form, this view was advanced in the former Soviet Union by Stalin's Congress of Soviet Writers, which decreed in 1934 that artists should create works of "socialist realism" in support of the Soviet state. The general idea of this decree was supported by some American writers of the Old Left, including the poet Mike Gold, whose proclamations for literature included the assertion that: "Every poem, every novel and drama, must have a social theme, or it is merely confectionary," and who attacked modernist writers by announcing: "We are not interested in the verbal acrobats—this is only another form of bourgeois idleness."[11] According to Stephen Spender, in *The God That Failed*, a seminal book edited by Richard Grossman and compiled from essays by former party members about international Communist Party attempts to tell artists what they ought to be writing, the "attitude of the Communists" was that "since poets and artists are not the best judges of the ideology which is an expression of the development of society, political theorists are in a position to dictate to them what society needs from their art."(268)

From the later years of the 20th century into the present, some postmodern theorists have also tended to conflate art and politics. Of course, this conflation occurs with far different and far less dogmatic intentions than those of the

1934 Soviet writers' congress, but I would argue that it can lead to a limited view of art nonetheless. There are a great number of different theories that can be said to fall roughly under the banner of postmodernism, but it seems possible to sketch some rough traits which these theories have in common. Along with rejecting Enlightenment-based notions of reason and universal values and championing difference, uncertainty, and aesthetic play, postmodern theorists have tended to delete the boundaries between various categories of intellectual exploration. In *The Postmodern Turn,* Steven Best and Douglas Kellner describe this point: "A new emphasis is evident on deconstructing boundaries within and among different disciplines in the postmodern turn. Hence, Derrida attacks the distinction between philosophy and literature, Foucault works across various disciplinary boundaries such as history and fiction, and pop art challenges the barriers between art and everyday life."(258)

The American school of poetry that has most strongly reflected postmodern theory has undoubtedly been the "Language poets," a group that once operated largely on the margins of the U.S. poetry world, but that has grown extremely influential in many American literary circles, including many university English departments. In "Contemporary Poetry, Alternate Routes," critic Jerome McGann advocates for the unique importance of language poetry by arguing that non-narrative or anti-narrative forms of poetry are necessary to resist co-optation by the dominant political order, whereas "narrative is a form of continuity; as such, its deployment in discourse is a way of legitimating established forms of social order."(259) McGann's assertion that a non-narrative art is alone capable of resisting political appropriation by the capitalist culture industry is reminiscent of Theodor Adorno, except that where Adorno celebrated this art form's ability to remain above or outside the political fray, McGann goes a step further and calls Language poetry "textual activism," eliminating the separation between Language poetry and the political arena, so that in this line of thought anti-narrative

Introduction

or non-narrative poetry dogmatically becomes the only style of political verse that can ever be sufficiently radical or effectively activist enough. Along these lines, the poet Charles Bernstein has written: "Regardless of 'what' is being said, use of standard patterns of syntax and exposition effectively rebroadcast, often at a subliminal level, the basic constitutive elements of social structure."(140) Another Language poet, Ron Silliman, criticizes "referential fetish," while correlating "the nature of capitalist reality" with "the imposition of narrative"—both of which are described as imperialistic. (129-31)[12]

But are continuity and narrative always supportive of the conservative status quo, and is discontinuity always a progressive political act? Aren't narrative and reasoned arguments needed to develop the basic principles of unity and solidarity required to build effective political movements? And what about the deconstructive tool that is the paper shredder, which has allowed many an establishment politician and corrupt corporate executive to destroy evidence of exploitative behavior and criminal misdeed? Or the famously indeterminate non-narratives (like Donald Rumsfeld's "known unknowns" and "unknown unknowns") constructed by the George W. Bush administration to assure that no high-ranking officials would personally be blamed for approving or designing the sort of torture that took place at Abu Ghraib and so-called CIA "black sites"? Or the slick montage-style TV commercials that have become highly popular as corporate product advertisements, in which it is sometimes nearly impossible even to figure out what product is being plugged until the very end of a commercial? The left literary critic Terry Eagleton insightfully notes that it is politically naive to think that art, of either the narrative or anti-narrative variety, can by itself resist political appropriation:

> How idealist to imagine that *art,* all by itself could resist incorporation! The question of appropriation has to do with politics, not with

> culture; it is a question of who is winning at any particular time: If *they* win, continue to govern, then it is no doubt true that there is nothing which they cannot in principle defuse and contain. If *you* win, they will not be able to appropriate a thing because you will have appropriated them.
>
> (*Ideology,* 372, author's italics)

From the point of view of activism, just as history is a totality of continuities and discontinuities, so will successful opposition movements need to appreciate the potential benefits of both effective deconstruction and intelligent reconstruction.

In the first half of the 20th century, left theorists had engaged in spirited debates about the social implications of surrealism and other forms of international modernism, debates that remain fascinating for those of us interested in the relationship between poetry and politics and that I think will help illuminate the work of a poet like Allen Ginsberg. The Hungarian Marxist philosopher, Georg Lukacs, developed a theory of "social realism" that was far more nuanced than the crude "socialist realism" pushed by the 1934 Soviet writers' congress.[13] Focusing primarily on the novel, Lukacs criticized literary modernism as politically naive, and praised critical realist literature in which, through organic interactions between characters, readers were able to experience the deepest social meanings and contradictions of the day. Lukacs believed that the avant-garde's formal experimentation simply reproduced the surface appearance of reality under capitalism—a reality full of ruptures and fissures—while it left society's underlying essence unexamined. He believed that art's main mission was to help readers comprehend their social reality, rather than to replace that reality with an imagined literary world. Unlike the Soviet congress, Lukacs did not call for portrayals of socialist heroes or even necessarily working-class characters. For Lukacs, even a well-done, in-depth portrayal of the capitalist class would better enable readers to grasp the underlying sources of the daily problems they encountered, and readers would then presumably be more likely to join organizations working for progressive change.

The debates that Lukacs had with other left theorists of his time can help us to understand many of the ideas that have energized a wide range of the works we admire today. Lukacs helped illuminate the power of 19th century realist novels, but his dismissal of modernism's liberating possibilities was arbitrarily constrictive, as opponents like the playwright Bertold Brecht and the philosopher Ernst Bloch argued. In Bloch's view, Marxists who attacked experimental modernism for a lack of realism were making both a theoretical and practical mistake. In practical terms, Bloch felt that anti-modernists discouraged young people from joining left movements by promoting the belief that progressive social change required a sacrifice of the imagination. To the contrary, Bloch asserted that socialists ought to nurture the imagination more than capitalists, who generally consign the human imagination to "hollow spaces."(159) Since, according to Bloch, the project of the left is to create a better world out of the present one, reality for the left ought to be understood as "reality plus the future within it."(162) Because the desired human world had not yet arrived, it could not be reduced to empirical perception or narrative realism. Experimental montage or surrealist imagery, by creating meanings which did not yet exist in the actual world, could, in Bloch's compelling phrase, offer "anticipatory illuminations"(160)—hints or sketches of future potential—in a way that realist writing could not. Myra Jehlen similarly highlights the importance of the literary imagination when she writes that "literary visions can be said to transcend when they see past their immediate situations."(LC, 52) For Ernst Bloch, modernism's "anticipatory illuminations" offer a look a little beyond the present—as did, I will argue, key parts of Ginsberg's poetry. By lauding the contributions of modernist imagination and experimental techniques in a way that does not negate the also-valuable contributions of more representational modes, Bloch refused to allow aesthetic criteria to become dogmatically subordinated to any political party or literary school's imperatives.

Here in the early part of the 21st century, it seems instructive to study the robust, past debates that took place around questions of literature and politics. And yet, from a distance and by embracing more generous theories, like those of Ernst Bloch, we can also recognize how the narrowness of certain critical views has sometimes limited the ability of readers to appreciate literature written in styles viewed as "other." We can now hopefully begin to take a less dogmatic approach to questions of political poetry. Perhaps the ability of different poetic schools to work together in the years ahead might even in some small way help to prefigure new models of working in more unified, broad coalitions for progressive political change?

One progressive philosopher who has attempted to develop a more nuanced and flexible view of the relationship between art and politics is the contemporary theorist, Jurgen Habermas. According to Habermas, under postmodern theory "*all* genre distinctions are submerged in one comprehensive, all-embracing context of texts."(PDM, 190) This "false pretense of eliminating the genre distinction between philosophy and literature," according to Habermas, only "robs both of their substance."(PDM, 210) Instead, Habermas embraces a Kantian notion of sphere-differentiation, where the boundaries between disciplines are seen as drawn in dotted lines, something like semi-permeable membranes. Terry Eagleton describes this view as maintaining a "necessary differentiation of the cognitive, moral and cultural spheres," which are seen as "interrelated but not conflated." (*Ideology*, 406) In other words, art and politics are conceptually seen as different spheres which can interact, overlap, embrace, or stand apart in different historical contexts and different geographical locales.

Under this philosophy of sphere-differentiation, one is able to discuss a variety of possible relations between art and

Introduction

politics without reducing the intrinsic possibilities or demands of either one of these spheres to the other. The idea thus allows for different criteria to be used when looking at politics and at culture: In the words of Stephen Bronner, "The object, in short, must generate its categories of inquiry."*(Critical Theory,* 329) For the purposes of looking at poetry, I would argue that this sort of category-differentiation is necessary if we are to appreciate fully the complexity and aesthetic pleasure of literature without imposing dogmatic political expectations on it—but without sacrificing our political views to the realm of aesthetics. Along these lines, we can express appreciation for poets (like Ezra Pound or T. S. Eliot, in my own case) who advocate a politics with which we disagree, without having to sympathize with their politics. And we can also appreciate artistic explorations of paradox and undecideability—even while asserting that reason, determinate judgments, and appeals to historically contextualized universal values are desirable for the political realm, so that, for example, activist groups can develop agreed-upon principles of unity, and so that policy-makers can argue for progressive legislative reforms by making the case that one particular reform would further equitable or ecologically sustainable goals more than another reform. It is not that reason and determinate political judgments are thereby rigidly excluded from the aesthetic realm or that no political question will ever merit ambiguous responses: it is merely that the criteria for valuing each realm will be seen as potentially different.

With a more flexible and complex criteria for judging art, we should be able to appreciate poems written in a wider variety of literary styles. In Bronner's succinct phrase, we ought to be able to appreciate both the "exposure of repression and the illumination of utopia."(*Critical Theory*, 175) Or, in the poignant words of the Chilean "antipoet" Nicanor Parra, from "Letters from the Poet Who Sleeps in a Chair": "Young poets / Write any way you want to / In whatever style you please / Too much blood has gone under the bridge / To go on believing—I believe— / That only one road is right: / In poetry everything is permitted."(23)

When the spheres of politics and poetry are seen as interrelated but not conflated, the dynamic complexity of those interactions becomes fascinating to study when a skilled poet challenges conceptual boundaries by writing "political poetry." Adrienne Rich, who has probably theorized questions of politics and poetry as well as any other recent U.S. poet, described the issue of looking for this complexity as: "not a matter of dying as a poet into politics....but of something else—finding the relationship."(*Found There*, 21)

* * *

The arbitrary idealization, promoted by the New Critics, of a poetic sphere left relatively uncontaminated by political thought was a relatively recent phenomenon, beginning in the 19th century. In the 18th century, well-known poets like Alexander Pope and John Dryden took it as a given that one of the poet's obvious roles was that of political commentator or social satirist. Thus, for the late poet Denise Levertov, the question of whether poetry that includes polemical content can be good poetry was "strictly a modern question, having its roots in the Romantic period but not really troubling anyone until the late nineteenth century."(162) The aversion to political poetry, having arisen during the late 19th century, was later exacerbated during the Cold War. In a sense, New Criticism's dogmatic bias against all political art can be viewed as a theoretical Cold War mirror to the Communist Party's literary dogmatism which demanded a specific form of political art, socialist realism. Of course, poets throughout the 19th century and early 20th century, from progressive poets like Blake and Shelley to more conservative ones like Eliot and Pound, continued to express social beliefs in their verse, but nonetheless an anti-political attitude grew among influential literary critics and poets, including many of those influenced by T. S. Eliot's own theoretical writings.

Introduction

Since the ascendancy of feminist, postmodern, and new Marxist theories in the late 20th and early 21st centuries, there has been a noticeable increase in the willingness of critics to discuss the political content of literary works. But how does one maintain a concern for a political poem's literary quality? As Myra Jehlen notes, "Opinions as to what constitutes literary value may differ widely but the issue is always present."(*Literary Criticism*, 50-51) For Levertov, questions like "whether it is poetic" and not simply "versified ideas," and whether it succeeds in "engag[ing] our aesthetic response" were paramount—and she insisted that these questions be asked not just of political verse, but also of psychological and autobiographical poems, as well as poems about "spring, love, death, a rainbow."[14] Rejecting both automatic embrace and *a priori* rejection of political poetry, Adrienne Rich asks similarly for a thoughtful aesthetic appraisal in the case of political verse: "Why do so many poems full of liberal or radical hope and outrage fail to lift off the ground, for which 'politics' is blamed rather than a failure of poetic nerve?" (*Found There*, 232) What Levertov and Rich are referring to is the question of literary value, what Myra Jehlen defines as "the effectiveness and vitality of a text."(*Literary Criticism*, 50) Elsewhere Jehlen perceives that "what we call greatness.... is an exceptional plenitude of vision." *(Literary Criticism*, 51)

Allen Ginsberg was a poet who displayed exceptional vision. This volume will explore some of the literary tools and strategies, political ideas, social observations, and imaginative leaps that Ginsberg used to achieve or convey that vision. For Jurgen Habermas, art or literary criticism entails a "bridging function" (*Philosophical Discourse*, 208), helping to draw out the emancipatory potential of an artwork for readers. This book will attempt to perform this sort of bridging function for the political poems of Allen Ginsberg, hopefully helping to illuminate various ways in which Ginsberg turned his social ideas and perceptions into memorable poetry.

The Poetry and Politics of Allen Ginsberg

* * *

In any library with a decent-sized poetry collection, one can find plenty of books that look at the intricacies of English-language poetry's traditional forms and meters and the varied ways in which well-known poets through the centuries have used those traditional elements. Although he wrote most of his best work in free verse, Allen Ginsberg knew these traditional forms and meters as well as most American poets of his time. After all, Ginsberg had grown up as the son of a traditional lyric poet, Louis Ginsberg, who used to recite poems aloud in their home. One can easily hear Allen's innate grasp of traditional English-language poetry meter and rhyme by reading his blues or ballads, such as "Airplane Blues" or "September on Jessore Road," or by listening to the moving way in which he put Blake's *Songs of Innocence and Experience* to music.

On a personal note, I was always impressed with how many poems Allen Ginsberg seemed to be able to recite by heart. When he would ask me if I knew a poem by Shelley or Milton, he would often recite a dozen or so lines as a way of describing more specifically which poem he was talking about. During my studies with Ginsberg at Naropa Institute in Boulder, Colorado in 1980, where I took his class on William Blake and where I did a one-month poetry apprenticeship with him, Ginsberg was passing out to students a photocopied sheet which he had compiled and labeled, "A Synopsis of Metrical Systems." This sheet listed the commonly studied English-language poetry meters, based on stress patterns over two or three syllables (iambus, trochee, anapest), as well as less commonly used metrical variations based on stress patterns over four and five syllables (proceleusmaticus, choriambus, anaclastic). Even when Ginsberg was setting aside many of the traditional notions of poetic meter in his own work, it was always clear that he was choosing to utilize *some* traditional formal tools, like assonance and alliteration in "Howl," and that he had most of the remaining notions of poetic meter and form in his poetic toolbox for those moments when he wanted to pick them up.

In this volume, I will take an occasional look at the way Ginsberg used some of the more traditionally discussed poetic techniques, but I want to look mainly at poetic tools and strategies in a different way, one that I think will better help illuminate some of the various ways in which Ginsberg made his political explorations effectively poetic. It is possible to categorize such strategies in any number of ways, but below I would like to list eight general tools and techniques that, throughout Ginsberg's best work and throughout, I think, much of the best political poetry of our times, we can find used to heighten the poetic quality and resonance of social observations and ideas:

1) *Clear images / empirical perceptions / realist narrative.*

Ginsberg had learned from William Carlos Williams, among others, that the clear and interesting presentation of empirical detail was a basic tool of poetry. In "Spring and All," Williams had written "so much depends / upon / a red wheel / barrow / glazed with rain / water / beside the white / chickens."[15] Ginsberg used to tell his poetry students to write "close to the nose"—to describe clearly and accurately what was in front of them so that readers could see through the eyes of the poet. In this kind of poetry, it was through a poet's objectively portrayed observations that readers would be able to tell what a poet was subjectively seeing and thinking. Often citing Blake's phrase "minute particulars," Ginsberg urged students to notice what was unique about their observation: I remember him saying that if one was looking at a tree, for instance, one did not need to describe the entire tree, just what was odd about this one's leaves or branches—and the reader would then be able to picture the entire tree. One sees Ginsberg's use of such imagery in "Sunflower Sutra," where he notes "the gray Sunflower poised against the sunset, crackly bleak and dusty with the smut and smog and smoke of olden locomotives in its eye."(146)[16]

When I sent Ginsberg one of my earliest poems, one of the poets that he suggested I read was Charles Reznikoff, one of the most well-known of the group of poets known as the "Objectivists." Ginsberg appreciated the way that Reznikoff was able to craft emotionally wrought poems by simply presenting realist pictures or narratives, like this one from Reznikoff's long poem, "Holocaust":

> An S.S. commander saw him
> and asked where he had taken the wood,
> and the old man answered from a house that had
>   been torn down.
> But the commander drew his pistol,
> put it against the old man's throat
> and shot him. (11)

Whether in "Kaddish," where Ginsberg uses moving, realist narrative to describe heartrending moments with his mentally ill mother, or in a later poem like "Junk Mail" where, by simply listing the contents of his daily mail Ginsberg provides readers with a sense of the day's most urgent worldly events and social causes, Ginsberg had learned that "minute particulars" could effectively serve to ground even the most imaginative of works.

2) *Surrealism / Modernism*.

The Paterson doctor-poet, William Carlos Williams, appreciated for, among other things, furthering the use of American diction in U. S. poetry, was far more versed in international art movements than is sometimes acknowledged, including I think by Ginsberg, who seemed mostly interested in the doctor's empirical verses. After all, when Williams

Introduction

offered his image of the red wheelbarrow cited above, it was in the middle of a long poem, "Spring and All," which juxtaposed neatly condensed empirical perceptions with longer sections of playful, disjunctive imagery influenced by modernist art styles like cubism and surrealism.

Ginsberg, too, had studied these international modernist movements thoroughly, both in the realm of visual art and in the poetry worlds of French surrealism and Russian futurism. In "Free Union," the French poet Andre Breton had written a poem for his wife that uses a surrealistic stream-of-consciousness style:

> My wife with her sex of the mirror
> My wife with eyes full of tears
> With her eyes of violet panoply magnetic needle
> My wife with savannah eyes
> My wife with eyes of water to drink in jail[17]

Breton had theorized literary surrealism as a way to help bring together the evolving studies of psychoanalysis and leftist politics, and one can note here that Breton's associative imagery includes an imagined cure for prison thirst. One can also note the similarities between this section of Breton's "Free Union" and section IV of "Kaddish" where Ginsberg uses similar surrealistic free association imagery in relation to his mother's eyes.

The Russian futurist Vladimir Mayakovsky also showed ways in which unreal imagery could be used to highlight idealistic desires. In "An Extraordinary Adventure which Befell Vladimir Mayakovky in a Summer Cottage," the poet calls the sun out of the sky to have tea with him. After a slap on the back from the poet, the sun announces, "You and I, / my comrade, are quite a pair!" In the end, Mayakovsky knows the sun well enough to proclaim on the sun's behalf: "Always to shine.... / and to hell with everything else! / This is my motto— / and the sun's!"[18]

In the 1986 annotated edition of *Howl*, published with

photocopies of original drafts of the poem, and notes and correspondences related to the poem and its reception, Ginsberg included selections of poets that had influenced his poetry at the time of "Howl." Among those included were Mayakovsky and the French poets Apollinaire and Artaud. From French surrealism and Russian futurism, Ginsberg learned techniques for adding electric-like energy to his work, an excitement that could engage readers with its dynamic rhythms and that could also imply utopian desires, along the lines of Ernst Bloch's "anticipatory illuminations," through its use of imagery that does not yet exist in the actual world.

3) *Mythification.*

Mythification is somewhat related to surrealism in that it can move a poem beyond empirically based narrative. By mythifying current events or interpretations of history, a poet can impart an aura of timelessness to current events or ideas. The most famous instance of this in Ginsberg's poems is his use of "Moloch" in part II of "Howl." Ginsberg's use of this poetic tool drew on William Blake's invention of the character "Urizen" in Blake's long prophetic works. Ginsberg acknowledged that it was from Blake that he learned the poetic technique of taking "political details," and "magnif[ying] roles into cosmo-demonic figures." [19]

The impulse to mythify current events can also be seen in another of the most famous English-language poems of the 20th century, William Butler Yeats' "Easter 1916." In that poem Yeats memorialized the leaders of Ireland's Easter Rebellion through such poetic tactics as associating one (Patrick Pearse) with the mythical figure of Pegasus: "This man had kept a school / And rode our wingèd horse."[54] The end of Yeats' poem serves to provide a sense of eternal poetic relevance and a timeless, living existence to the named activists who in real life had already been put to death:

Introduction

> MacDonagh and MacBride
> And Connolly and Pearse
> Now and in time to be,
> Wherever green is worn,
> Are changed, changed utterly:
> A terrible beauty is born.[20]

It is this same strategy of mythification that Yeats employs when, in "The Second Coming," after noting that the "best lack all conviction, while the worst / Are full of passionate intensity," he asks: "what rough beast, its hour come round at last, / Slouches toward Bethlehem to be born?"(89)

4) *Demythification/Demystification/Historicization.*

In a mirror strategy, Ginsberg often deconstructs false myths promoted by the mainstream media or government institutions. Ginsberg's motive in these instances is to give readers a more accurate sense of history—or of the human values at stake in a given situation—than that which is being provided by establishment authorities. We can see this tool used frequently, for instance, in Ginsberg's most well-known poem opposing the Vietnam War, "Wichita Vortex Sutra," which is filled with shrewd and powerful historical perceptions that undermine the military and corporate media's propaganda justifying that unwarranted war. While generals tried to convey a sense that they were supporting a popular South Vietnamese army, Ginsberg's poem noted that even the CIA knew Ho Chi Minh would have easily won a democratic election if one had been held. While the media trivialized war casualty counts, Ginsberg humanized the victims by asking readers whether they have looked into the eyes of the dead.

This is the sort of historicization undertaken by Muriel Rukeyser when she went down to West Virgina and wrote her masterpiece long poem, "Book of the Dead," which takes an in-depth and poetic look at an industrial accident in which 2,000 men died because Union Carbide had them dig through a silica tunnel without the proper protective masks. In that poem, Rukeyser presented verbatim quotes from Congressional hearings in which the government decided to let Union Carbide go legally unpunished. As a humanizing counterweight to those callous government hearings, Rukeyser also presented historical testimony from surviving spouses, as well as stunning lines of poetry intended to break through common corporate rationalizations for making decisions based more on profit-maximizing motives than on considerations of human health and well-being. Rukeyser's poetic strategy of demythification is explicitly explained in her poem, "The Poem as Mask," where she declares: "No more masks! No more mythologies!"(122) Of course, a single poem can contain elements of both mythification and demythologization. In "The Poem as Mask," once Rukeyser has announced "There is no mountain, there is no god," (122) she can then and seemingly only then assert that "the god lifts his hand, the fragments join in me with their own music"(122) —that is, once Rukeyser announces that there is no external omniscient god, she can realize a new mystical idea of a divinity within. In a later chapter, I will look at the way Ginsberg's "Wichita Vortex Sutra" uses similar strategies of both demystification and re-mythification to oppose the Vietnam war.

5) *Personalization.*

By intertwining highly personal themes with social issues and historical moments, Ginsberg heightens the emotional intensity of political matters by concretely demonstrating their impact on individual human beings. One sees this most readily and effectively in "Kaddish," Ginsberg's long elegy for his mother, Naomi, where his mother's mental illness and his family's interactions are so tied up with world affairs that moving descriptions of Naomi's decline and Allen's responses necessarily carry social implications.

Introduction

Indeed, in many love poems—and also elegies—written for politically engaged persons, we see the emotional power of a poem carried partly by virtue of the connections made between the personal and political. In his beautiful poem, "In the Middle of This Century," Israeli poet Yehuda Amichai describes a war-ravaged environment in which "The earth drinks people and their loves / like wine, in order to forget."(30) In such a turmoil-filled society, love seems stronger because of its seeming ability to exist in opposition to the pitilessness of the world: "Desert dust covered the table / we hadn't eaten from. / But with my finger I wrote in it the letters of your name." (31) At the end of Amiri Baraka's love poem, "Ballad Air & Fire," he succinctly describes a connection between personal love and social activism: "what it was about, really. Life. / Loving someone, and struggling."[21]

Personalization can also embed political intentions within self-exploration, in that some personal struggles can be seen as attempts to assert subjective desires against an objectifying or dehumanizing culture, as when Ginsberg declares at the end of "America": "America, I'm putting my queer shoulder to the wheel." (CP, 156) In Judy Grahn's 1973 epic poem, "A Woman Is Talking to Death," the poet ends with a declaration that implies human subjectivity's triumph over an oppressive culture:

> wherever our meat hangs on our bones
> for our own use
> your pot is so empty
> death, ho death
> you shall be poor. (131)

This is the assertion of human worth against a repressive society that Adrienne Rich implies when she ends her poem "North American Time" with the line "and I start to speak again,"[22] and that Langston Hughes memorably declares when he says, "I, too, sing America."(46)

6) *Humor*.

As far back as Ovid and Catullus, poets well understood that humor helps make the political medicine go down, and helps engage readers or listeners in ideas they might not otherwise stop to consider. In poems like "America" and "Death to Van Gogh's Ear," Ginsberg helped re-introduce to poetry readers the realization that poetic humor could appear as an element in high-quality poetry and also that humor was not at all the opposite of seriousness of purpose. If one listens to the early live recording of Ginsberg reading "America" on *Holy Soul Jelly Roll!*, the audience laughter after many of the poem's lines is stunning—and it is clear that mid-1950s audiences were not expecting such humor in poems. Yet, when Ginsberg asks America, "When can I go into the supermarket and buy what I need with my good looks?"(CP, 154), it is clear that he is asking a comically phrased, but serious question about when the nation's economic system will become more just. The humor helps turn the line into quality, memorable verse.

Ginsberg's sense of poetic humor has clearly been one of his most lasting influences in the literary world. It influenced his immediate Beat Generation circle, as we can readily see in the inventive poems of Gregory Corso, whose poem "Marriage"—which begins, "Should I get married? Should I be good? / Astound the girl next door with my velvet suit and faustus hood?"(62) —became an instant hit in literary circles and with anthology editors, and who continued to write brilliant, funny poems like "I Gave Away" and "The Whole Mess...Almost" throughout his career. Or look at some lines from Pedro Pietri's poem, "Telephone Booth Number 905-1/2," which has also become a classic example in some circles of a highly serious theme conveyed in comic style. After calling his employer to say that he will not be coming to work that day, his employer asks the poet if he is sick, to which the poet responds:

Introduction

Photo of Allen Ginsberg and Gregory Corso in New York, 1995.
Photo by Eliot Katz.

"No Sir" I replied:
I am feeling too good
to report to work today,
if I feel sick tomorrow
I will come in early[23]

7) <u>Extending or subverting previous poetic traditions in interesting ways</u>.

In discussing the significance of William Blake lengthening John Milton's poetic line and using free verse instead of Milton's blank verse, Susan Wolfson notes that Milton had utilized blank verse in order to free poetry "from the troublesome and modern bondage of rhyming," and that the more radical Blake subsequently "raised the stakes, launching a revolutionary poetics in *Milton* (1804) that outdid Milton, by expressing heroic contempt for any 'tame high finisher of....paltry Rhymes; or paltry Harmonies'."(199) Ginsberg too realized that extending or altering poetic traditions could carry a social or political resonance. In "Howl," for instance, Ginsberg utilizes long lines in the tradition of Blake and Whitman, but he makes his own lines even longer than these cherished predecessors'. As I will discuss further in the next chapter, these long lines carry the implication of an even more radical project of freeing self and society from restrictive boundaries.

In addition to long free-verse lines, Ginsberg also utilizes and in some ways extends a variety of other formal traditions—including American blues and jazz, Old Testament concepts and rhythms, pastoral poetry, war verse, modernist montage—in ways that resound politically and that will be discussed further throughout this book.

Introduction

8) *Surprise*!

When Emily Dickinson was asked what constituted a great poem, she famously declared that she knew a poem was great when it made the top of her head feel like it was coming off. What Dickinson was getting at was the element of surprise, the element that—more than any other, I would argue—can make a poem feel aesthetically vital. That surprise can come in any number of ways—through thought-provoking insights, surprise phrasing, startling imagery, an unexpected way of looking at an event or object, an odd line break, novel wit or humor, an inventive sense of rhythm or form, or a provocative way of addressing previous poets and poetry traditions. When Adrienne Rich asks, as noted above, why much political poetry seems weak, I would answer because much of it seems rather flat and predictable, in both substance and language, as does much psychological poetry. Importantly, the question of whether a poem offers surprise to the reader is relevant whether the poem is written in the style of Language Poetry or narrative poetry. As Ginsberg's poetry evidenced, and as poets like Pope and Dryden well knew, even politically didactic poetry, so often disparaged by mainstream reviewers, can be effective when it is accompanied by surprising phrasing, imagery, or insight, so that as literary vehicles the poems are not merely reducible to their pedagogical effects, becoming mere "versified ideas." (Levertov)

The issue of surprise is, of course, a subjective one. What is new and surprising to one reader may not be to another. When we talk about poetry of extraordinary literary value, we are talking about poetry that will inspire surprise and wonder in a relatively large number of readers—or we think it would inspire that sense of wonder if a large number of readers were to see the work. Usually, though perhaps not always, the appearance of surprise will require that readers are already engaged with, and paying attention to, the text for other reasons in order to feel the surprise arrive. For that to happen, poets have to have a competent sense of the other items in a poet's toolbox, including a sense of poetic rhythm that can maintain a reader's attention or curiosity. When my friend Danny Shot first gave Allen Ginsberg a poem in 1976 after we saw him read at Rutgers University for the first time, Ginsberg sent Danny a postcard soon thereafter (in May 1976), which noted in part: "Another thing you gotta remember is each line should have some haiku or double joke or image or mad sound or Poetry in it, not be just flat prose."[24] In a poem like Ginsberg's "Howl," it is the inventive and endlessly surprising linguistic mix—nothing like "flat prose"—that has enabled the poem to continue sounding lively and relevant to so many successive generations. The surprise quality in Ginsberg's poems is what Helen Vendler observes when she writes: "his mind roams widely, in unpredictable ways....One can't widen consciousness in poetry by having it follow a programmed path." (*Part of Nature*, 100-101)

Because most readers are not expecting so forceful a question, it is a sense of surprise that I believe hits so many readers when Langston Hughes asks at the end of "Harlem (A Dream Deferred)": "Or does it explode?" (426) It is also what so intrigues readers when first coming across the modernist anti-narrative style of Gertrude Stein: "Red flags the reason for pretty flags / And ribbons. / Ribbons of flags."(164) It is the jolt felt by readers at the first line of Mayakovsky's "A Few Words about Myself": "I love to watch children dying."(57) It is the way Pablo Neruda makes readers look at war and political repression in new ways through a cubist-style variation in line breaks at the end of "I'm Explaining a Few Things," written in response to fascist violence during the Spanish Civil War:

> Come and see the blood in the streets.
> Come and see
> the blood in the streets.
> Come and see the blood
> in the streets![25]

Introduction

Surprise can also be created through the invention of words, as when Adrienne Rich titles a poem "Dreamwood,"[26] conjoining the material world with the realm of fantasy via language, or when Yehuda Amichai entitles a poem "Wildpeace,"(88) implying that he is calling for a peace arrived at through energetic activity by all parties, not the clichéd peace of "the wolf and the lamb."(88)

Surprise can come in the form of a stunning line or two, like this one from Adrienne Rich: "beauty that won't deny, is itself an eye" (*Atlas*, 24); or these two from Alicia Ostriker at the end of "The Volcano Sequence": "sometimes the stories take you and fling you against a wall / sometimes you go right through the wall."(119) In Jayne Cortez's "Tell Me," the surprising imagery comes from one line to the next in the form of biting surrealism addressed to an overly militarized society: "Tell me that the plutonium sludge / in your corroded torso is all a dream / Tell me that your penis bone is not erupting / with the stench of dead ants."[27] At the end of Andy Clausen's poem, "We Could," Clausen writes a striking line that is simultaneously a protest against religious fundamentalism and the ultimate act of embracing a deeply human spirituality: "We lick the Jewel in the Lotus / till it is human / then / We eat God alive!"[28] After 9/11, the Palestinian-American poet Suheir Hammad circulated a poem, "first writing since," on the internet that surprised readers with its incisive, close-to-home mix of mourning and emotionally charged complaint: "one more person asks me if i knew the hijackers. / one more motherfucker ask me what navy my brother is in. / one more person assume no arabs or muslims were killed." (100) And, in the early days of the Bush administration's unending, so-called "war on terror," rapper Michael Franti noted in a popular song called "Bomb the World," in a surprisingly compact couplet: "You can bomb the world to pieces / But you can't bomb it into peace."[29]

In his poem, "Many Have Fallen," Gregory Corso reminds readers that he once wrote a "frolicy poem called BOMB" in which he predicted that an atomic bomb would fall during his lifetime. He then notes later revelations that the U.S. tested nuclear explosions in the deserts of Utah, Nevada, and New Mexico in the 1950s, and marched soldiers toward the blasts to observe the after-effects. In the poem's last three lines, Corso strikingly asserts: "all survived /.... until two decades later / when the dead finally died." (182) The last line is accurate in a realist sense in that soldiers died cancer-ridden deaths years after this nuclear testing from radiation they had received at the time of the blasts, but it is the profound phrasing that makes my head, as a reader, metaphorically pop off, along the lines of Emily Dickenson's notion of powerful poetry. When all of the elements are in place, including the element of surprise, there is a sense that a poem has magic. Denise Levertov urges political poets to remember "poetry's roots in song, magic, and the high craft that makes itself felt as exhilarating beauty even when the content voices rage or utters a grim warning." (172)

Allen Ginsberg developed one of our time's most important poetic voices through an inventive mix of poetic and thematic explorations, and a rather large supply of literary magic. The eight tools and techniques enumerated above are meant to be flexible, and intended mainly to provide some new ways to talk about how Allen Ginsberg's (and other writers') political poems gain their literary vitality. In the following chapters, I will look closely at Ginsberg's poems themselves to explore their internal dynamics and also to examine their external dynamics—how they engage perceptively and imaginatively in dialogue with the world around him. I will also take a look at the way Ginsberg moved in his own life to put his political ideas into activist practice.

Chapter 2: "Howl": The Work Heard Round the World

By now, most Ginsberg readers know that many of his earliest reviewers were less than enthusiastic. Fellow poet John Hollander famously criticized *Howl and Other Poems* for an "utter lack of decorum of any kind."(26) In a letter to the poet, Ginsberg's former Columbia professor Lionel Trilling wrote: "I'm afraid I have to tell you that I don't like the poems at all....There is no real voice here. As for the doctrinal element of the poems, apart from the fact that I of course reject it, it seems to me that I heard it very long ago and that you give it to me in all its orthodoxy, with nothing new added."[1] While M.L. Rosenthal found moments worth complimenting, he nevertheless judged Ginsberg's poems: "all too destructive and therefore mistaken."(31)

One of the most prescient early reviews of *Howl and Other Poems* was written by the San Francisco poet, Kenneth Rexroth, in 1957. Rexroth predicted that, "if he keeps going," Allen Ginsberg would become "the first genuinely popular, genuine poet in over a generation."(33) Rexroth criticized early reviews, even some of the favorable ones, for misreading "Howl" as a "destructive" poem: "Nothing goes to show how square the squares are so much as the *favorable* reviews they've given it. 'Sustained shrieks of frantic defiance,' 'single-minded frenzy of a raving madwoman,' 'paranoid memories,' 'childish obscenity'—they think it's all *so* negative." (32; author's italics) Against those interpretations, Rexroth countered with a rather different and more perceptive view of Ginsberg as a rescuer of important literary and utopian traditions: "It isn't at all violent. It is *your* violence it is talking about....Once Allen is through telling you what you have done to him and his friends, he concerns himself with the unfulfilled promises of *Song of Myself* and *Huckleberry Finn*, and writes a sutra about the sunflower that rises from the junk heap of civilization." (32-33)

Why was it difficult for so many readers of the day to see, even at a basic level, what the poems were doing? First, of course, there was ideological resistance to Ginsberg's leftist politics. And then there was the matter of Ginsberg's poetic style: his work re-awakened poetic traditions many literary scholars hoped would remain asleep. In 1961, Harvey Shapiro pointedly described these literary stakes: "Maybe the major reason for the resistance to Ginsberg is that he opens questions many poets and critics have an interest in considering closed." (90) As Shapiro noted, the influential critic R.P. Blackmur had, in a 1952 *Kenyon Review* article, pronounced the apocalyptic and surrealist traditions finished and announced the future domination of the "school of Donne." According to Shapiro, "When I first went to school to the quarterlies there was little doubt about the way American poetry was to go. Blackmur summed it up in an essay in *Kenyon Review* in 1952 ('Lord Tennyson's Scissors: 1912-1950'). The Apocalyptic and Violent school (Lindsay, Jeffers) and the other school of anti-intelligence (writers in *transition* who copied French poets like Apollinaire) were finished. The dominant school was to be the 'school of Donne' (described at one point as writers of 'a Court poetry, learned at its fingertips and full of a decorous willfulness called ambiguity')." (90-91) "Now," wrote Shapiro, "largely because of Ginsberg's work, we are not so sure. It will all have to be fought out again." (91) In a 1972 interview, Ginsberg framed the matter in similar terms: "The academic people were ignoring Williams and ignoring Pound and Louis Zukovsky and Mina Loy and Basil Bunting and most of the major rough writers of the Whitmanic, open form tradition in America." (*Composed*, 93)

It would be an exaggeration to proclaim that the school of "rough writers" has now outraced the "school of Donne" on the American academic track. But, certainly, contemporary theory has helped underscore the need to appreciate diverse literary endeavors, and even to replace the rigid boundaries between schools with porous fences. This has helped make it possible for an ever-widening range of U.S. and international literary scholars and anthology editors to acknowledge Ginsberg's poetry as among the most important of recent times.

Allen Ginsberg's groundbreaking poetry lifted off from the literary and social environment of mid-1950s America. For young, curious, and progressive intellectuals attempting to make sense of mid-1950s reality the need to develop new and alternative ways of seeing must have been desperately apparent. Politically, while Soviet atrocities of the Stalin era were becoming more widely known, the repressive atmosphere within the U.S. was growing more intense. Rigid Cold War ideologies forged a militaristic U.S. foreign policy that included engagement in the Korean War as well as various Third World interventions. In several instances, such as Iran in 1953 and Guatemala in 1954, the CIA was involved in the covert overthrow of democratically elected, left-leaning governments.

Cold War thinking also led to civil liberties-infringing domestic policies that chilled democratic dissent at home. Historian Howard Zinn describes the wide net cast by national attempts to inhibit dissent:

> Truman's executive order on loyalty in 1947 required the Department of Justice to draw up a list of organizations it decided were "totalitarian, fascist, communist or subversive .... or as seeking to alter the form of government by unconstitutional means." Not

> only membership in, but also "sympathetic association" with, any organization on the Attorney General's list would be considered in determining disloyalty.
>
> <div align="right">(<i>Twentieth Century,</i> 135)</div>

The 1950 Internal Security Act, sponsored by the McCarthy-led congressional Republicans, required the registration of organizations found to be "Communist-front." Between 1947 and 1952, over six-and-a-half million people had been investigated, and hundreds of domestic groups appeared on federal watch lists, including: "the Chopin Cultural Center, the Cervantes Fraternal Society, the Committee for the Negro in the Arts, the Committee for the Protection of the Bill of Rights." (*Twentieth Century,* 131-35) As Stephen Bronner observes, in the climate of McCarthyite paranoia, "often the very attempt to criticize the existing order became tantamount to treason and commensurate with communist leanings." (*Moments,* 93) On June 19, 1953, McCarthyite repression reached new heights with the execution of Julius and Ethel Rosenberg. As I.F. Stone put the matter succinctly in June 1954, "On the altar of security as thus established all else is to be sacrificed." (82)

Cold War limits on expression made evident only one of the gaps between America's liberal ideals and its less-than-liberal reality. Joe McCarthy had not only demonized political dissent; he had also denounced homosexuality. After McCarthy's criticism of the State Department for employing gays, the Senate in 1950 conducted an investigation into the employment of "homosexuals and other sex perverts" in the federal government, and in 1953 President Eisenhower signed an executive order that required the government's gay employees to be fired. Local police department raids on gay and lesbian bars and private parties were also common in the early 1950s.

Another obvious gulf between America's ideals and its daily reality was visible in the area of civil rights. A country that had only a decade earlier fought against the racist policies of Nazi Germany nonetheless fostered official racist policies of its own, in the form of Jim Crow laws, until 1954 when the Supreme Court finally struck down the doctrine of "separate but equal" in *Brown v. Board of Education.* Yet, even in 1954, as Zinn notes, the Supreme Court did not insist on an immediate change in practices but asked only for integration with "all deliberate speed." In fact, according to Zinn, as of 1965, three-quarters of Southern school districts remained segregated. (*Twentieth Century,* 152) The year 1955 saw the unfortunate acquittal of Emmett Till's murderers, as well as the beginning in December of the historic Montgomery bus boycott inspired by Rosa Parks, both of which effectively highlighted the era's entrenched racism. One hundred years after "Song of Myself," Walt Whitman's poetic vision for an enlightened and inclusive American democracy was a far cry from the view one saw on the nation's streets.

Cold War pressures demanded both ideological and cultural conformity. Alan Trachtenberg describes the day's dominant cultural images: "closed doors and drawn shades of suburban ranch-style houses joined the 'man in the gray flannel suit' as defining images of the conventional middle-class life." (300) The resultant sense of isolation which often ensued from those closed doors and drawn shades was framed as the inevitable fruit of social success.

For many young people opposed to such constricting political and cultural pressures, a sense of crisis was exacerbated by a real and growing apocalyptic fear of nuclear annihilation. Nuclear technology had become even more highly developed after atomic bombs were first dropped on Hiroshima and Nagasaki near the end of World War II. By the middle of the 1950s, nuclear weapons were routinely described as part of America's standard war arsenal. After an October 1954 speech by Field Marshal Lord Montgomery, I.F. Stone wrote: "It is sometimes assumed that we will not use nuclear weapons unless the enemy does. But Montgomery made clear....that we would use nuclear weapons for defense against attack, whether that attack was atomic or not. The decision has been made, the armed forces shaped, for atomic war." (88) In 1955, working under the belief that the potential use of nuclear weapons was entering a particularly urgent and dangerous phase, ten major American scientists and philosophers released an anti-nuclear statement, known as the Russell-Einstein Manifesto, named after two of its renowned signers, Bertrand Russell and Albert Einstein. That manifesto included the following warning, "Remember your humanity, and forget the rest." American leaders ignored such peace-activist calls for nuclear disarmament and instead promoted a national climate of Cold War-related fear, under which American school children pulled coats over their heads in school cafeteria drills that were still taking place in my own childhood school years of the mid-1960s. I.F. Stone captured the general apocalyptic threat felt by many: "The die that may mean the destruction of civilization is not only cast but loaded in advance." (89)

By the mid-1950s, varied segments of the left were energetically working to come up with new ideologies and strategies for opposing America's militaristic political environment and for building progressive alternatives. In his book, *If I Had a Hammer: The Death of the Old Left and the Birth of the New Left,* the historian Maurice Isserman explores, in depth, five of the important progressive tendencies that took shape in the 1950s. First, following the death of Stalin in 1953 and increasing revelations about the extraordinary levels of repression and murder that had occurred under his rule, the U.S. Communist Party began to allow and even encourage more public debate about left theory among its rank and file members. Secondly, the 1950s saw the rise of more determined organizing by democratic socialists like Max Schachtman who were deeply opposed to the "actually existing socialism" of the Soviet bloc and who were therefore committed to building left organizations that were simultaneously anti-capitalist and anti-communist. Michael Harrington, whose highly influential book, *The Other*

America, chronicled the story of poverty in the U.S., was a student of Schachtman's and later a cofounder of Democratic Socialists of America. Thirdly, new journals of the democratic left were created, the most influential being *Dissent,* founded by Irving Howe in early 1954. The 1950s also saw the growth of American pacifism as an influential movement against war and nuclear weapons, with the formation of several new groups expressly dedicated to nonviolence, including the National Committee for a Sane Nuclear Policy (SANE). In 1955, some of the key leaders of this movement—including Dorothy Day, A. J. Muste, Dave Dellinger, Ralph DiGia, Bayard Rustin, and Jim Peck—organized the first major act of group civil disobedience in the 1950s, coming together outside of City Hall in Manhattan and refusing to take shelter during a mandatory Civil Defense drill.[2] Lastly, Isserman describes the 1950s left as a period in which youth groups like the Student League for Industrial Democracy (SLID) took on new prominence, a factor that would help lead to the birth in the early 1960s of Students for a Democratic Society (SDS), the most influential group of the 1960s New Left.

Of course, the 1950s also saw the growth in numbers and influence of the modern civil rights movement, led by mid-decade by Martin Luther King, Jr., who had traveled to Montgomery to help organize the bus boycott. And, partly because economic conditions had not yet led working classes throughout the world to take power as some of the more orthodox Marxists of earlier eras had predicted, there was new importance being placed on the role of psychology and culture in shaping social conditions and institutions. French existentialists like Sartre and Camus were widely read, as was the social psychologist Erich Fromm, who is largely credited with introducing Americans to the philosophical ideas of the young Karl Marx—the Marx of *Economic and Philosophic Manuscripts of 1844,* who had focused on such topics as alienation. Fromm had written several popular books, including *Escape from Freedom* (1941), that focused on the social character of personal psychology and that helped popularize radical critiques of media and popular culture. These new philosophical and activist energies were in the air—and in left publications—in the years immediately preceding Allen Ginsberg's writing of "Howl." That poem beautifully captured the new oppositional energies of the time, and through Ginsberg's own literary skills and imagination, helped amplify these energies for generations to come.

"Howl" also helped create new progressive energies in the poetry world by challenging the New Critics' more impersonal and politically conservative aesthetics. In the realm of literature, opposition to industrial forms of capitalism had been ongoing since the Romantics. The early modernist experiments that followed were consistently anti-capitalist, albeit from diverse philosophical positions ranging from democratic-socialism to communism to fascism. In *The Politics of Modernism*, Raymond Williams observes the wide-ranging, protest-oriented ideas that could be found in the work of international modernists:

> In remaining anti-bourgeois, its representatives either chose the formerly aristocratic valuation of art as a sacred realm above money and commerce, or the revolutionary doctrines, promulgated since 1848, of art as the liberating vanguard of popular consciousness. Mayakovsky, Picasso, Silone, Brecht are only some examples of those who moved into direct support of Communism, and D'Annunzio, Marinetti, Wyndam Lewis, Ezra Pound of those who moved towards Fascism, leaving Eliot and Yeats in Britain and Ireland to make their muffled, nuanced treaty with Anglo-Catholicism and the celtic twilight.
>
> (*Politics*, 34)

But by the 1950s, international modernism had lost much of its oppositional energy. As Raymond Williams puts it,

"Modernism quickly lost its anti-bourgeois stance, and achieved comfortable integration into the new international capitalism." (*Politics*, 35) James Breslin describes this phenomenon as it appeared specifically in relation to American poetry: "a particular phase of modernism—that identified with Eliot and the New Criticism in America—had achieved a powerful hegemony which successfully domesticated modernism." (*Modern*, 13)

According to Breslin, the influence of T. S. Eliot—who had in 1927 proclaimed himself a "classicist in literature, royalist in politics, and anglo-catholic in religion"[3]—on American poets of the fifties concerned matters of literary form and style. It was an influence "associated with a specific set of attitudes and values, subtly defining the expectations of many readers and editors as well as writers of poetry; and this influence was transmitted most powerfully by the New Critics." (*Modern*, 15) As Breslin writes, "By the mid-fifties, Ransom's 'Criticism, Inc.' had arrived." (*Modern*, 17) The result was the privileging of: "Literary works, registering but not resolving contradictions," literary works that had "become self-reflexive, autonomous objects—not expressions of human emotion or criticisms of life." (*Modern*, 18) In *The Sacred Wood*, T. S. Eliot had declared: "Poetry is not a turning loose of emotion, but an escape from emotion; it is not the expression of personality, but an escape from personality." (58) Eliot's prosaic declarations—which, as a major poet, he was smart enough to ignore in many of his own best poems—were funneled by Ransom's *Criticism, Inc.* into a call for studying the methods by which poetry, according to Ransom, "secures 'aesthetic distance' and removes itself from history." (232)

Of course, the suppression of certain ideas can often reap unintended consequences. By undermining modernism's contentious spirit, America's New Critics unwittingly helped clear the path for a new poetry of energetic opposition to emerge. As Breslin observes: "ironically, it was largely the New Critics like Ransom and the young formalist poets he was praising who, by reducing modernism to an orthodoxy, helped make it into a doctrine that could be assailed by the new generation of poets." (*Modern*, 22)

Allen Ginsberg, steeped in left politics and alternative literary traditions, grew to oppose the whole gamut of 1950s political and cultural conformity, developing a poetry that—against New Critical dogma—was both deeply personal and quite willing to say what was on his mind about the world around him. His poetry would not be a poetry devoid of literary tradition, but one that would extend traditions that were well outside the dominant New Critical canon of the mid-1950s. In a 1954 letter to his brother, Eugene Brooks, Ginsberg had written: "I never saw the possibility of political poetry before but the international political situation seems to me to have at last palpably revealed its final necessary relation to moral or spiritual justice." (*Letters*, p. 99) Although I am not quite certain how literally we ought to take this statement of Ginsberg's to his brother, that he was only now first thinking about the possibility of political poetry—since Ginsberg had already put some politics into his poetry before 1954, since he was quite familiar by then with a wide range of political poets from Blake and Whitman to the political poets published in left journals like *The Masses* and *The New Masses,* and since he was certainly well-versed in a long pre-1950s history of domestic and international political injustices that had served as subject matter for important works of art and literature—I do think this can be seen as a noteworthy comment by Ginsberg of his express desire to begin writing the even more explicitly political works that would soon emerge in such essential mid-1950s Ginsberg poems as "Howl" and "America."

Ginsberg developed one of the 20th century's most important poetic voices through an inventive mix of literary and thematic explorations. In terms of style, he imaginatively integrated, expanded, and revised Whitman's long-lined oratory, William Carlos Williams' concern for American diction and cadence, Emily Dickinson's incisive and paradoxical condensations, African-American blues lyrics and bebop jazz rhythms, Biblical anaphoric phrasing and apocalyptic imagery, William Blake's techniques for channeling and depicting the imagination, Eastern verse forms, classical comedy and tragedy, and international modernism, especially French surrealism and Soviet futurism. In the arena of form, Ginsberg fulfilled Ezra Pound's dictum to "make it new" in the way that directive is interpreted by Frank Lentricchia: "Pound's famous avant-garde directive, 'make it new,' really means 'make contemporary what is old.'" (204)

Additionally, Ginsberg's expansion of poetry's oral tradition helped raise poetry off the page and into the public ear. His poetic voice was (and still is, thanks to various recording technologies of the last sixty years) an oral one as well as a written one, effectively helping to re-unite language with the body. Indeed, Ginsberg deserves primary credit for the exponential growth of poetry readings that first appeared in the late 1950s through the 1960s, and that has exploded more than ever since the last decade of the 20th century. This is especially significant in a consideration of poetry and politics, since in this television-and-internet age of so much stay-at-home entertainment, the resurgence of poetry readings has created new public spaces that provide additional opportunities for social meetings and public discussions, especially among young people. It is also important for our own period in which rising discontent is often coupled with a sense of political hopelessness that Allen Ginsberg's poems view social reality as mutable, dependent on human actions, and potentially open to dramatic improvement.

* * *

Allen Ginsberg grew up in an urban, working-class neighborhood of Paterson, New Jersey. According to biographer Michael Schumacher, "Allen's earliest friends were from poor working-class neighborhoods; he grew up among blacks and fellow Jews, witnessing the vile effects of racial prejudice and anti-Semitism." (8) Poetry and left-wing politics were always central to the Ginsberg household. Naomi, Allen's mother, who had emigrated from Russia at age 10 in 1905, was active in Paterson's Communist Party and would take Allen to local Party meetings where he would hear such noted left speakers from the time as Scott Nearing and Israel Amter. His father, Louis, was a widely published lyric poet who introduced Allen to poetry at an unusually early age. Schumacher notes that "Even as a toddler, he was exposed to poetry. Louis would move about their....apartment, reciting from memory the poetry of Dickinson, Poe, Shelley, Keats, and Milton as he did his daily chores." (7)

Ginsberg entered Columbia University in 1943 at age 17, and studied with a number of well-known literature professors, including Lionel Trilling, Mark Van Doren, and Raymond Weaver. In those years, he began writing rhymed, metaphysical verses in the style of poets like Marvell, Wyatt, and Blake. He also wrote some satirical lyrics for a Columbia University humor magazine. And he began to meet members of New York's bohemian subculture, some of whom would later become known along with Ginsberg as the Beat Generation, including Jack Kerouac and William Burroughs.

One of the first friends he met at Columbia was Lucien Carr, a classmate in Lionel Trilling's course. Carr was two years older than Ginsberg, and he introduced Ginsberg to New York's underground street life. Ginsberg met William Burroughs in 1944. Burroughs had graduated from Harvard University seven years earlier and was a grandson of the famous inventor of the adding machine. Even at a relatively young age, Burroughs had a fairly full history behind him, one that included short stints in the Army and in a psychiatric hospital, as well as the use of narcotics. Slightly older and more globally well-read, Burroughs encouraged Ginsberg's literary efforts and introduced him to the works of international writers who were not yet being studied much in American universities, including Kafka, Celine, Baudelaire, and Blake.

It was also at Columbia University that Ginsberg met Jack Kerouac, who had entered the school on a football scholarship. Ginsberg was impressed by Kerouac, who was the first athlete Ginsberg had met that seemed sensitive about life and knowledgeable about poetry. Ginsberg soon fell in love with Kerouac, and it was Kerouac to whom Ginsberg first opened up about being gay. As one of Ginsberg's biographers, Barry Miles, writes: "He believed Jack's tolerance gave him 'permission' to open up and talk about it."(55) Together, Kerouac, Ginsberg, and Burroughs enthusiastically studied alternative intellectual and cultural traditions that would later, in large part due to their own efforts, enter into America's popular culture.

Ginsberg would meet Neal Cassady, the hero of Kerouac's *On the Road* in 1946, and the poet Gregory Corso in 1950 at a Greenwich Village bar. Through the 1950s, many interesting writers came to be part of the circle we know today as the Beat Generation: Joyce Johnson, Elise Cowan, Herbert Huncke, Leroi Jones/Amiri Baraka, Hettie Jones, Bob Kaufman, Janine Pommy Vega, Gary Snyder, and others. These writers mutually inspired each other to search for a "New Vision" and more humane social arrangements, as well as new literary styles for fiction and poetry. In *Naked Angels*, John Tytell notes: "The Beats saw themselves as outcasts, exiles within a hostile culture, freaky progenitors of new attitudes toward sanity and ethics." (4-5) Tytell observes that, although the Beat Generation "lacked any shared platform such as the Imagist or Surrealist manifestos," it nonetheless "cohered as a literary group" since the "work of one informed the approach and style of another—in the way that Kerouac's prose line and aesthetic of spontaneity affected Ginsberg's poetic." (3)

In terms of stylistic influence, it was about 1948, as a result chiefly of having read the manuscript of Kerouac's first novel, *The Town and the City*, that Ginsberg realized that he wanted to move beyond his early experiments with rhymed verse. Those early rhymed metaphysical poems were often, however, passionate and haunting, such as these lyrics from the opening stanza of "A Mad Gleam":

> Go back to Egypt and the Greeks,
> Where the Wizard understood
> The spectre haunted where man seeks
> And spoke to ghosts that stood in blood.
>
> (CP, 24)

While Ginsberg's early experiments with rhymed verse, published in *Gates of Wrath* and *Empty Mirror*, were certainly not the poems that stamped his impact on American literature, they do show early evidence of his poetic curiosity, his grounding in traditional forms, his desire to explore large human themes, and his willingness to try on a variety of poetic voices. In "On Reading William Blake's 'The Sick Rose'," for instance, we see Ginsberg as a 22-year old poet taking literary risks in attempting to augment the work of a visionary poet and artist who would remain a lifelong influence, and trying to tackle such weighty, time-honored themes as immortality, death, and the existence of god:

> What everlasting force confounded
> In its being, like some human
> Spirit shrunken in a bounded
> Immortality, what Blossom
> Gathers us inward, astounded?
> Is this the sickness that is doom?
>
> (CP, 14)

Ginsberg's passionate attempts in poems like "Mad Gleam" to explore human mystery and paradox recall his early poetic influences, such as Thomas Campion (1567-1620) ("But fools do live, and waste their little light, / And seek with pain their ever-during night,"[4]) and Andrew Marvell (1621-1678) ("What magic could me thus confine / Within another's grief to pine?"[5]). One can easily imagine that the skeleton in Ginsberg's "Complaint of the Skeleton to Time"—"Take the thoughts that like the wind / Blow my body out of mind.... / But leave my bones alone" (CP, 25) —is a skeleton rescued from another of Ginsberg's early influences, Thomas Gray (1716-1771), who had noted that "Some frail memorial" is erected for the purpose of "these bones from insult to protect."[6] One can see in these poems early signs of a young poet with talents and energies trying to find a voice capable of building upon what he felt were important literary themes and traditions. Of course, one rarely knows at such an early stage how or whether such talents and energies will develop.

Ginsberg received a letter from William Carlos Williams in early 1950 that criticized his rhymed lyric mode: "In this mode, perfection is basic"[7]. "Perfection is basic" is, I would contend, a clear overstatement,[8] but Williams' note nonetheless helped spur Ginsberg to think and work harder to develop a more evolved and original poetic style.

Even before the letter from Williams, Ginsberg had already begun, in 1949, with his poem "Paterson," to experiment with free verse and with American speech idiom. "Paterson" begins with the poet reflecting upon the difficulty of understanding one's own true desires in a society obsessed by gross materialism: "What do I want in these rooms papered with visions of money?" (CP, 48) Here, Ginsberg veers away from the Elizabethan-rhymed style of his earlier lyrics and utilizes a longer, Whitmanic-length, free-verse line:

> How much can I make by cutting my hair? If I put
>   new heels on my shoes,
> bathe my body reeking of masturbation and sweat,
>   layer upon layer of excrement
> dried in employment bureaus, magazine hallways,
>   statistical cubicles, factory stairways.
>   (CP, 48)

"Paterson" accuses America's dominant culture of placing

unhealthy and arbitrary limits on human emotions and sexuality. Targets of reproach include factories, bad psychiatry, department store bosses, war, and repressed sexual desire. Addressing themes that would be further explored in "Howl," "Paterson" proposes madness and drugs as simultaneously an alternative to, and the result of, contemporary social trappings: "I would rather go mad, gone down the dark road to Mexico, heroin dripping in my veins, / eyes and ears full of marijuana." (CP, 48) Unlike "Howl," this pre-"Howl" poem ends pessimistically with Ginsberg expressing a preference for gory escapist death rather than the more distasteful choice of participating in a conformist, industrial society: "blood streaming from my belly and shoulders," laid out "by the bayoux and forests and derricks leaving my flesh and my bones hanging on the trees." (CP, 48-49) As I will argue shortly, one of the key advances of "Howl" will be the way in which Ginsberg is able to envision a path beyond his earlier poem's depressing choice of either resignation or escape.

By 1953, Ginsberg was experimenting more widely with different forms of free verse and with the inclusion of American speech diction, initiating the sorts of experiments that would soon alter the nation's poetry map. In "The Green Automobile" (1953), he examines the role and power of poetic vision, using a four-line cascading form that employs American jargon and humor:

> If I had a Green Automobile
>   I'd go find my old companion
>   in his house on the Western ocean.
>   Ha! Ha! Ha! Ha! Ha!
>   (CP, 91)

In the repetition of "Ha! Ha!," we can see Ginsberg beginning to venture into ecstatic language as one way to express fantasy and possibility—the "ha ha's" would soon turn into the "holy holy's" of "Footnote to Howl." Imagination in the form of the green automobile "which I have invented /

imagined and visioned" (CP, 91) enables a spiritual union to take place between two friends living on opposite ends of the continent, a union that can be seen as a precursor to the solidarity with Carl Solomon expressed in the third section of "Howl." "The Green Automobile" shows Ginsberg exploring the relationship between imagination and the material world, and using a mix of conversational and lofty diction that would become his hallmark by the decade's end.

* * *

"Howl" (1955-56) was Ginsberg's breakthrough poem that combined fully developed poetic and political explorations. In the nearly sixty years since the poem's publication, it has deservedly become one of the most widely read and influential poems of the 20th century. As one can tell from early audience reactions—the bursts of laughter and applause on early recordings—, "Howl" astonished even those familiar with Ginsberg's work up until that time, stunning readers and listeners with its linguistic and oratorical energy, its striking imagery, its mix of empirical perception and surreal imagination, its extension of previously undervalued literary precursors, its dynamic willingness to explode widely accepted cultural and political dogma, its assertions of honest selfhood and sexuality against a repressive culture, and its relentless search for a more fulfilling life-world.

"Howl" is structured like many meaningful projects in politics, psychology, or science. A problem is first examined, so that it can be identified. Once the problem is identified, a solution is proposed—and, if the solution seems like a potentially effective one, the project's designer celebrates.

Formally, one notices immediately that "Howl" extends the long lines of Blake, Whitman, and biblical psalms. Interestingly, if one looks at the 1986 *Annotated Howl*, one can see that the long-lined form of the poem's first section developed gradually over several subsequent drafts. This compelling line-lengthening is probably Ginsberg's major stylistic contribution to American verse forms. I do not want to claim as any kind of universal theory that formal poetic innovations will always carry a particular political significance, since similar poetic forms can be used to promote a wide variety of political ideas. But, in the case of "Howl," as I have already described in the previous chapter, I believe that Ginsberg's extension of the line length used by his predecessors, Blake and Whitman, carried an implication of an even more radical project than theirs: as the lines continually refuse to stop at the right-hand margin of the page, they imply a strenuous effort to free the poetic line, and by extension the culture at large, from restrictive boundaries. Ginsberg titled an essay from 1961 with a quote from Plato— "When the Mode of the Music Changes, the Walls of the City Shake."[9] In that essay, he wrote that conventional form is too symmetrical and pre-fixed. His line-lengthening was thus meant to break out of the imprisonment of "pre-fixed" forms by swinging the gates of the city's walls open even further than Whitman had swung them. When that original 1961 essay was published decades later in *Deliberate Prose*, Ginsberg added an author's note that included his belief in the connection between political liberty and more open-ended poetic forms, his belief in "a political liberty that could only be defended by undaunted, free, bold humorous imagination, open field mentality, open field poetics, open field democracy. The closed forms of the older poetry, it seemed to me, were ostrich-head-in-sand-like. It seemed to me that breakthroughs of new poetry were social breakthroughs, that is, political in the long run." (*Deliberate Prose*, 253)

In my pointing out that this line-lengthening was an important Ginsbergian contribution to literary forms, I do not want to suggest that he was the first to use lines of this length, nor even the first to utilize them with an implied political intent. In the 1930s, some of the leftist poets published in journals like *The New Masses* and in anthologies like *Proletarian Literature in the United States*, edited by Granville Hicks and Mike Gold, used lines that also extended Whitman's. Kenneth Fearing's poem protesting both capitalist economics and personal conformity, "No Credit," contained lines that were quite similar in length to the lines in the first section of "Howl":

> only Steve, the side-show robot, knows content; only Steve, the mechanical man in love with a photo-electric beam, remains aloof; only Steve, who sits and smokes or stands in salute, is secure. [10]

In the Hicks and Gold anthology, Richard Wright's "Between the World and Me," describing a lynching, and Mike Gold's "A Strange Funeral in Braddock," about the death of a steel worker, also feature lines of the approximate length and shape of many of the lines in Part I of "Howl":

> My voice was drowned in the roar of their voices, and my black wet body slipped and rolled in their hands as they bound me to the sapling. [11]

> And he forgets to be as hard as steel and remembers only his wife's breasts, his baby's little laughters and the way men sing when they are drunk and happy.[12]

Another poem written before "Howl" that utilized lines of approximately the length and shape of "Howl" was Margaret Walker's compelling 1937 civil rights poem, "For My People":

> For my people blundering and groping and floundering in the dark of churches and schools and clubs and societies, associations and councils and committees and conventions, distressed and disturbed and deceived and

> devoured by money-hungry, glory-craving leeches, preyed on by facile force of state and fad and novelty, by false prophet and holy believer.[13]

I am not sure which of these poems or poets Ginsberg may have read before writing "Howl," but because he grew up in a left household with a poet father, it seems likely that he had seen many of these long-lined poets from the 30s and 40s in left journals and working-class poetry anthologies of his youth. Indeed, interestingly, in "When the Mode of the Music Changes, the Walls of the City Shake," Ginsberg alludes to this wing of the American poetry tradition, while adamantly asserting that his influences in coming up with the long lines of "Howl" were not Fearing and the proletarian poets:

> How often have I seen my own work related to Fearing and Sandburg, proletarian literature, the 1930s—by people who don't *connect* my long line with my own obvious reading: Crane's *Atlantis*, Lorca's *Poet in NY*, Biblical structures, psalms and lamentations, Shelley's high buildups, Apollinaire, Artaud, Mayakovsky, Pound, Williams, and the American metrical tradition, the new tradition of measure. And Christopher Smart's *Rejoice in the Lamb*. And Melville's prose-poem *Pierre*. And finally the spirit and illumination of Rimbaud. Do I have to be stuck with Fearing (who's alright too) by phony critics whose only encounter with a long line has been anthology pieces in collections by Oscar Williams?
>
> (*Deliberate Prose*, 249)

As a poet with obvious social convictions, why would Ginsberg be so resolute at the time in distancing himself from proletarian poets like Kenneth Fearing, even as he was sure to add in that Fearing was a capable poet? I say "at the time" because later, when writing endnotes for the 1986 *Annotated Howl*, Ginsberg described his line-lengthening this way: "to expand the line beyond that of Christopher Smart, as on occasion Whitman did, and the modernist Kenneth Fearing, more loosely. Paragraphic prose poetry by Rimbaud and St.-John Perse provided more electric model." (*Original Draft Facsimile,* 130) The key phrases here are "more loosely" and "more electric." Even though the long lines of some of these earlier leftist poets may well have been part of Ginsberg's poetic consciousness before "Howl," he seems to have felt that they had not utilized the long lines to their fullest potential in terms of poetic quality—that those earlier poets' lines were too flat or prose-like for his own more energetic poetic tastes. In a 1976 postcard which I cited in my earlier chapter that Ginsberg had sent to my friend Danny Shot, Allen had warned Danny to make sure his line would "not be just flat prose." In "Howl," the formal contribution that Ginsberg gave to American literature was to develop a long line that seemed new and different—more densely packed and more electric.

Infused with the rhythms of Kerouac's recent prose and bebop jazz—the latter carrying, among other things, an implicit rejection of 1950s racial segregation through its embrace of an African American-invented musical form—as well as an expert use of traditional poetic elements like alliteration and assonance, the long lines of "Howl" sparkled with vitality, and held together as fully energized units tightly packed with a mix of lively perceptions, dazzling imagination, humor, and resourceful wordplay capable of keeping readers and listeners thoroughly engaged as if hooked for the long haul to the poet's voice. In lines like "storefront boroughs of teahead joyride neon blinking traffic light, sun and moon and tree vibrations in the roaring winder dusks of Brooklyn, ashcan rantings and kind king light of mind," (CP, 134) we feel the excitement of a lengthy improvisational riff typical of the burgeoning contemporary jazz scene, and it makes sense when Ginsberg himself says that he was thinking of the musician Lester Young's "Lester Leaps In," along with Kerouac's recent prose, when initially contemplating the poem's oratorical rhythms.[14] Marjorie Perloff contrasts the consistently forward flow of Whitman's long lines with Ginsberg's rhythms that feel more like "a bumping and grinding that vocalizes the poet's feverish intensity." (209)

While magnifying the projects of poetic innovators like Whitman and Williams[15], "Howl" uses assonance ("ashcan rantings," "light of mind") and alliteration ("hollow-eyed and high," "battered bleak of brain all drained of brilliance") to provide rhythm within the long lines and another traditional device, anaphora, to connect the long lines of Part I to each other. Walt Whitman had incorporated the biblical technique of anaphora to provide a rhythmic device for some of the free verse of "Song of Myself":

> Through me many long dumb voices,
> Voices of the interminable generations of slaves,
> Voices of prostitutes and of deformed persons,
> Voices of the diseased and despairing, and of thieves and dwarfs[16]

Ginsberg uses anaphora—the repetition of "who"—in a similar fashion, as a way to build connections and a rhythmic momentum between the lines and themes of Part I. Other poetic elements adopted in Howl" include 20th-century modernist forms, especially French surrealists and Russian futurists, whose work Ginsberg had been reading in recent years, as well as the kinds of biblical forms and themes, including apocalyptic ones, that William Blake had previously embraced as part of his visionary notion of poet as radical community prophet.

In "'Howl' Revisited: The Poet as Jew," Alicia Ostriker observes that the notion of a poet-prophet has always been a rather diversely interpreted literary idea:

> The notion of the poet as prophet is a loose one. From the Greek prophetes, interpreter or proclaimer, or one who speaks for a deity, the term has been used in the English tradition since the late eighteenth century to denote a variety of sublimities opposed to neoclassic rationality. Jean Wojcik and Raymond-Jean Frontain define a "prophetic" stance in Western art as implying private vision, an insistence on the righteousness of the prophet and the corruption of his society, passionate and hyperbolic language, social radicalism, stylistic obscurity or incoherence, and "obsession, fine or frenzied," as "with every technique of language he can muster, the prophet delivers a message that never arrives."
>
> ("Howl" Revisited, 28)

Ostriker then insightfully notes the parallels between "Howl" and the Lamentations of Jeremiah. In a 1965 interview with Tom Clark, Ginsberg asserts that prophecy works "because it touches a common key….what prophecy actually is is not that you actually know that the bomb will fall in 1942. It's that you know and feel something which somebody knows and feels in a hundred years."[17]

In extending the traditions of Blake and Whitman—one hundred years after Whitman's "Song of Myself"—, Ginsberg re-energized a prophetic tradition in poetry that has since become more widely acknowledged in part because of the ways in which a poem like "Howl" reshapes our ideas about literary history and about the social and political potential of poetry.

* * *

"Howl" begins with one of the most quoted opening lines in American poetry: "I saw the best minds of my generation destroyed by madness, starving hysterical naked." As Alicia Ostriker notes, after the poem's first line, the poet immerses his own self into the intensely described fabric of the poem:

> After the initial "I saw," the first-person singular pronoun evaporates. The "I" releases itself, or is released, into its material....we have no sense of him as a controlled being apart, capable of observing, interpreting, judging, explaining. Instead of shaping, he appears to let himself be shaped, spontaneously and irrationally, by his "visions." In other words, Ginsberg "becomes what he beholds."
> (Blake, Ginsberg, 120)

Ostriker's citation ("becomes what he beholds") refers to Los, the poet-prophet figure of William Blake's epic poems. In each of Blake's long prophecies, as Ostriker observes, the prophet undergoes a "descent into the sickness of our life." (Blake, Ginsberg, 118) Indeed, after the initial "I saw," Ginsberg tosses aside traditional poetic cautions—like the then-dominant New Critical notion of poetic detachment—and descends relatively unshielded into the social turbulence of his day.

Ginsberg's relinquishment of self, his descent into turmoil, in the first section of "Howl" is illuminating on many levels, not merely the social. In literary-biographical terms, we can see his willingness to dive into the belly of the American beast as a literary act of commitment for a 1950s U.S. poet who rejects the choice of escapism, a choice taken by several of Ginsberg's key predecessors, including T.S. Eliot and Ezra Pound, who each moved to Europe. It also shows an evolving ability to move beyond the escapism of his own earlier poetry described above in "Paterson."

In psychological terms, we might read this allegorical descent as an attempt to work through difficult or painful emotional issues instead of avoiding or denying them. Rather than the more popular Freud, it might be suggestive to discuss the psychological dynamics of "Howl" in Reichian terms, since Ginsberg had engaged in Reichian psychotherapy in 1948, having been introduced to Wilhelm Reich's visionary and controversial work by William Burroughs several years earlier. Reich's theory of character analysis included the assertion that people develop a character "armor" which segregates one's daily behavior from one's natural, and healthier, human instincts. According to Reich, "The surface layer of social cooperation is not in contact with the deep biologic core of one's selfhood; it is borne by a *second*, an intermediate character layer, which consists exclusively of cruel, sadistic, lascivious, rapacious, and envious impulses." (*Mass Psychology*, p. xi) For Reich, the armor is theorized dialectically. On the negative side, it keeps a person distanced from his or her own natural qualities, and reduces a person's capacity for pleasure. Yet it simultaneously plays some positive roles by at least temporarily protecting an individual from being too severely affected by otherwise traumatic experiences with the external world. In Reichian terms, Ginsberg's symbolic act of self-descent in part I of "Howl" depicts a therapeutic maneuver to shed his human character armor—to move into the world unprotected in order to see it with an unobstructed view, and to work through traumatic elements and experiences in order to reach a more natural and pleasurable state of being.

Like Reich's idea of character armor, the view of madness expressed in the first line of "Howl" is also dialectical. Ginsberg had grown up with, and taken care of, a mentally ill mother who was often the source of frustration, sadness, and embarrassment. And yet, Naomi Ginsberg was simultaneously capable of acute social insights and a spirited brand of activism, capabilities that her son deeply admired as he watched her help organize Communist Party events in working-class Paterson, New Jersey. From his complex relationship with his mother, Ginsberg seems to have sensed early in life that the psychological trauma that could drive someone toward paranoia, depression, or psychosis could also catalyze extraordinary passion, shrewd political thinking, and brave personal deeds.

This early perception of what we might call a madness/transcendence dialectic was later confirmed in his college-age encounters with bohemian literary figures like William Burroughs and Carl Solomon, both of whom, along with Ginsberg himself, spent some time in psychiatric hospitals. The dialectic becomes one of the major organizing themes of "Howl," in which, as James Breslin notes, "an exhausting and punishing *immersion* in the most sordid of contemporary realities issues in *transcendent* vision." (*Modern to Contemporary*; 97; author's italics)

On the political level, by plunging the self into social turbulence at the beginning of "Howl," Ginsberg is able to look behind America's curtains of conventional propriety and denial to see and feel how repressive aspects of culture are actually affecting people, particularly young people around the poet's age who were longing for more fulfilling lives and a more welcoming society. The exploration includes an energetic examination of both worldly details and metaphysical imagination—in so doing, Ginsberg finds a way to connect his Williams-influenced concern for empirical observation with his Blake-influenced interest in prophetic imagination. Breslin notes that it is this dynamic linking of "the visionary and the concrete, the language of mystical illumination and the language of the street" (*Modern to Contemporary*; 97) that will empower the poet to reach transcendent insights.

Diving into the world, the poet of "Howl" sees "the best minds" of his generation grappling desperately to overcome deep feelings of frustration, alienation, depression, and a wide range of unfulfilled desires. The Holocaust-survivor psychiatrist Viktor Frankl labeled this sort of spiritual crisis "existential frustration" or "existential vacuum," where existential refers to the striving for meaning in one's personal experience. (See 123-28) Frankl believed that existential vacuum was widespread in the twentieth century, and he believed that it was a byproduct of conformism and totalitarianism. Writing originally in 1945, Frankl claimed that a survey revealed that 25 percent of his European students at the time showed a marked degree of existential vacuum, but "among my American students it was not 25 but 60 percent.... Such widespread phenomena as depression, aggression and addiction are not understandable unless we recognize the existential vacuum underlying them." (129) With Frankl's observations in mind, it becomes easy to see why "Howl" hit a nerve, and probably why it continues to hit a nerve, among such a broad section of American youth looking for more significance or meaning in life.

Because of this existential frustration, people are, according to Frankl, "even ready to suffer, on the condition, to be sure, that....suffering has a meaning." (136) In developing the idea of suffering as part of the search for meaning, Frankl utilizes a double-sided notion similar to Ginsberg's conception of madness: "suffering is not always a pathological phenomenon; rather than being a symptom of neurosis, suffering may well be a human achievement, especially if the suffering grows out of existential frustration." (124-25) In Frankl's view, shaped by his own concentration camp experiences, "everything can be taken from a man but one thing: the last of the human freedoms—to choose one's attitude in any given set of circumstances, to choose one's own way."(86)

Of course, Ginsberg's post-WWII best minds are not in a concentration camp; they are free not only to choose an attitude but to act, in a nation with constitutionally protected freedoms, in order to try to find meaning in their lives. Their wide-ranging responses to existential frustration range from healthy, energetic efforts to achieve self-integration to rash, self-destructive acts to stifle the pain. To find a nonconformist existential fulfillment, Ginsberg's compatriots look to alternative spiritual and literary traditions ("seeking visionary indian angels who were visionary indian angels," "who studied Plotinus Poe St. John of the Cross telepathy and bop kabbalah"); to jazz ("who lounged hungry and lonesome through Houston seeking jazz"); to drugs ("Peyote solitidies of halls"); and to sexual exploration ("who copulated ecstatic and insatiate"). Impatience with status quo and self leads Ginsberg's best minds to frenetic travel that in the double-edged spirit of Part I is clearly preferable to staying put, but that does not quite succeed in resolving his protagonists' weighty needs:

> who barreled down the highways of the past journeying
> to each other's hotrod-Golgotha jail-solitude watch
> or Birmingham jazz incarnation,
> who drove crosscountry seventytwo hours to find out if I
> had a vision or you had a vision or he had a vision to
> find out Eternity
> who journeyed to Denver, who died in Denver, who came
> back to Denver & waited in vain.
> (CP, 137)

As John Tytell recognizes, there is a "propelling, torrential quality" (19) to Ginsberg's long lines, a torrential quality that perfectly undergirds the vigorous endeavors described.

Amid such a torrent, it only makes sense that empirical perceptions would often seem blurred. It may be tempting to see the images and events described in Part I as empirical perception: after all, the section begins with a declaration of witness ("I saw"). But even a cursory glance at the imagery of Part I ("who disappeared into the volcanoes of Mexico leaving behind nothing but the shadow of dungarees and the lava and ash of poetry scattered in fireplace Chicago") reveals that the witnessing of "Howl" is a rather expressionistic one. This is not literal testimony, but a fusing of the real and the surreal. The "I saw" of "Howl" looks at the real world, but it also looks beyond it ("their heads shall be crowned with laurel in oblivion"). It witnesses the outward acts of real people ("who jumped off the Brooklyn Bridge this actually happened"), but it also impressionistically attempts to transmit a compendium of inner psychic adventures ("who ate the lamb stew of the imagination or digested the crab at the muddy bottom of the rivers of Bowery").

The Port Huron Statement, the 1962 document penned mostly by Tom Hayden that became the manifesto of Students for a Democratic Society (SDS), begins with a line whose rhythm seems reminiscent of the opening lines of "Howl": "We are people of this generation, bred in at least modest comfort, housed now in universities, looking uncomfortably to the world we inhabit."[18] The SDS statement goes on to describe the day's social environment in the clear language of political history and philosophy:

> When we were kids the United States was the wealthiest and strongest country in the world: the only one with the atom bomb, the least scarred by modern war, an initiator of the United Nations that we thought would distribute Western influence throughout the world. Freedom and equality for each individual, government of, by, and for the people—the American values we found good, principles by which we could live as men. Many of us began maturing in complacency.
>
> As we grew, however, our comfort was penetrated by events too troubling to dismiss. First, the permeating and victimizing fact of human degradation, symbolized by the Southern struggle against racial bigotry, compelled most of us from silence to activism. Second, the enclosing fact of the Cold War, symbolized by the presence of the Bomb, brought awareness that we ourselves, and our

friends, and millions of abstract "others" we knew more directly because of our common peril, might die at any time.[19]

I include this excerpt from the beginning of the Port Huron Statement to highlight some potential distinctions between the language of quality poetry and the language of a quality political essay. The goal of the Port Huron Statement was to develop an effective organizing tool that would persuade large numbers of young people, by virtue of its compelling logic and accuracy, to consider joining SDS. In "Howl" Part I, historical accuracy is only one of a number of concerns—with others including an exploration of emotional, spiritual, and artistic dynamics.

In the simultaneously realist and surrealist catalog of Part I, a few of Ginsberg's "best minds" try left-wing protest in order to overcome their growing sense of social alienation: "who distributed Supercommunist pamphlets in Union Square weeping." (CP, 135) In this line, as indicated in an endnote to the *Annotated Howl*, Ginsberg was thinking of a 1955 peace rally with such diverse participants as Dorothy Day, Bayard Rustin, Judith Malina, and A.J. Muste. Additionally, some best minds "burned cigarette holes in their arms protesting the narcotic tobacco haze of Capitalism." (CP, 135) Yet, overall in Part I, political protest seems only a small part of his protagonists' struggles to obtain self-fulfillment, and there is little explicit emphasis in Part I on political repression as a root cause of his friends' despair, loneliness, impatience, and rage.

Indeed, "Howl" Part I is not heavily political in a traditional pre-1950s leftist sense. The group that Ginsberg unites under the banner of "best minds" is not a traditional class-based collective on the left. Rather, Ginsberg has poetically developed—by symbolically connecting people through the anaphoric repetition of "who"—an alternate basis for unity, a grouping of young people united in their desperation for more existentially meaningful lives. Significantly, this new assemblage that Ginsberg has created—based on generational concerns about spirituality, psychology, and culture, as well as politics and the economy—prefigures what would a decade later become a widespread American youth counterculture and a youth-led New Left.

Whether political, spiritual, or cultural, the energetic attempts to find fulfillment, salvation or enlightenment in the poem's first section—although viewed largely by the poet with considerable empathy or admiration and as far preferable to passive acceptance of a toxic status quo—ultimately prove unsuccessful, at least for the moment. Later, after lessons are drawn from the various explorations, the sufferings of Part I will prove transformative. But, for now, people get "busted in their pubic beards" and end up experiencing "waking nightmares" in their search for redemptive dreams. Attempts at escapism prove fruitless. Those who bid to remove themselves from society's material restraints end up with alarm clocks falling "on their heads every day for the next decade." (CP, 137) As for the peace activists in Part I, those engaging in the sort of civic participation that social psychologists like Erich Fromm were suggesting was necessary to combat alienation, the Pentagon bomb-makers squash their outspoken efforts: "the sirens of Los Alamos wailed them down." (CP, 135)

Near the end of Part I, the last shred of hope for improved conditions seems to disappear: with the "last fantastic book flung out of the tenement window," "the last door closed," and "mother finally ******." (CP, 138) It is at this moment, when the poem's narrative exudes a dire pessimism, that the poet shifts focus, turning attention directly to the problem at hand, in this case toward the explicit issue of poetic technique. In the structure of the poem, it is this reflection on poetic technique and poetic imagination that inspires the emergence of new substantive possibilities.

At the end of Part I, Ginsberg begins to recognize—in poetry's wide-ranging stylistic toolbox, which obviously includes the imagination as one of its most important tools—

the possibility of hope, the potential of creating alternative, redemptive spaces within a constrictive society. By using surreal imagery ("the ghostly clothes of jazz"), modernist montage ("hydrogen jukebox"), and suprarational discourse ("mother finally ******"), the poet can create "incarnate gaps in Time & Space through images juxtaposed." (CP, 138) In other words, poetry can construct "gaps" within dominant culture, since it can portray elements or images that do not yet exist in the actual world (but only in the "archangel of the soul"). These are Ernst Bloch's "anticipatory illuminations," described in the previous chapter, portending the possibility of a future world transformed for the better out of the present.

For the author of "Howl," in appropriating Blake's idea of the poet's prophetic role, poetic imagination and experimentation become understood as means to envision healthier social and psychological possibilities. Part I ends by alluding to Jesus' last words on the cross. The implication is that a psychic sacrifice, accomplished through an unarmored, self-relinquishing poetic immersion into the social disorder of the day—ripping away the curtains of denial in order to take an honest look at one's world and one's place in it—offers the best hope of self and social transformation.

In addition to providing anticipatory illuminations, the technique of modernist montage also invites audience participation in the creation of meaning. Because montage does not contain a clear narrative logic, it requires, as Ginsberg notes in the liner notes to *Holy Soul Jelly Roll!*, a "mind interpreting sense to it."(Liner Notes, 8) Or, in the words of Stephen Bronner, modernist forms of art can "foster individual responsibility insofar as the audience is made to take part in the active construction of something new." (*Of Critical Theory*, 175) The jazz rhythms of the poem may similarly encourage this sense of building a dialogue between poet and reader, as Richard Quinn argues in discussing bebop jazz and the poetics of Beat improvisation: "As consumers, listeners took the musical statements offered by the musicians, considered these statements through an engaged intellect and feeling, and made the music personally meaningful. As such, the music both expressed its own internal meaning and became a dialogic material for the creation of additional meaning." (153)

The work's modernist language and bebop rhythms thus seem to urge readers to see themselves as part of a kind of dialogue that helps shape the ultimate meanings of the poem. Ginsberg's "best minds," after all, refer only in part to his personal friends and acquaintances—and to his own autobiography as Marjorie Perloff observes.[20] Because the catalogs of Part I do not name names, readers are free to find places in which to insert their own identities and desires into the text. We might even say that, because it encourages reader participation, the poem implicitly entreats its audience to choose whether to sympathize with the countercultural community Ginsberg is creating or with the dominant institutions from which that community is rebelling. Some readers may even see how the poem's vast progressive energies can move beyond even its own author's comprehension, which may help explain, for one example, why "Howl" has been cited by so many contemporary feminist poets as inspirational, even though it admittedly did not explore dominant gender dynamics in the way that it explored so many other important issues of the day. By nurturing readers' subjectivities and sense of choice, the poem's modernist elements offer additional challenge to the sort of institutional pressures toward conformity that have been driving the poem's protagonists mad.

* * *

Just what is it that has been driving the poem's protagonists mad? Where did these institutional pressures originate? Part II of "Howl" begins: "What sphinx of cement and aluminum bashed open their skulls and ate up their brains and imagination?" Now that Ginsberg has undertaken a full-immersion tour of his contemporary society, exploring symptoms of alienation and desperation among his generation, he is able to define the social source of those symptoms.

Part II displays a radical shift in the poet's approach. Rather than continue to narrate or describe, here the poet analyzes and declares. This section is also far more explicitly political than the first section. In the process of narrating the experiences of his protagonists in Part I, Ginsberg created an implicit countercultural community. Now that the poet is drawing lessons and uncovering the causes of a community's maladies, the focus moves to an even more collective and public level.

In this section, various sources of repression are grouped together and named Moloch, after the Canaanite fire god who was worshiped by the sacrifice of children, as mentioned in the biblical books of Joshua, Kings, and Jeremiah. James Breslin notes that, in "Howl," the figure of Moloch "stands broadly for authority—familial, social, literary." (*Modern to Contemporary,* 101) Along these lines, Tony Trigilio writes that Ginsberg "builds systems that, paradoxically, attempt to undo the dominant impulse toward system-building." *(Prophecies, 174)* But, although Trigilio, as a member of the Beat Studies Association, has written some of the most important and insight-filled recent scholarly work on Ginsberg's poems[21], I think it would be a mistake to fit Ginsberg's ideas into a kind of postmodern "anti-system" theoretical framework. Rather than opposing all notions of "authority" and "system-building," it seems to me that it is the particularly repressive characteristics of actually existing authority and systems that Ginsberg is criticizing. Along these lines, the radical social psychologist Erich Fromm in *Escape from Freedom* had distinguished between "rational authority" (as in a healthy teacher-student relationship or in a democratically accountable governing institution) and "inhibiting authority," in which "superiority serves as a basis for exploitation." (163) Ginsberg, I would argue, does not rule out the hoped-for possibility of developing far more humane and democratic systems in the future. Indeed, in many ways it is the vision of just such a long-term possibility that I would argue seems to drive so much of "Howl," as well as Ginsberg's later work. In a 1965 interview with Tom Clark, Ginsberg made this point about system-building explicit: "Another century has gone, technology has changed everything completely, so it's time for a new utopian system." (*Spontaneous Mind,* 33) In "Death to Van Gogh's Ear!," Ginsberg similarly describes this view—in humorous and poetic terms that are nonetheless substantively clear:

> fortunately all the governments will fall
> the only ones which won't fall are the good ones
> and the good ones don't yet exist
> But they have to begin existing they exist in my poems.
>
> (CP, 176)

As many literary scholars have pointed out, there are clear similarities between Allen Ginsberg's Moloch and William Blake's Urizen ("Times on times he divided, & measur'd / Space by space in his ninefold darkness"[22]). Each is a figure that embraces an instrumental reason divorced from human emotion and imagination. It is the instrumental and exploitative character of present institutional structures, rather than any inherent notion of authority or system-building, that leads to social injustice and that can contribute to self-fragmentation.

As mentioned earlier, the 1950s were years in which wide segments of the American left were re-evaluating received ideas. As the subtitle of historian Maurice Isserman's book, *If I Had a Hammer*[23] indicates, it was the decade that saw the death of the old left and the creation of the new. Many key figures on the left, from Frankfurt school theorists like Adorno and Horkheimer to the American writer Dwight McDonald, were focusing more attention on the roles played by culture and psychology than had the more orthodox left of previous eras. As early as 1944, Dwight McDonald had written in *Partisan Review:* "The deadening and warping effect of long exposure to movies, pulp magazines and radio can hardly be overestimated." [24] According to Isserman, by the 1950s, "Learning to understand mass culture thus seemed to many intellectuals a matter of political self-defense, even of survival." (*Hammer*, 99) In the second issue of *Dissent* magazine, Erich Fromm noted how psychological issues ought also to be considered paramount: In America, Fromm contended, he found growing numbers of psychological "automatons," the sort of person who "never experiences anything which is really his....whose smiles have replaced laughter; whose meaningless chatter has replaced communicative speech; whose dulled despair has taken the place of genuine pain." [25]

One of the most influential social analysts of the mid-1950s was the radical sociologist C. Wright Mills, author of such popular "Howl"-era volumes as *White Collar* and *The Power Elite*. Although Ginsberg mentions reading Mills in a letter to his father in 1961 (*Family Business,* 145), I am not sure whether he had read Mills by the time of "Howl." But Mills' political ideas were circulating in progressive publications and in the activist environment Ginsberg inhabited, and it was Mills who is largely credited with popularizing the term "New Left" in the United States. It is also interesting to note that Mills was the subject of graduate theses written by two of the early cofounders of SDS, Tom Hayden and Bob Ross.

Many of the ideas of C. Wright Mills parallel, and can help illuminate, those ideas found in "Howl," especially in the poem's Part II. Mills rejected, as inadequate for the 1950s era, much of orthodox Marxism's economics-privileging language and analysis, including the old left idea that the working class would necessarily be the main agent of social change. Yet Mills insisted on the need for more radical ideas than those offered by the tradition of American liberalism: "the liberal ethos, as developed in the first two decades of this century by such men as Beard, Dewey, Holmes, is now often irrelevant, and....the Marxian view, popular in the American 'thirties, is now often inadequate. However important and suggestive they may be as beginning points, and both are that, they do not enable us to understand what is essential to our time." (*White Collar*, p. xx)

In Mills' opinion, a new, broad "power elite" was now "in command of the major hierarchies and organizations of modern society. They rule the big corporations. They run the machinery of the state and claim its prerogatives. They direct the military establishment." (*Power Elite*, 4) Observing post-WWII pressures toward personal conformity, Mills described a new white collar class in which "the malaise is deep-rooted; for the absence of any order of belief has left them morally defenseless as individuals and politically impotent as a group." (*White Collar*, xvi) At work, white-collar people "sell not only their time and energy but their personalities as well. They sell by the week or month their smiles and their kindly gestures, and they must practice the prompt repression of resentment and aggression." (*White Collar*, xviii)

Mills argued that capitalist bureaucracies had usurped human freedom in the name of instrumental reason: "rationality seems to have taken on a new form, to have its seat not in individual men, but in social institutions which by their bureaucratic planning and mathematical foresight usurp both freedom and rationality from the little individual men caught in them." As a result, average people become psychologically alienated and politically distrustful or apathetic: "Estranged from community and society in a context of distrust and manipulation; alienated from work and, on the personality market, from self; expropriated of individual rationality, and politically apathetic—these are the new little people." (*White Collar*, xviii) Mills believed that young people would play an important role in new movements for social change and he contended that "to be politically conscious, either in loyalty or insurgency, is to see a political meaning in one's own insecurities and desires, to see oneself as a demanding political force, which, no matter how small, increases one's hopes that expectations will come off." (*White Collar*, 327) In this Millsian sense, it is the exploration of the psychological effects of contemporary society on his generation in "Howl" Part I that enables Ginsberg's more politically conscious analysis and declarations in Part II.

Although sometimes people from different parts of the ruling class might intentionally work together or conspire, the notion of aggregating different elements of the ruling class into a single group does not always imply conscious intention or conspiracy. Cornel West writes that C. Wright Mills believed "the ruling elite—political, economic, and military big shots—live and revel in a cultural form of life that cements them into a group characterized by coordinated actions, unified interests, and a highly limited range of opinions and outlooks." (*American Evasion,* 129) Ginsberg, like Mills, believed the power elite were cemented by common interests into a group, and he named this group Moloch.

Of the Moloch section of "Howl," Alicia Ostriker writes: "In Blakean terms, Ginsberg is 'giving a body to Error'." (Blake, Ginsberg, 121) In this poet-prophet tradition, one cannot cast out error until one has defined it and given it a material shape. In "The Four Zoas," Blake's poet-prophet figure Los:

> began the binding of Urizen day & night in fear
> Circling round the dark Demon with howlings
>   dismay & sharp blightings
> The Prophet of Eternity beat on his iron links &
>   links of brass[26]

Note that Blake's poet-prophet figure Los is able to bind, and help transform, Urizen, through "howlings"!

As mentioned earlier, Ginsberg acknowledged that he learned from Blake the poetic technique of mythification, of taking "political details," and "magnif[ying] roles into cosmo-demonic figures." [27] For Ginsberg, Moloch becomes a literary figure capable of carrying a clear social critique through its tying together of various present-day institutions, and simultaneously capable of mythologizing that critique to suggest a universal and timeless relevance.

If "Howl" were a piece of political or philosophical prose, we might be tempted to say that the use of such a mythic metaphor at the core of a political critique shows simply that the writer is being ahistorical. According to Jurgen Habermas, "Demythologization that does not break the mythic spell but merely seeks to evade it only brings forth new witch doctors." (On *Society*, 45) But Habermas was speaking here about political essays and I have earlier discussed my own belief, following theorists like Habermas and Eagleton, that different criteria ought to be used for judging art and politics. Again, take a look at the way in which existing institutions in need of improvement are spelled out more clearly in the Port Huron Statement:

> And if these anxieties produce a developed indifference to human affairs, do they not as well produce a yearning to believe there is an alternative to the present, that something can be done to change circumstances in the school, the workplaces, the bureaucracies, the government?[28]

Because he is writing a poem and not a political essay, Allen Ginsberg does not need to list such institutions as school, workplace, and government. Rather, he uses the poetic technique of mythification to such an effective degree that the "Moloch" section of "Howl" continues to echo with readers six decades after it was written, particularly in a United States that, as a result of the Bush administration's various responses to 9/11 and the Obama administration's willingness to continue at least some of the previous administration polices, has seen new forms of militarism, like long-distance drone bombings, combined with new forms of surveillance and restrictions of civil liberties—as well as lingering fundamentalist Christian ideas still held by many Americans about science and culture.

While Ginsberg's criticism of Moloch utilizes a mythification technique, this does not mean it cannot also include identifiable social criticism regarding his own American era. By giving a body to error, Ginsberg is able to reveal the cause of his compatriots' existential frustration to be a set of intertwined, oppressive aspects of religious, sexual, familial, political, artistic, historical, and economic institutions. As the biblical Moloch ate children, unaccountable modern institutions devour healthy human subjectivities and bodies.

Pointing out the chasms that remain between American reality and American ideals one hundred years after Walt Whitman's "Song of Myself," the poet of "Howl" declares that the country that presumes to nurture individuality and informed political citizenship actually obliterates these: "bashed open their skulls and ate up their brains and imaginations!" (CP, 139) America has not groomed liberal democratic subjects, but has allowed industrialism to fashion nonhuman, conformist mentalities ("Moloch whose mind is pure machinery!"). Professing to promote the rule of law and universal moral values, America actually imprisons people for irrational reasons ("Moloch the incomprehensible prison!"), and reveals immoral tendencies through its lust for militarism ("Moloch whose fingers are ten armies!"). The United States creates toxic governing structures ("Moloch the stunned governments!") and builds factories that pollute the country's natural ecology ("whose smokestacks and antennae crown the cities!"). And furthermore, the supposedly freedom-loving America actively suppresses healthy sexuality ("whose fate is a cloud of sexless hydrogen"). (CP, 139) Here, in connecting politics and sex, Ginsberg seems once again influenced by Wilhelm Reich, who, in books like *The Function of the Orgasm* and *The Mass Psychology of Fascism,* consistently expressed the view that sexual repression left people psychologically unhealthy and open to an irrational support for authoritarian political leaders.

While the Moloch section of "Howl" highlights the gap between America's ideals and its reality, it further implies that our founding ideals are in need of a radical update: "Howl" Part II derides nationalism ("spectral nations!"), challenges a core value of liberal individualism by equating Moloch with "Solitude!," and takes consistent and energetic aim at profit-oriented, capitalist economics and the financial hardships that result: "Moloch whose blood is running money!", "Moloch whose soul is electricity and banks!", "Moloch whose poverty is the specter of genius!" (CP, 139)

If part of what makes quality poetry interesting is the way in which it can inventively extend prior literary traditions, then another part is the way in which it can subvert the work of past influential writers—sometimes by embracing aspects of a literary predecessor and then inverting some of his or her key ideas. In "Howl," Ginsberg uses some of the imagery of T. S. Eliot, whose poem "The Wasteland" was certainly the most well-known and influential long American poem of the first half of the 20th century. In "The Wasteland," modern society is presented as waterless and dry, and rocks are used as symbols of social sterility: "Here is no water but only rock." (42) Earlier, in T. S. Eliot's poem, "The Love Song of J. Alfred Prufrock," this symbolic sterility is embedded within the protagonist's very name. In "Howl," Part II, we see similar imagery: "Moloch whose love is endless oil and stone," "granite cocks," "Mad generation! down on the rocks of Time!" Thus, "Howl" adopts T. S. Eliot's critique of a sterile society, and even some of the same kinds of rock-related imagery, but by the poem's end Ginsberg will subvert T. S. Eliot's project by using this imagery to convey a far more progressive political vision for overcoming that social sterility.

Like William Blake and C. Wright Mills, Ginsberg attacks an instrumental reason and a hyper-rationalized judgment that is devoid of compassion: "Moloch the heavy judger of men!" (CP, 139) Ginsberg shares Blake's concern for elevating beyond instrumental rationality by unifying reason with compassion and by creating a rapprochement between mind and body. For Ginsberg, hyper-rationality has led to self- and social-disintegration. The resultant social ills evident in the 1950s technological age have now become objectified in the new atomic weapons of mass destruction, the "monstrous bombs!" No longer is the fear of a life-annihilating apocalypse purely speculative or allegorical. As the SDS students at Port Huron would write just seven years later: "Our work is guided by the sense that we may be the last generation in the experiment with the living."[28] Thus, while the use of a metaphor, Moloch, to identify the source of multiple social oppressions can on one hand be said to avoid historical specificity, we can also see that the mythification simultaneously enables Ginsberg to present a long-reverberating social critique that focuses a spotlight on the interconnected worlds of political, psychological, cultural, and militaristic repression.

* * *

Once the source of repression is identified, the possibility of transformation can be envisioned. And, again in the tradition of William Blake, Ginsberg writes with the assumption that what a visionary poet can imagine can one day be made real. As Ginsberg later says in "Death to Van Gogh's Ear!" about good governments: "they have to begin existing they exist in my poems." (CP, 139) Or, as Blake had said in "The Mental Traveller," "For the Eye altering alters all." (501) Although Ginsberg's poet friend, Carl Solomon, at the end of Part III physically remains in Rockland, Ginsberg's optimistic gesture in the third section of "Howl" is to envision alternatives to the existing world that one day might be actualized, a keen assertion that—although changing society is not easy—the world is mutable and dependent on human actions. Or, as the global justice movement succinctly put it during its

Global justice movement rally.
Photo by Eliot Katz.

demonstrations against the World Trade Organization in Seattle in 1999 and at follow-up rallies against corporate globalization during ensuing years, "Another world is possible."

"I'm with you in Rockland" is Part III's anaphoric assertion of solidarity, the tonic to Moloch's "solitude" that will help free the confined Carl Solomon, and by extension help alleviate the actual and existential suffering of America's repressed subjects. In his biography of Ginsberg, Michael Schumacher offers a lively description of Solomon, a well-traveled dadaist poet with a leftist background who is well positioned to carry the social-symbolic weight of the third section of "Howl":

> Two years younger than Allen, Solomon boasted of experiences Allen could only imagine. A brilliant student, Solomon had skipped four grades in public school and had attended a high school for the academically gifted. At fifteen, he had entered the City College of New York and joined a Marxist organization called the American Youth for Democracy. Two years later, in 1945, he joined the merchant marine, and he spent the next couple of years alternating his time between the merchant marine and school. In 1947, while stationed in France, he left his ship and attended a reading given by French Surrealist writer Antonin Artaud, gaining an appreciation for Artaud's literature, as well as his distrust in any form of psychiatry.... Fascinated by the idea of gratuitous crime, and prompted by an almost suicidal nihilism, he stole a peanut butter sandwich from Brooklyn College cafeteria and showed it to a policeman, hoping his actions would land him in a mental institution....On his twenty-first birthday, he

arrived at the Psychiatric Institute asking for a lobotomy. The hospital refused. The day Allen met him, Solomon was emerging from a coma brought on by insulin shock treatment. (116)

In Part I, a countercultural youth collective had been envisioned through formal means—the syntactic parallelisms and the anaphoric repetition of "who." In Part III, the desire for solidarity is made explicit and becomes a model for the sort of collective social effort that could potentially improve human conditions by challenging Moloch's large-scale, multilayered isolation and repression.

In "Howl" part III, Carl Solomon is detained in Rockland, described as an "armed madhouse," an instrumentally rational institution where "the faculties of the skull no longer admit the worms of the senses." By describing Rockland in such heightened imagistic language, Ginsberg turns Rockland into a mythified figure like Moloch, except in this case readers know that Rockland is a real hospital. [29] In America's psychiatric hospitals, as in society as a whole, authoritarian solutions are no solutions: "I'm with you in Rockland / where fifty more shocks will never return your soul to its body again from its pilgrimage to a cross in the void." (CP, 141) Social institutions have wrenched body from mind, and the medical establishment's prescriptions are mean-spirited and ineffectual. Thus, as in Part I's opening line, madness is once again viewed dialectically, and Solomon's mad perceptions are seen as semi-accurate: "where you accuse your doctors of insanity." (CP, 141)

The expression of interpersonal solidarity asserts a view of the self in relational terms, a view of healthy subjectivity as healthy inter-subjectivity, of healthy independence as requiring a sense of interdependence. Ginsberg's commitment to inter-subjectivity and interdependence distinguishes him from more politically conservative poets like Ezra Pound and T. S. Eliot who preceded him. Describing the absence of an interest in solidarity by Pound, literary critic Frank

Lentricchia writes that Pound was not looking for "a solidarity of individuals—but an epic hero to combat conspiracy; and Mussolini was just over the horizon." (56) For T. S. Eliot, according to Lentricchia, a community merely meant "the literary tradition since, and proceeding from, Homer." (259) Ginsberg instead had the desire to build a community of living, breathing human beings, and his sense of solidarity included an extra dose of compassion for those who were marginalized by the dominant institutions.

The poet's empathy in Part III of "Howl" is largely articulated in a personal way, but it does include broader political references as well. Carl Solomon plots "the Hebrew socialist revolution" (CP, 141), and "twentyfive thousand mad comrades all together singing the final stanzas of the Internationale" (CP, 141) are envisioned before Solomon's ultimate redemption can occur. This is not to claim that Ginsberg implies a specific political program or ideology in the poem. There is no sorting out varied left traditions like anarchism, syndicalism, progressive populism, or democratic socialism. (By the mid-1950s, there was overwhelming information widely available about the crimes of Stalin, long highlighted by Ginsberg's Debsian socialist father, so that Soviet-style communism was seen by Ginsberg not as falling within the honest arena of left traditions but as a betrayal of those traditions. That is why his activists in Part I distribute "Supercommunist" rather than "Communist" pamphlets; why he praises the "fifth International" in the "Footnote to Howl," while the Fourth International had been the last one to have actually taken place; and why his poems were able to be embraced by young, dissident writers in Eastern Europe during the Cold War.) There is no choosing in "Howl" among particular anarchist, labor, or democratic-socialist groups, parties, or platforms. And yet, while there is no fixed ideology or specific program advanced in the poem, its historical references and social criticisms align it clearly within a general arena of leftist traditions. In this way, as I will discuss further in a later chapter, I would argue that Ginsberg's political philosophy was more pragmatic than rigidly ideological, or that it was "ideologically flexible" within a clear spectrum of left traditions—exhibiting a consistent belief in values such as engaged citizenship, accountable institutions, peace, compassion, environmentalism, economic fairness, gay rights, civil rights, and civil liberties, but not worrying about seeking a narrowly defined political philosophy. After he had seen the ideological dogmatism that led to severe repression in the Soviet Union and that undermined the efforts of America's Old Left—and that, importantly, created family friction between his own Communist mother and democratic-socialist father—it is not surprising that Allen should have remained less rigid in these ideological matters.

The envisioned freeing of Carl Solomon from Rockland takes place in the longest line of Part III, appropriately, since long lines in "Howl" imply a desire to break free from boundaries: "where we wake up electrified out of the coma by our own souls' airplanes roaring over the roof they've come to drop angelic bombs the hospital illuminates itself imaginary walls collapse   O skinny legions run outside   O starry-spangled shock of mercy the eternal war is here   O victory forget your underwear we're free." (CP, 141) Here, we should note that Ginsberg has taken and transformed the biblical idea of apocalypse, creating in the words of Tony Trigilio "an apocalypse without fatalism" and "apocalypse as a mode of consciousness." (*Prophecies*, 16) For Ginsberg in this section of "Howl," apocalyptic release is viewed as earthly, beneficial, humorous, and emanating from "our own souls" and from human solidarity rather than from an external divine entity as in the biblical Revelation ("Salvation *belongs* to our God who sits on the throne, and to the Lamb"[See Revelation 7:10]) and in opposition to the quite fatal apocalyptic threat of the world's growing nuclear arsenals. The elevated mythic diction of Part III contains worldly relevance: "starry-spangled" as an adjective preceding the idea of mercy alludes to the U.S. national anthem and suggests a more compassionate spirit as central to U.S. needs;

and "imaginary walls collapse" implies the need to end the sort of dualizing, Cold War-type political thinking that has built the Berlin Wall as well as the madhouse walls. Rather than the shock of shock treatments, it is the quality-shock of mercy or empathy that would enable freedom. The walls that collapse can also signify a Reichian character armor that precludes individuals from being in touch with their own core subjective needs and wants. In this way, the poem links the process of working through one's own psychological repression, in order to free one's mind, with the struggle for a liberating politics.

Seven years later, the manifesto of Students for a Democratic Society would similarly assert a link between interpersonal solidarity and psychological health. For SDS, the "participatory democracy" they advocated included the principle that "politics has the function of bringing people out of isolation and into community, thus being a necessary, though not sufficient, means of finding meaning in personal life."

In the last line of Part III, the liberating aspect that results from the spiritual solidarity between Ginsberg and Solomon is imagined as physical reality, in watery imagery that unites the sea with the American highway: "I'm with you in Rockland / in my dreams you walk dripping from a sea-journey on the highway across America in tears to the door of my cottage in the Western night." (CP, 141) Once more playfully using T. S. Eliot's imagery of rocks and water, Ginsberg adopts Eliot's conception at the end of "The Wasteland" of redemption through charitable compassion (Eliot's "data" and "dayadhvam"), but he also importantly inverts Eliot's ideas by offering a more optimistic vision than "The Wasteland," by embracing far more progressive notions of psychological and sexual desire, and by favoring leftwing political traditions.

* * *

While Ginsberg's poetry has often been criticized by conservatives or centrists for his progressive views (with aesthetic arguments sometimes used to mask what are at bottom political disagreements), a rare critique was leveled in the mid-1990s from an influential political writer on the left that seems instructive to address here. In "Why Johnny Can't Dissent," Thomas Frank—whose perceptive and bestselling 2004 book, *What's the Matter with Kansas*, looks at why so many white working class residents of middle America have often in recent years voted Republican—argued that countercultural challenges, as exemplified by Ginsberg, to America's corporate-dominated sensibilities were no longer liberatory. According to Frank, capitalism had changed, and corporate advertising by the mid-1990s was no longer attempting to induce personal conformity as it had in the 1950s, but was instead perfectly comfortable promoting products as helping consumers in a "Ginsbergian search for kicks upon kicks."[30]

As long as citizens remained politically inactive consumers, corporate culture would encourage expression of individuality and would no longer press for acquiescence of dress or ideas. According to Frank, even some of America's top corporate gurus, like Tom Peters, had adopted Beat-influenced rhetoric: " 'Revolution,' of course, means for Peters the same thing it did to Burroughs and Ginsberg, Presley and the Stones in their heyday: breaking rules, pissing off the suits, shocking the bean-counters." (38) He writes further: "Turn on the TV and there it is instantly....dreadlocks and ponytails bounding into Taco Bells....Corporate America, it turns out, no longer speaks in the voice of oppressive order that it did when Ginsberg moaned in 1956 that *Time* magazine was 'always telling me about responsibility'." (33) Frank concluded that by the late twentieth century a corporate co-optation of Ginsberg's message had occurred, and that this was possible only because Ginsberg wrote poetry in the first place that was insufficiently meaningful to resist.

Frank's critique of Ginsberg is erroneous, I would argue, on several grounds—chiefly because it is based on a terribly reductive and misleading reading of Ginsberg's poetry. As we have just seen in Part III of "Howl," Ginsberg's message can in no way be limited to Frank's notion of "breaking rules, pissing off the suits, shocking the bean-counters,"—even if it is no doubt true that many people in business suits were indeed shocked or upset when encountering "Howl" for the first time in the mid-1950s. But Frank's reading of the poem ignores the important notion of solidarity as most powerfully expressed in "Howl" Part III, and also fails to highlight the passionate critique in "Howl" of militarism and capitalism's economic exploitation, as well as Ginsberg's ensuing four-plus decades of writing and activist work, detailed throughout this book, on behalf of a wide range of human rights and ecological causes.

Frank also problematically assumes that, if culture is absorbed by some mainstream elements, it is the fault of the artist for not being radical enough. But, as Terry Eagleton persuasively argues, it is naive to think that "*art*, all by itself" can "resist incorporation." According to Eagleton, "If *they* win, continue to govern, then it is no doubt true that there is nothing which they cannot in principle defuse and contain. If *you* win, they will not be able to appropriate a thing because you will have appropriated them." When it comes to the effectiveness of oppositional art, Eagleton concludes that, ultimately, "the question of integration stands or falls with the destiny of a mass political movement." (*Ideology*, 372)

Frank's argument also makes the theoretical mistake of assuming that any stance which corporate culture attempts to display is automatically repressive. If one takes culture seriously, as I know Frank does, then it seems worth acknowledging that, chiefly as a result of the progressive movements of the 1960s and 1970s, the modern American cultural environment has largely been a far more open one than the conformity-urging culture of the 1950s—with an important exception, I would add, of the immediate aftermath of 9/11, when bands like the Dixie Chicks lost their radio airplay and one of the most progressive cable TV news shows, MSNBC's "Donahue," was canceled. Since the 1960s, the vast majority of people who have publicly disagreed with government policies have generally been able to speak their minds without fear of arrest or of being called in front of HUAC-style government committees—despite the admitted occasional overreach of officially sanctioned surveillance programs or despicable government attempts to punish a select few heroic whistleblowers like Edward Snowden, who formerly held positions with official access to embarrassing information about harmful or even criminal policies that the government hoped to keep secret. And although there are still far-too-common and serious back-steps like police shootings of innocent black youth, and although there is certainly much more work to be done to completely eliminate institutional discrimination, there has since the 1950s been much concrete forward movement nationally, including legislatively, around issues of racism, sexism, and homophobia, and there is far more social acceptance than in the era of "Howl" of open and honest sexual expression and discussion.

Such cultural improvements have not led to a widespread economic transformation, and economic inequality and deep poverty remain entrenched social problems. But it is important to acknowledge that, as a result of social movements of the 1960s and 1970s, American culture has generally become far more open and tolerant than it was in the 1950s, which is why corporate advertising campaigns have been altered to appeal to more rebellious sensibilities. If contemporary corporate managers have, as Frank argues, adopted some Beat-influenced rhetoric, then it seems to me this is partially a sign that Ginsberg's poetry and the work of other Beat Generation writers has positively affected mainstream culture and public consciousness to such an extent that even corporations have decided to respond by changing the style of their appeals. Rather than criticize Ginsberg and other Beat Generation writers for having at least somewhat helped to open up the culture, it seems to me that it would behoove those of us on the left to occasionally celebrate our victories, even our partial ones. Sure, as long as large corporations hold sway, it is impossible to stop them from trying to co-opt countercultural energies for more conservative or for more plainly commercial reasons, but we can challenge those attempts by offering fuller pictures of our own (and, in this case, Ginsberg's) social visions.

Along those lines, I felt at the time that it was important to challenge Lee Siegal's 2010 article in a *New York Times Book Review* comparing Ginsberg's views with those of the modern right-wing American Tea Party, an article which I addressed in the previous chapter. Following the publication of Lee Siegal's 2010 review, I wrote and sent a letter to the editor of the *New York Times Book Review*, and when it was not published there, I sent it around to some literary websites that posted it. I noticed that a number of similarly purposed letters defending Ginsberg and other Beat Generation authors also appeared on various literary and political websites. But, as Terry Eagleton argues, only by building significant mass political movements can we ensure that the energies of oppositional art are not defused by the dominant power structure. And it deserves to be said here that Ginsberg's poetry has done as much as anyone's to inspire people working in these kinds of mass social movements.

Furthermore, after 9/11, when high-ranking members of the Bush administration announced that people ought to watch what they say and what they do, and when some mainstream media reporters began to criticize musicians and actors for speaking out against the Iraq war, it became apparent that the protest against conformity in "Howl" will continue to find renewed relevance at different and critical points in contemporary times and into the future.

Thomas Frank is right that the Culture Industry's version of "rebelliousness" provides an insufficient basis for effective political opposition. But rather than reject the countercultural impulses to which such corporate strategies often appeal, it would seem far more helpful to stretch those countercultural ideas further, by articulating additional social needs and possibilities that would help constitute more effective political strategies. Ginsberg's "Howl" focuses on many of these additional social needs, including, for instance, the needs for more economic fairness and more peaceful foreign policies. Crucially, one of those additional needs for building effective social movements would be the notion of solidarity that is presented so forcefully in "Howl" Part III. As Jurgen Habermas contends, it is the "power of solidarity" in the form of effective political movements that may potentially "be in a position to assert itself against the systematically integrating steering media of money and power." (*Philosophical Discourse*, 364)

* * *

Once Carl Solomon is imagined freed, Ginsberg celebrates. The first line of the final section of "Howl," "Footnote to Howl," depicts pure ecstasy, with "Holy!" repeated fifteen times. As Part III had transformed the apocalyptic qualities of the biblical Revelation so that sudden change was viewed as positive, and as emanating from within and from interpersonal solidarity rather than from an external deity, the "Footnote to Howl" appropriates the "Holy, holy, holy" of Revelation (See Revelation 4:8), and applies the description to humanity and the living world rather than to an all-powerful god.

In relation to the poem's four-part structure, arduous explorations of current reality, the use of the poetic imagination, and the expression of interpersonal solidarity have freed the poet from psychic and institutional repression and have made such rapture possible. Basically, this is a dramatic portrayal of pure, well-earned joy—logical argument is no longer needed and no longer the goal. In a Blakean sense, Ginsberg at this point in the poem has reached a poetic New Jerusalem, in which ultra-rationality and hyper-judgmentalism can be cast aside in favor of far more compassionate alternatives: In the words of the historian E. P. Thompson, "To create the New Jerusalem something must be brought in from outside the rationalist system, and that something could only be found in....affirmatives of Mercy, Pity, Peace and Love." (221)

In psychotherapy terms, Ginsberg has broken through denial and worked through difficult issues in order to achieve a healthier psychological state: In Reichian terminology he has broken through the character armor to reach the biological core, where humans are "essentially honest, industrious, cooperative, loving." According to Reich, "the biologic core of man has been without social representation. The 'natural' and 'sublime' in man, that which links him to his cosmos, has found genuine expression only in great works of art." (Mass Psychology, xi-xii) "Howl," I would argue, is one of those artworks.

Having broken free from psychic and institutional repression, Ginsberg is able to see the divine within all: to celebrate body and soul, the phenomena which modern society values ("Holy the solitudes of skyscrapers and pavements!") as well as that which society often abhors or marginalizes ("Holy the jazzbands marijuana hipsters peace peyote pipes & drums!"). (CP, 142) As the body and soul are declared holy, so are both the sea and the desert, as the sort of wet-versus-dry symbolism of T.S. Eliot is here both embraced and transcended. The oral energies of the poem—the long-breathed rhythms—further contribute to uniting poetic ideas with the body, as readers reciting the poem aloud, or listening to it being recited, will physically feel a glimpse of the ecstasy being celebrated. In this new holistic state, Ginsberg can redeem his friends and even his "mother in the insane asylum," since he now understands dramatically what Blake meant when he exclaimed at the very end of "Marriage of Heaven and Hell": "every thing that lives is Holy." (195) Ginsberg offers his readers the Blakean poet-prophet formula, whereby what is imagined can one day be made real: "Who digs Los Angeles IS Los Angeles!" (CP, 142) Even the source of social oppression has an aspect of worthiness within: "holy the Angel in Moloch!" (CP, 142)

As mentioned earlier, in a rhetorical flourish that is extraordinarily shrewd for those of us interested in the poem's political implications, Ginsberg inventively celebrates a utopian socialist gathering that has not yet taken place: "holy the fifth International." (CP, 142) The First International (1864-1872), with Karl Marx playing a leading theoretical and organizational role, had been a loose international federation of left-wing and working class groups representing a range of different (and fiercely debated) progressive philosophies. In subsequent Internationals, positions and debates had hardened. Since there has not yet been a fifth International, Ginsberg here in the "Footnote to Howl" is thus envisioning a utopian International beyond the philosophical arguments between theorists such as Marx and Bakunin that marked the First International, and beyond the Soviet-centered debates that marred subsequent formations. In his notes to the *Annotated Howl*, Ginsberg observes that there were four workers' internationals (1864, 1889, 1919, 1938) and that the "Fifth International of workers, entrepreneurs, peasants and indigenous communities of world has not yet assembled to propose survival norms in era of imperial private and state monopoly capital's near-absolute and potentially suicidal power."(146) In "Howl," a young poet wisely imagines the possibility of refashioning a left historical legacy—one that furthers human freedoms in the spirit of the original socialist project rather than restricting them as in the "actually existing socialism" of the mid-1950s Soviet bloc.

The witnessing of society that began the poem with an initial "I saw" has been transfigured into a witnessing of, and an urging toward, a better future. There is no comprehensive political program or platform offered here. But for all of those who have descended into existential frustration or suffered because of political injustice, "Howl" witnesses and then envisions a potential path out—through increased political consciousness, psychological exploration, spiritual enlightenment, artistic imagination, and human solidarity.

At the poem's close, Ginsberg also celebrates internationalism, praising foreign cities: "Holy Paris Holy Tangiers Holy Moscow Holy Istanbul." His inclusion of Moscow takes more than a tacit jab at 1950s U.S. Cold War ideology. For the mid-1950s U.S. left, there was considerable debate about how to frame discussions over the Soviet Union. In *If I Had a Hammer*, Maurice Isserman describes a falling-out that took place between C. Wright Mills and the journal *Dissent* when Mills argued with Irving Howe that Howe's continuing insistence that the American left always be explicitly anticommunist was becoming "obsolete." (117) A similar debate took place in 1962, when the young organizers of SDS refused to accept Michael Harrington's entreaties to include a clear statement condemning Soviet communism in their Port Huron Statement—instead, SDS criticized America's restrictive Cold War mentality, with its absurd level of military spending, and observed that "anticommunism" has often been used by conservatives as a rationale for opposing "liberalism, internationalism, welfarism, the active civil rights and labor movements." Like Mills, Ginsberg always recognized the severely repressive aspects of Stalinism and never tried to rationalize them away, but—because he saw the mirror problems in the West of poverty, militarism, and McCarthyism, and because he valued socialist ideals—he refused in "Howl" to replicate the dominant Cold War mentality of the day, one more way in which the ideas in "Howl" prefigured, and helped influence, those of the New Left. And finally, contrary to the destructiveness or pessimism that some of Ginsberg's early critics saw in the poem, "Howl" ends with one of the most unabashedly optimistic and faith-filled lines of 20th-century American poetry. If one has the courage, energy, and persistence to uncover the sheets of denial that can surround both the social and psychological status quo, one can see the "supernatural extra brilliant intelligent kindness of the soul!"

Today, after more than a decade's worth of conflicts

involving the U.S. military, including both large-scale wars and smaller-scale drone bombing campaigns; economic policies that have generally become more regressive in recent decades through both Republican and Democratic administrations; the backsliding of civil liberties and an increase in domestic surveillance; and ever-worsening environmental dangers from pollution to climate change; the radical legacy of "Howl" remains as relevant as when it was first published.

Fortunately, it is still true that young people who read "Howl" quite often come away with a strengthened belief that it is possible to create a far more just and equitable world. Sixty years after "Howl" was written, the poem continues to inspire writers and activists around the world with its passionate commitment to get to the root of what ails us and its visionary insistence (via both form and content) on the viability of a more humane future. For many young poets, and some established ones as well, the poem provides a generous assortment of literary strategies for turning political ideas and observations into memorable poetry. Like some previous 20th century long poems, including Muriel Rukeyser's "Book of the Dead," Langston Hughes' "Montage of a Dream Deferred," William Carlos Williams' "Spring and All," or Pablo Neruda's "Canto General," "Howl" demonstrates that a poet does not have to choose a single poetry path or style—i.e. realism or surrealism, narrative or anti-narrative, elevated diction or American speech. One can embrace multiple interests and mix them in original, personal, and surprising ways.

If we conceptualize poetry and politics as differentiated categories that interrelate and overlap in various ways in different historical and geographical eras and contexts, then the question for a political poet is how to write poems of literary value while pushing against the poetry-politics boundaries so that one's literary efforts might help at least in some small ways to enlighten consciousness, illuminate public issues, stir public dreams and desires, improve ideological climate, aid political movements, or otherwise help alter the social landscape. Denise Levertov addressed the question of poetry's potential to help transform society in this way: "I don't think one can accurately measure the historical effectiveness of a poem; but one does know, of course, that books influence individuals; and individuals, although they are part of large economic and social processes, influence history." (169) If one is to make a political-poetic mark and inspire people around the globe to work toward a more progressive future, it helps to have written inspired poems like "Howl."

* * *

For the rest of his life, Ginsberg's poetry would continue to be filled with the kind of insightful criticisms of existing society and the visionary insistence on the potential of creating social change that Ginsberg initially developed in "Howl." In later years, as will be discussed in subsequent chapters, he would also become a dedicated activist working to help further the progressive causes addressed in his poems. But before looking at his poems from ensuing decades, I would like to look briefly at two other poems from his influential early book, *Howl and Other Poems,* to see some of the ways in which he experimented with different poetic styles to express his evolving social perceptiveness.

In "America" (1956), Ginsberg's political critique is more direct than in "Howl." Here, rather than incorporating mythological tropes like the Moloch figure in "Howl," Ginsberg uses comedy and satire to demythologize or demystify dominant culture's political propaganda, and he asserts radical history and personal desires against the mainstream discourse of government and mass media. "America" acquires its poetic quality and energy chiefly from its unique combination of humor and politics as part of its project of historicization, a project that insists on returning to America's historical memory some key radical activists and movements (Wobblies, Trotskyites, Scottsboro Boys,

Mother Bloor, Scott Nearing, Paterson silk strikes) that had been left out of too many of mainstream culture's (e.g. *Time, Reader's Digest,* high school history texts) typical portrayals of American history.

In terms of its humor, as mentioned earlier, if one listens to the early live recording on *Holy Soul Jelly Roll!*, one can immediately tell from the audience laughter that this was a poetry completely unexpected at the time. Alicia Ostriker credits Ginsberg's humor in part to his Jewish upbringing and the Jewish comedic tradition, writing that Ginsberg is willing to "schpritz shamelessly alongside Henny Youngman and Lenny Bruce." ("Howl" Revisited, 28) These days, one can attend a bar or cafe poetry reading in almost any city in America and see at least a few poets reading poems that mix politics and humor—yet another sign of the continuing influence of Ginsberg's work—but this was quite a fresh mix for American poetry of the mid-1950s. As Saul Alinsky reminds us in *Rules for Radicals,* comedy can help make the medicine go down: "through humor much is accepted that would have been rejected if presented seriously." (xviii)

As far as alternative American history goes, in recent decades we have had Howard Zinn's brilliant *A People's History of the United States,* which has become something like an historical bible for the American left.[31] Zinn's success, with over a million copies sold, has also opened the door for many other progressive historians to get their works more widely published. Today, of course, we also have the Internet with its widely available sources of alternative news and analysis, and a growing number of progressive radio new shows, including Amy Goodman's "Democracy Now," which reaches over a million listeners every weekday. While some progressive analyses and histories were certainly being published in the U.S. in both books and periodicals in the mid-1950s, we need to remember when reading "America" that these views and histories were not nearly as widely available as they are today, a reality that provided additional intellectual punch to readers of the poem.

The poem begins with the contention of a parasitic relationship between American society and the poet's selfhood, "America I've given you all and now I'm nothing" and quickly criticizes American policy using language calculated to bring readers to both shock and laughter: "America when will we end the human war? / Go fuck yourself with your atom bomb." (CP, 154) Ginsberg's outrageous discourse here is certainly calculated to challenge what James Breslin has referred to as New Criticism's preference for a "rhetoric based on propriety and reasonableness." (*Modern to Contemporary*, 49) The intellectual trick on readers aghast at the phrase "go fuck yourself" appearing in a poem is that the line forces an audience to rethink notions of vulgarity—that is, which is really more vulgar: the phrase "go fuck yourself" in a poem or the actual atom bomb hovering in constant threat over society? While the comedy of "America" is often slapstick, it is clearly intended to urge readers into more thoughtful modes of political reflection.

The poem's critique of capitalist economics is simultaneously funny and serious: "When can I go into the supermarket and buy what I need with my good looks?" (CP, 154) It takes a stab at America's mainstream media: "Are you going to let your emotional life be run by Time Magazine?" (CP, 155) —even as Ginsberg himself admits that he also reads *Time*. Such lines, grounded as they are in "minute particulars" (Blake's phrase), help make political philosophy seem as urgent and personal as they actually are, since they goad readers into considering the way social and cultural institutions affect their own daily behavior. By so doing, "America" invites a broad readership, including many readers who are not yet as politicized as the author, to consider more radical interpretations of American history. This broad appeal is enhanced both by the poem's comedy and by an American speech diction that offers itself as an accessible alternative to mainstream "objective" newspeak on the one hand and to stale Old Left rhetoric on the other.

The social analysis in "America" is grandly

comprehensive. Using satire, the poem (perhaps helping to pave the way for John F. Kennedy just four years later?) reproaches the nation's religious bigotry ("My ambition is to be President despite the fact that I'm a Catholic."), its repression of dissent ("America free Tom Mooney....Sacco and Vanzetti must not die"), and its Cold War foreign policy ("The Russia wants to eat us alive. The Russia's power mad.") In the tradition of 18th-century poetry of social criticism (e.g. Pope, Dryden), the poem is not afraid to be didactic; it ventures easily between the didactic ("save the Spanish Loyalists") and the parodic ("Her wants our auto plants in Siberia"). (CP, 155-56) When the poem is didactic, it is inventively so, since as we have seen Ginsberg is always concerned with making sure that his poetic lines do not sound like "flat prose." For instance, "America" utilizes a cagey historical gamesmanship by asking America to save the Spanish Loyalists two decades after the fact, and by declaring "what a good thing the [Communist] party was in 1835." (CP, 155) Of course, 1835 predates the founding of the Soviet Communist Party and even predates Marx and Engels' writing of *The Communist Manifesto*. The line thereby urges readers to think of a time well before Stalin had the chance, through his repressive and murderous policies in the Soviet Union, to despoil both the name of the political party and even the name of the political philosophy. In other didactic moments, the poem imaginatively interconnects the personal with the political: "You should have seen me reading Marx. / My psychoanalyst thinks I'm perfectly right."

By recalling renowned anarchists, communists, socialists, and trade union organizers and bringing them back to America's historical record, this poem, like "Howl," alludes generally to a broad arena of leftist traditions, without advocating for any single ideology or party line within the wider left. This is another example of Ginsberg's political pragmatism or ideological flexibility. And, like "Howl," "America" simultaneously decries the U.S. for betraying its own liberal democratic ideals (by arresting dissent, institutionalizing racism, repressing individualism, and publishing disinformation) and also criticizes those ideals from a more radical stance committed to recovering leftist history from prevailing cultural erasure. Again, this strategy of historicizing or demystification is a different strategy for writing powerful political poetry than the mythologizing strategy of the Moloch section of "Howl." In "America," Ginsberg goes so far in his urging of historicization that he includes, as the poem's second line, the date on which the poem was written, and the exact amount of money in his pocket at the time.

It is important to remember that this championing of an honest left history was courageously being written during an era when the American left was still facing serious and widespread government repression. Although Joe McCarthy had finally been censured by the U.S. Senate in December 1954, the House Un-American Activities Committee (HUAC) hearings were still being held. And extreme anti-anticommunism—not only in terms of criticizing the Soviet Union but also in terms of suppressing activists in the U.S.—was not only the property of conservative Republicans. Hubert Humphrey, then considered a young leader of the liberal wing of the Democratic Party, had introduced a Senate bill in 1954 to imprison members of the U.S. Communist Party.

In "America," the nation is not viewed as an external entity, but rather as a collective whose fate is literally linked with the poet's own: "It occurs to me that I am America. / I am talking to myself again." (CP, 155) This is another line that is meant to be taken both comically and seriously. On the serious side, the struggle with America over national policies is seen in part as a struggle for the consciousness of its individual citizens. This reflects a growing sense in the mid-1950s of the centrality of ideology in determining social relations. If this were an essay and not a poem, it might be fair to argue here that these two lines are misleading, since in reality Allen Ginsberg has not personally been involved in developing the onerous social policies that the poem indicts. But again, as poetry, the lines exhibit a powerful pull on readers because they imply a utopian possibility in which the nation becomes a collective whose fate really could be linked with the democratic desires and decisions of its citizens. About a decade earlier, the African-American poet, Langston Hughes, had written similarly, "I, too, am America," and it is also possible to read Ginsberg's lines as drawing on the words of his predecessor to assert that gay Americans, like black Americans, ought to have full equality and democratic rights in the U.S.

"America" is thus hopeful as well as satiric. In refusing to surrender to the opening line's depressed emotional state, and in moving from that state into a lengthy and lively social investigation, the poet prefiguratively constructs the prospect of a more democratic America. As "Howl" envisioned the potential of individual and social transformation, so "America," which began with "now I'm nothing," ends optimistically with a renewed assertion of subjectivity against a dehumanizing culture: "America I'm putting my queer shoulder to the wheel." Within a culture then suffused with institutionally sanctioned homophobia, the poet refuses to keep his sexual identity suppressed. And since the poet can assert "I am America"—as Walt Whitman had asserted in "Song of Myself" that "every atom belonging to me as good belongs to you" and Langston Hughes had asserted "I, too, sing America"—by extension other democratic citizens can challenge institutional restrictions on their own personal desires, and by so doing, transform those institutions into more democratically accountable entities.

In many ways, this striking last line of "America" did successfully move the nation's cultural institutions. Along with the celebration of gay sexuality in "Howl," it helped to inspire the future gay rights movement. In his book, *The Gay Metropolis: 1940-1996,* Charles Kaiser observes that Ginsberg and other Beat writers were influential in large part because they were the first American writers to present gay themes as hip: "Kerouac, Ginsberg and the rest of the Beats, as they called themselves, were far more important for what they stood for than for whom they slept with....In this postwar period, they were the first group of American writers ever to portray homosexuality as hip—a huge step forward for all those who continued to accept society's definition of this orientation as an illness, a crime, or both."(100) Bob Rosenthal, who worked as Allen Ginsberg's secretary for the last two decades of Ginsberg's life, has written that during his first ten years of work, not a week went by without their office receiving a letter thanking Ginsberg for helping him or her come out of the closet.[32]

Additionally noteworthy is the way in which that last line seizes the mantle of American poetic tradition from William Carlos Williams who averred, in the concluding line of the "pure products of America" section of *Spring and All,* that there was "no one to drive the car." (133) Ginsberg's resolution expresses the possibility of an imaginative, politically daring poet with a keen sense of humor helping to steer America's social and cultural future in a more humane and progressive direction.

Restoring human subjectivity within a dehumanizing environment is also the focus of "Sunflower Sutra" (1955), a dense and complex poem that, remarkably, was composed in only twenty minutes. Like "Howl," this is a poem with Blakean influences, recalling Blake's "Ah Sun-Flower," whose verses were ingrained into Ginsberg's consciousness after he had had an auditory vision/hallucination in 1948 of William Blake reading to him while he was lying in bed. In addition to recalling Blake, this poem appropriates an American pastoral figuration, which the literary critic Leo Marx calls a "machine-in-the-landscape," [33] a literary device, like the Joads' tractor in *Grapes of Wrath,* which signifies industrialism's toxic intrusion on human life. The machine-in-the-landscape figure which Ginsberg employs in "Sunflower Sutra" is the Southern Pacific locomotive, which has turned Ginsberg's sunflower into "a gray Sunflower poised against the sunset, crackly bleak and dusty with the smut and smog and smoke of olden locomotives." (CP, 146)

The description of industrial consumer-capitalist images which this sunflower stirs in Ginsberg is intense and horrifying: "Hells of the Eastern rivers, bridges clanking Joes Greasy Sandwiches, dead baby carriages, black treadless tires forgotten and unretreaded, the poem of the riverbank, condoms & pots, steel knives, nothing stainless, only the dank muck and the razor-sharp artifacts passing into the past." (CP, 146) In contemporary culture, engines have subsumed the human, body and all, and we are left with "skin of machinery," "milky breasts of cars," and "sphincters of dynamos." In symbolic opposition to the machine-in-the-landscape, the sunflower serves as symbol of pre-industrial purity in the modern world, "a sweet natural eye to the new hip moon." (CP, 146)

In the face of industrialization, the sunflower is in drastic need of regeneration. For Ginsberg, human forces, not outside religious ones, are viewed as potential redeemers. The implicit rejection of an external deity to rescue nature helps place the poem within the tradition of Buddhist wisdom literature—thus the "sutra" of the poem's title. For Ginsberg, an attentive perceptiveness, engaged imagination, and increased self-awareness are seen as capable of salvaging both nature and the human soul from a devouring brand of industrialism, since "we're all golden sunflowers inside." (CP, 147) Like the "Footnote to Howl," this assertion of a divine-like quality within is the Blakean moment of the poem which justifies the allusion to Blake's "Ah, Sun-Flower." As Tony Trigilio notes about Blake: "scholars generally agree that the prophetic path to redemption in Blake is inward." (*Prophecies*, 47)

Of course, for Ginsberg an inward path is not the opposite of an outward one, since it is possible to work at the same time on increasing one's personal self-awareness and enhancing interpersonal solidarity. In "Sunflower Sutra," it is significant that Ginsberg does not go out into nature alone but with a human companion, his friend and fellow writer,

Jack Kerouac. As in the Carl Solomon section of "Howl," human solidarity and inter-subjectivity, not a Thoreau-like transcendental isolation, help make possible the visionary transformation of nature and society. The poem ends with an inventive, deep- and long-breathed redemption that includes a jazzed-up succession of juxtaposed images:

> —We're not our skin of grime, we're not our dread bleak dusty imageless locomotive, we're all golden sunflowers inside, blessed by our own seed & hairy naked accomplishment-bodies growing into mad black formal sunflowers in the sunset, spied on by our eyes under the shadow of the mad locomotive riverbank sunset Frisco hilly tincan evening sitdown vision.
> (CP, 147)

Both in its substantive rescuing of intrinsic human beauty, and in its stylistic use of modernist phrasings that—in the sense of Ernst Bloch's "anticipatory illuminations"—offer a glimpse of personal and social realities that do not yet exist in the actual world, "Sunflower Sutra," like "Howl," beautifully expresses a utopian yearning for unrepressed human and social possibilities. Here again, Ginsberg's dazzling poetic imagination is on full display, and it is easy to see why the verses in "Howl and Other Poems" struck a dynamic chord in the minds of so many mid-1950s American readers, and why those same verses continue to inspire millions of readers across the planet today.

Chapter 3:
Politics and Family History:
Kaddish and Other Poems

Following *Howl and Other Poems*, Ginsberg's next major work was "Kaddish" (1957-59), the long elegy for his mother, Naomi. While "America" and "Howl" had each linked political themes with psychological ones, "Kaddish" takes this connection in new and far more personal directions. I do not want to claim that one should read "Kaddish" primarily as a political poem since the dramatic power of the poem comes primarily from its psychological intensity, from the dramatic exposition of a son emotionally and candidly witnessing his mother's crisis-filled life and processing her death. But since Naomi Ginsberg's life was steeped in politics, the exploration of this mother-son relationship, and of the grieving process following her death, could not help but become charged with political content.

Indeed, the political character of Naomi's life enhances the psychological power of the poem: her story achieves elevated importance because it is intimately wrapped up with the stories of nations. About the melding of the personal and the social in modern Polish poetry, Czeslaw Milosz has written: "a peculiar fusion of the individual and the historical took place, which means that events burdening a whole community are perceived by a poet as touching him in a most personal manner." (94) This description perfectly fits the case of Allen Ginsberg's "Kaddish," where the poet has both perceived and felt larger social forces bearing down on his own family.

The death of his mother propelled Ginsberg to delve into childhood and family issues and memories, shattering matters of personal and familial denial as "Howl" had helped burst the nation's cultural and political denial. Allen Ginsberg's teenage years, in which he was forced to participate in medical decisions regarding his mentally ill mother that are usually reserved for adults, clearly left a mark in the poet's belief in candid revelation as necessary for emotional healing, and do much to reveal the origins of Ginsberg's lifelong dedication to compassion and forgiveness. Politically, as the poem narrates his upbringing by a Communist mother and an anti-Stalinist, democratic-socialist, lyric-poet father, it reveals how the deeply personal grew inextricably intertwined with the worldly social.

Because of his parents' differing views regarding left traditions, and because of the general suppression of socialist thought in 1950s America, Ginsberg's family reflections offer a rare, revealing portrait of an oft-forgotten segment of post-WWII America. Naomi Ginsberg was a Russian immigrant who had come to the United States at age ten. In Paterson, New Jersey, she was an active member of the U.S. Communist Party, taking Allen as a child to Party summer camps and local cell meetings. At Camp Nicht-Gedeigat, a summer camp in upstate New York, Stalinist purges were trivialized, and capitalism as well as non-Stalinist left alternatives to capitalism, such as Trotskyism, were criticized. Like too many other American and international leftists of her time who remained members of various international Communist Parties affiliated with the U.S.S.R., despite ever-growing evidence of Stalin's vast crimes and repression, Naomi Ginsberg had maintained a faith in a Soviet-style Communism that had idealized workers' rights in theory and that had in actuality played a major military role, at much human sacrifice, in defeating Nazi Germany. In Naomi's extreme paranoia, as "Kaddish" attests, the forces of Western capitalism, Hitler's Nazism, and Trotskyist socialism would often end up merged, all equally seeking to undermine Soviet politics and thereby persecute Naomi personally. Furthermore, Naomi's psychiatric illness often caused her to believe that her own relatives, and even her husband Louis, were aiding her political opponents in their quest to increase her suffering. As her son saw it, Naomi's internally contrived paranoia was exacerbated by the actual history of Cold War-era anti-communist hysteria, including FBI spying, McCarthyite blacklists, and the general harassment of a wide variety of left-wing movements, most of which, of course, were not affiliated with the U.S. Communist Party, and certainly not with the Soviet Union. Ginsberg's personal grieving process over Naomi's death would thus become in part an investigation of the Cold War environment that he felt contributed to his mother's illness.

Titled after the Jewish mourner's prayer, "Kaddish" attempts to carry on that prayer's purpose of using ritual to reconcile with death, and also carries its traditional Hebrew rhythms—rhythms that Ginsberg revised by adding measures of African-American blues: "So the cadence all through the poem's based on davening rabbis do to move the spirit and body when chanting the mourner's Kaddish, somehow connected with the near-Aramaic cantillation of Ray Charles."[1] As is almost always the case, when Ginsberg appropriates traditions, he infuses his project with interesting twists.

The very act of appropriating the mourner's Kaddish for a highly personal poem is transgressive, since in traditional Judaism, the prayer is recited in public services with a minimum number of Jewish men (a *minyan*) present, focuses on God and the Jewish community, and does not include any explicitly personal material directly related to the deceased. In fact, it lacks any mention whatsoever that a human being has died. Here are a few lines from the traditional prayer in translation:

> Glorified and sanctified be God's great name
> throughout the world, which He has created

> according to His will. May he establish His kingdom within your lifetime and within the lifetime of the whole house of Israel, speedily and soon, and let us say, Amen.....
>
> May the Creator of heavenly peace bestow peace upon us and all Israel, and let us say, Amen.[2]

As a politically progressive poet, Ginsberg was not one to let established institutional doctrines prevent him from exploring important personal and worldly-social material, so he was quite willing to use the tradition of the mourner's Kaddish to develop an intensely personal literary work that would include shocking family revelations, and implications about world politics, that went obviously far afield from the traditional ritualized prayer. By revising the traditional Mourner's Kaddish, Ginsberg makes the point that our social rituals, in place for centuries, are in need of update, including the insertion of a far deeper level of personalization and candor. In a 1966 essay, "How *Kaddish* Happened," Ginsberg describes his process of writing the poem. He began with some of the less-personalized sections, but "then I realized that I hadn't gone back and told the whole secret family-self tale—my own one-and-only eternal child-youth memories which no one else could know—in all its eccentric detail. I realized that it would seem odd to others, but *family* odd, that is to say, familiar—everybody has crazy cousins and aunts and brothers." (345)

In its attempt to tell "the whole secret family-self tale," especially in the second section, "Kaddish" functions, perhaps even more than "Howl," as a poem of witness in addition to being a powerful elegy. In *Testimony: Crises of Witnessing in Literature, Psychoanalysis, and History*,[3] Shoshana Felman describes this highly personalized nature of witnessing—a witnessing that, despite its private aspects, also includes the need to speak to the public at large on behalf of what has been witnessed:

> Since the testimony cannot be simply relayed, repeated or reported by another without thereby losing its function as a testimony, the burden of the witness....is a radically unique, noninterchangeable and solitary burden.... And yet, the *appointment* to bear witness is, paradoxically enough, an appointment to transgress the confines of that isolated stance, to speak *for* and *to* others." (3)

As a poet who had already achieved a certain status as a public figure, Allen Ginsberg may certainly have felt the sense, upon hearing of Naomi's death, that he was now appointed to speak for her. Or perhaps it would be more accurate to say that he had been appointed to speak for both of them, since as Scott Herring notes, "In important ways, their relationship is not a matter of dependence or guardianship. They form, rather, an alliance." (551-52)

In structure, "Kaddish" shares many traits with "Howl." As in the earlier poem, Ginsberg immerses himself in an environment of madness in order to explore, comprehend, and redeem it. In this case, the environment is largely a familial one—albeit a family environment teeming with political concern and urgency. The poem begins with long lines resembling those of "Howl," which soon thereafter take a paragraph-like shape. Again, the thematic purpose of the long lines seems to be to challenge conventional boundaries of poetic investigation—the paragraph-like form of the lines assists in this endeavor since it adds a new line shape to surprise even those who had already read "Howl."

In "Kaddish," the lines seem choppier, more condensed or economical than the lines of "Howl," punctuated throughout by dashes reminiscent of Emily Dickinson ("Because I could not stop for Death—/ He kindly stopped for me—...."[4]). The short, choppy phrases of "Kaddish" give the reader a sense of the fragmented life the poem describes—a fragmentation that is nevertheless connected to a whole poem and a whole, even though ill, psyche. As in Dickinson's poems, the dashes here seem to signify Ginsberg's psychic swerves. We might say they are psychic turn-signals, letting readers know the poet is about to take his search for memories or reflections in a new direction. They also suggest modernist elliptical spaces in which readers are able to find room to add their own interpretations of the poem's meanings. Shoshana Felman observes that bearing witness, like talking to a psychiatrist, requires a listener—that "it takes two to witness the unconscious." (15)

The first section of "Kaddish" sets the scene, beginning with an acknowledgment of Naomi's death and the poet—as is often Ginsberg's strategy—situating or grounding himself psychically and geographically: "Strange now to think of you, gone without corsets and eyes, while I walk on the sunny pavement of Greenwich Village." (CP, 217) As he sets himself for the task before him, Ginsberg ponders prior literary elegies and classical representations of death: "And read Adonais' last triumphant stanzas aloud—wept, realizing how we suffer." (CP, 217) He recalls both Eastern and Western traditions: "remember, prophesy as in the Hebrew Anthem, or the Buddhist Book of Answers." (CP, 217) Ginsberg knows that one of the ways in which a poem can take on extraordinary literary vitality is to extend prior literary traditions in meaningful new ways. Here it is as if Ginsberg is surveying literary and religious traditions of elegy in the hope that, by so doing, he might stumble upon a way to extend those elegiac traditions that will feel both personally and poetically meaningful, inspired but not limited by those memorable elegies that have come before.

Ginsberg soon begins a stroll, where observed details stir childhood memories. The poem's elevated intensity lifts off from those empirical details, those Blakean "minute particulars":

> No more of sister Elanor, —she gone before you—
> we kept it secret—you killed her—

> or she killed herself to bear with you—an arthritic heart—But Death's killed you both—No matter—....
> or Boris Godunov, Chaliapin's at the Met, hailing his voice of a weeping Czar—by standing room with Elanor & Max—watching also the Capitalists take seats in Orchestra, white furs, diamonds.
>
> (CP, 218)

As Part I winds down, evocations of Dickinson's poems about death are mixed with phrases taken from the traditional mourner's Kaddish: "Magnificent, mourned no more...." The new elegy Ginsberg is writing attains part of its emotional and literary power through the inventive way in which it shows an American poet attempting to come to grips with his mother's death by creating a new, contemporary ritual—one that can include elements of his family's religious traditions, but that must also include the tradition of great American poets: "Jehovah, accept. / Nameless, One Faced, Forever beyond me, beginningless, endless, Father in death. / ....Death, stay thy phantoms!" (CP, 220)

After ending the first section with the Dickinsonian "Death, stay thy phantoms!" Part II plunges headlong into an exploration of family madness, filled with both comedy and tragedy, in an apparent attempt to acknowledge and come to some sort of resolution about Naomi's death. One understands why Harvey Shapiro calls this section "the heart of the poem." (88) Here Ginsberg records, for instance, at age 12, taking Naomi on a three-hour bus ride to a Lakewood institution, "All the time arguing," while Naomi describes her suspicions that doctors have placed three big sticks in her back, and that Grandma is out to destroy her with Louis "under her power." Ginsberg reveals episodes of Naomi's psychic terror, with her "hiding under the bed screaming bugs of Mussolini." The empirical descriptions are stunning, as are the internal questions that Ginsberg recalls thinking about during those teenage years: "Would she hide in her room and come out cheerful for breakfast? Or lock her door and stare thru the window for sidestreet spies? Listen at keyholes for Hitlerian invisible gas?" (CP, 221) This is Ginsberg showing the poetic power that can be attained with clear imagery and realist narrative when that imagery and narrative are conveyed in a manner that is both lively and unpredictable.

Because Ginsberg recalls lines from precursors as part of his strategy of developing a meaningful contemporary ritual, some of his descriptions contain literary allusions that seem worth highlighting. At one point, Ginsberg recalls traveling with Naomi and passing bridges, where they might see old artifacts lying by the streambed. One of the items that Ginsberg lists "seeing" is a "Pocahontas bone," an image that seems to be partly a surreal vision and partly an allusion to Hart Crane's poem, "The Bridge," in which Pocahontas had been a major character. In that earlier poem, Hart Crane had searched energetically for a symbolic image that might help him reconcile American history with American ideals, past with present, humanity with nature, man with woman, white Americans with the peoples they have oppressed, and human with divine. Crane asks the Brooklyn Bridge to be his muse, hoping that the powerful symbolic image he is looking for might come not from classical literature but from the history and products of America. In "Kaddish," as Ginsberg is recalling scenes and artifacts from his past, he seems similarly to be hoping that he will be able to recall or come up with an image that might enable him to reconcile the human—in this case, his mother—with the divine in order to help give meaning and consolation regarding his mother's demise. It is as if Ginsberg is looking for all of the tools that he can possibly collect—family memories, previous poetic elegies, religious traditions, historical items, personal visions—in order to attempt to redeem Naomi's memory by the end of the poem.

In telling his mother's story in part II, Ginsberg acts both as a testifying witness to Naomi's life and as Naomi's own voice, since she is no longer around—and was not in any case sufficiently healthy—to tell her own story. Because of the selectivity of memory and the possibility of faulty memory, we as readers ought to understand that Ginsberg's account will be a partial one. It is Naomi's story, and yet in crucial ways it cannot be Naomi's story, not the whole of it and not the complete truth of it. As Felman writes, in testimony "the speaking subject constantly bears witness to a truth that nonetheless continues to escape him, a truth that is, essentially, *not available*, to its own speaker....The testimony will thereby be understood, in other words, not as a mode of *statement of,* but rather as a mode of *access to,* that truth." (15-16)

The truth Ginsberg is seeking, then, is an impressionistic one, rather than a full literal rendering of Naomi's biography. The truth to which Ginsberg's particular testimony begins to explore will be shocking to readers, and it is that shock which functions as a countervailing force to a danger foreseen by Adorno in literary testimonies, the possibility that the aestheticization which inevitably results from placing a traumatic history into a literary form may serve to smooth over, and thereby trivialize, the suffering of the victim. Shoshana Felman describes Adorno's warning in this regard, as well as his later recognition that the best response to such a possibility is to write "against" the nearly unavoidable aestheticization of literature:

> "The aesthetic principle of stylization," writes Adorno, "….make[s] an unthinkable fate appear to have had some meaning; it is transfigured, something of its horror is removed. This alone does an injustice to the victims." …..In Adorno's radical conception, ….all of writing….now has to think, to write against *itself*. (34)

The shocking nature of the "Kaddish" narrative seems to

fulfill this Adorno prescription since it shows Naomi, and the mother-son relationship, at times in raw and disturbing states that one would not normally expect to see in a poem meant to elegize a loved family member.

In Naomi's story as described in Part II, political history wraps itself around the family at almost every turn. Allen remembers Naomi reading Communist fairy tales to youths. He recalls his own youthful desire to be a "revolutionary labor lawyer....inspired by Sacco Vanzetti, Norman Thomas, Debs." (CP, 222) Paterson daily life is recalled as a mythified political struggle: "The madmen struggling over Zone, Fire, Cops & Backroom Metaphysics." (CP, 224-25) As Mike Newberry notes: "It is not just for his mother that he says 'Kaddish,'....nor for himself alone; but for America, as he sees it, the America of 'Money! Money! Money! shrieking mad celestial money of illusion!'" (101)

At one point in Part II, Allen remembers how Naomi, in a paranoid state, feared "The enemies approach." Those enemies were fused together as the FBI, Zhdanov, Trotsky, Uncle Sam, Uncle Ephraim, and Aunt Rose. Later, the gang of enemies is recapitulated as: "Hitler, Grandma, Hearst, the Capitalists, Franco, Daily News, the '20s, Mussolini, the living dead." (CP, 229) Once, coming home from a hospital stay, Naomi suspects "poisoned money" and "mysterious capitalism" are at work. The point of many of these recollections seems to be that Naomi's paranoia includes large chunks of delusion, but also some nuggets of keen perception concerning the exploitation and threats to freedom apparent in pre- and post-WWII America. As Scott Herring has noted: "There are various shades of paranoia in 'Kaddish,' levels of fear in Naomi that range from the wildly irrational to the rather sensible." (537) In Allen's view, wrapped up within Naomi's madness, one could find significant traces of a deep-rooted and totally admirable sense of justice. About two pages from the end of Part II, Ginsberg remembers that Naomi had had a stroke several years before her death in June, 1956, nostalgically contrasting his mother, before her stroke and before her progressing mental illness, with his idyllic earlier memory of a "Communist beauty" with "promised happiness at hand." (CP, 231) Beauty is importantly seen here both as a physical trait and as an assertion of idealistic politics.

After her stroke and after her worsening mental illness, Naomi fails to recognize her own son when he visits her in the hospital after a two-year absence. The following year, in June 1956, by telegram, Ginsberg received news of his mother's death, and two days later a letter from Naomi arrived. His mother wrote:

> The key is in the window, the key is in the sunlight at the window—I have the key—Get married Allen don't take drugs—the key is in the bars, in the sunlight in the window.
>
> Love,
your mother
(CP, 232)

In the context of the poem the key seems to be, like Hart Crane's Brooklyn Bridge, finding a symbol that would enable humans to touch the divine and to thereby achieve an integrated psyche and a more healthy social life. Naomi would like to believe she has passed along this ability to her son. As the poem will show, Ginsberg is grateful for his mother's visionary gift in that it adds a powerful visionary tool to his literary repertoire and seems to provide one more possible way for him to connect psychologically with his mother beyond the grave—but, of course, he will reject her specific prescriptions to get married and to avoid drugs. The remainder of the poem in some ways is a dramatic portrayal of Ginsberg's various attempts to grasp the metaphorical key.

Once Ginsberg has explored the madness, he can begin to attempt reconciliation with his mother's death and with her life. As earlier, he continues coming back to the traditional mourner's Kaddish as his base—"Magnified Lauded Exalted the Name of the Holy One Blessed is He!" (CP, 233)—

and then adds elements that were not a part of traditional religious rituals but that are meaningful in his own personal life. In Ginsberg's "Kaddish," unlike in the biblical tradition, homosexuality is proclaimed a divine quality: "Blessed be He in homosexuality!" (CP, 233) As he had years earlier recognized the angel in Moloch, in the "Hymmnn" section of "Kaddish," Ginsberg blesses elements of his mother's pain since these elements are also seen as crucial to her humanity: "Blessed be you Naomi in Hospitals!.....Blest be your bars!.... Blest be your stroke! Blest be the close of your eye! Blest be the gaunt of your cheek! Blest be your withered thighs!" (CP, 233) The same body that reveals Naomi's emotional suffering also provides a reminder of the preciousness of human life. When reading "Kaddish" and its portrayal of Naomi's suffering, the critic Helen Vendler is reminded of the words of John Keats: "Do you not see how necessary a World of Pains and troubles is to school an Intelligence and make it a soul?"(Soul Says, 13)

But where the "Hymmnn" section of "Kaddish" roughly compares to the "Holy" section of "Howl," in this highly personal poem, the resolution is not quite settled. Making this point clearly is the fact that Ginsberg undertakes two more sections in order to contemplate issues and emotions that are not yet resolved: "O mother / what have I left out." (CP, 234) Among other lingering emotions, Allen wonders whether he had empathized sufficiently with Naomi's illness while she was alive:

> only to have seen her weeping on gray tables in long wards of her universe
> only to have known the weird ideas of Hitler at the door, the wires in her head, the three big sticks rammed down her back, the voices in the ceiling shrieking out her ugly early lays for 30 years,
> only to have seen the time-jumps, memory lapse, the crash of wars, the roar and silence of a vast electric shock.
>
> (CP, 233)

Kaddish

Strictly speaking, most of these images, as Naomi's private memories, would have been unavailable to her son's observations. The fact that Ginsberg nonetheless laments his not seeing them highlights the frustrating and incomplete nature of witnessing. While memories prove useful to the grieving process, they also reveal their limitations. Even with extraordinary candor, Ginsberg is not able to witness or to recollect quite enough to reconcile himself to his mother's death. These passages illustrate the dialectical nature of ritual, which is simultaneously necessary and inadequate, even when personally relevant elements are added to the more traditional texts.

Thus the poem continues in Part IV, with Ginsberg utilizing as metaphor Naomi's physique, particularly her eyes, in lines that convey a sense of history and that also add a Breton-like layer of surrealism:

> with your eyes of America taking a fall
> with your eyes of your failure at the piano
> with your eyes of your relatives in California
> with your eyes of Ma Rainey dying in an ambulance
> with your eyes of Czechoslovakia attacked by robots
> with your eyes going to painting class at night in the
>   Bronx.
>
>   (CP, 235)

With the phrasing, "your eyes of America taking a fall," rather than "your eyes that saw America taking a fall," Naomi's eyes are shown both to have seen social forces at work and to have been partially constructed or shaped by those same social forces. Naomi's body has been victimized ("with your eyes of ovaries removed / with your eyes of shock / with your eyes of lobotomy"), and at the same time it has been actively involved in the fray to improve humanity ("with your voice singing for the decaying overbroken workers.") As a symbol, the poetic inclusion of Naomi's body, including her eyes, further underscores the social aspects of the poem—the deterioration of Naomi's body parallels the deterioration of an America in moral decline as a result of its myopic and repressive Cold War policies. Thus, Ginsberg says farewell both to his mother "with a long black shoe," as well as to his mother with "Communist Party and a broken stocking" and with her "belly of strikes and smokestacks." (CP, 234) This is the kind of embodied identification between person and history that Gregory Corso would play with a decade later in the first line of his moving elegy for Jack Kerouac, "Elegiac Feelings American": "How inseparable you and the America you saw yet was never there to see." (125)

Does the ending of "Kaddish" present the same level of resolution and hopefulness as the ending of "Howl"? I would say not, but I do think it achieves the level of reconciliation with the death of a loved one that is usually possible in the time following that death—a reconciliation that is inevitably partial and incomplete. In the Jewish tradition from which the Kaddish springs, the impossibility of achieving a total reconciliation with death has resulted in centuries-long disagreements among religious scholars about the proper way to conceptualize what happens after death. According to Kolatch: "As we study the variety of views expressed about life in the hereafter, it becomes evident that it is impossible to integrate them into a whole and label them as *the* Jewish view. There are diverse, distinct beliefs about the nature of the soul, the meaning of resurrection, and the nature of existence after death." (267)

The traditional Mourner's Kaddish ends: "May the Creator of heavenly peace bestow peace upon us and all Israel, and let us say, Amen."[5] Like Ginsberg's poem, the traditional ritual addresses the death of a loved one by including a wish for the health of a collective. Ginsberg's poem, with its recognition of intersubjectivity and publicness, appropriates this aspect of the traditional ritual, even as its worldly focus rejects the nationalist dimension of the historical Kaddish. I think it is fair to say that the poem's attempt to salvage

Naomi's life implies as well an effort to redeem a deteriorating society ("America taking a fall," "Czechoslovakia attacked by robots," "starving India"). Like "Howl," this poem, with its heavy emphasis on bearing witness and candid memory, seems to be aimed as much toward improving the future as it is toward resolving the past.

In the last section of "Kaddish," the graveyard scene, Ginsberg moves into more metaphysical territory, as if the poem and the grieving process cannot conclude until some sort of spiritual comprehension has been reached. The section's rhythm is structured through an anaphoric repetition which begins each line—a repetition that alternates between "Lord Lord" and "caw caw," the latter identified in the first line as the sound of a crow. The ostensible effort, the reason for shifting back and forth between Lord and crow, is to search for some meaningful symbolic connection between the earthly and celestial:

> caw caw my eye be buried in the same Ground
>   where I stand in Angel
> Lord Lord great Eye that stares on All and moves in
>   a black cloud
> caw caw strange cry of Beings flung up into sky over
>   the waving trees
> Lord Lord O Grinder of giant Beyonds my voice in a
>   boundless field in Sheol.
>
>   (CP, 235)

Actually, "search" may be too strong a word here, since there seems to be no organized thematic exploration for an effective symbolic resolution, but rather a succession of emotions and surreal or abstract thoughts. In "How *Kaddish* Happened," Ginsberg acknowledges this structure-by-association rather than by logic-driven narrative: "Standing on a streetcorner one dusk another variation of the litany form came to me—alternation of Lord Lord and Caw Caw .. and I went home and filled in that form with associational data." (346) It is as if Ginsberg here in the final section is hoping to stumble across some way to process his mother's death that will finally feel meaningful, as according to kabbalistic tradition: "Whoever delves into mysticism cannot help but stumble, as it is written: 'This stumbling block is in your hand.' You cannot grasp these things unless you stumble over them."[6]

In the beginning of "Kaddish," Ginsberg writes that he has read "Adonais' last triumphant stanzas aloud." In personal conversations that I had with Ginsberg in later years, he often used to cite Shelley's "Adonais" as one of his favorite elegies. Shelley's memorable elegy for Keats was filled with clearly stated suggestions for how the living might take comfort despite the death of such a young and talented poet: Keats' work would be remembered for a long time—"his fate and fame shall be / An echo and a light unto eternity." In addition, Keats' death would end the suffering the young, ill poet had been experiencing in life—"From the world's bitter wind / Seek shelter in the shadow of the tomb." And furthermore, death would unite Keats with other divine elements in the universe: "No more let Life divide what Death can join together."[7]

In "Kaddish," Ginsberg does not seem to be able to offer clearly articulated lessons that would feel truthful to the ending of this dramatic poem or that would feel meaningful in relation to the tragic end of his mother's life, but he does seem to arrive at some similar lessons by means of symbolic and literary language. By the end of the section, "Lord Lord" and "caw caw" have been used to express a diversity of emotions, including praise, grief, acceptance, and awe. In the penultimate line, Ginsberg implicitly recognizes that he is not soon going to stumble over any clear metaphysical lessons, and so he praises "all Visions of the Lord." (CP, 238) "All Visions" I take to mean the entire range of beliefs in what may lie beyond human comprehension. In such a state of awe, there is no way to rationalize death, and so the poem's last line reaches a reconciliation that is not a clearly stated reason for the poet to take comfort in his mother's passing, but rather a purely symbolic resolution that conjoins the earthly and celestial through a beautifully rhythmic linguistic juxtaposition: "Lord Lord Lord caw caw caw Lord Lord Lord caw caw caw Lord." (CP, 235)

In Ginsberg's mid-fifties' journals, there is a poem called "Elegy for Mama," written November 24, 1957, which appears to have served in part as draft material for "Kaddish." In his journal, Ginsberg tries to picture Naomi in the afterlife: "—and find you? / Naked, singing folk songs among the / smelly tendrils of roots of trees?" (396) Significantly, there is no such afterlife image in the conclusion of "Kaddish"—as if such an image would have felt false, an insincere attempt to narrate a full closure.

In the Kabbalah, the individual letters that make up words are believed to have their own life energy or magic. In the last line of "Kaddish," it is as if Ginsberg attempts to redeem Naomi's life and death, not through reasoned comfort nor an imagined afterlife, but purely by setting together a magical combination of letters and words in order to reach a symbolic assertion of connection between the earthly and the divine. Daniel Matt describes the relationship between the earthly and divine worlds, as that relationship appears in the Kabbalah, this way: "There is a secular world and a holy world, secular worlds and holy worlds. These worlds contradict one another. The contradiction, of course, is subjective. In our limited perception we cannot reconcile the sacred and the secular, we cannot harmonize their contradictions. Yet at the pinnacle of the universe they are reconciled." (153)

Naomi's symbolic redemption is augmented by the literary allusion of the last section. Ginsberg's crow recalls the thrush of Walt Whitman's "When Lilacs Last in the Dooryard Bloom'd," the thrush whose song inspires Whitman to realize—as Shelley had explicitly realized in "Adonais" and as we eventually do in most cases when a friend or loved one dies after an illness—that death ends life's sufferings. In Whitman's elegy, "They themselves were fully at rest, they suffer'd not, / The living remain'd and suffer'd." (280)

Although Ginsberg does not make this point directly at the end of the poem, by evoking Whitman's elegy for Lincoln, "Kaddish" implicitly acknowledges the end of Naomi's suffering and elevates the significance of her life by placing her in a Lincolnesque position as subject of an important American elegy.

It is also important to think of Naomi's death in a post-World War II context in which, as Scott Herring notes in his essay on "Kaddish," "Ginsberg was a member of the first generation of young Jewish intellectuals forced to come to grips with the murder of six million Jews." (536) In Herring's compelling view, Ginsberg's "Kaddish" becomes "not just an elegy for a single woman but for all the dead of the Holocaust." (536) Certainly, the poem includes many references to ways in which Hitler functioned as a major source of Naomi's illness, and Herring is right that, in elegizing a Jewish Communist, the poem is elegizing "the very sort of person whom the Final Solution was intended to destroy." (541) It also makes sense that if the poem is partially an elegy for the six million Jews who died in the Holocaust, it would end on a note that does not offer any clear, rationalized comfort.

But although there is no clear comfort at the poem's end, I do think that one of the projects of "Kaddish" has been to undertake an in-depth and uncensored effort to redeem Naomi's political idealism and her hope for a better future. In "Kaddish," the poet has mourned the death of a "Communist beauty" with "promised happiness at hand." He has paid tribute to his mother for passing along a dream: the key in the window that Naomi has left behind, and that "should be left behind," the key that is available to those who learn to use their poetic imaginations to "take / that slice of light in hand—and turn the door—and look back see / Creation glistening." (CP, 234) The poem has viewed the breakdown of Naomi in relation to the Stalinist legacy in Russia and to Cold War policies of the United States, as well as to her continuing fear of Hitler's Germany. Viewed in this context, I think it is fair to say that Naomi's symbolic redemption exhibits a broad refusal on the poet's part to let her utopian dream ("promised happiness") of a better world die without at least showing a deep commitment to keeping its legacy alive.

In terms of Ginsberg's personal life, even if the poem cannot offer the explicitly comforting lines of a poem like Shelley's "Adonais," the act of witnessing, of giving testimony, will likely aid the healing process. What Shoshana Felman says about psychoanalysis and pedagogy is also true about poetry, that it can often help to enable change by virtue of its performative elements and Ginsberg's providing testimony on behalf of his mother is the kind of powerful performance that can aid in both self- and social-healing.

* * *

Several other poems which appeared in Ginsberg's book, *Kaddish and Other Poems,* seem worth discussing for the way they deal with political themes.

Like "America," "Death to Van Gogh's Ear" (1958) is a poem that uses humor, surprise phrasings, and unique or eccentric insights to take explicit aim at then-current economic, political, and military policies. The poem comically suggests placing a representation of Van Gogh's ear on America's cash bills—instead of American presidents or other historic American figures—under the perhaps naive belief that the problem of economic exploitation might be attenuated simply by including a symbol of widely acknowledged artistic brilliance on the currency. The poem also offers some of Ginsberg's most witty, insightful, and directly prophetic lines about the potential of political verse to help reshape a nation:

> the day of the publication of the true literature of the
>   American body will be the day of Revolution
> the revolution of the sexy lamb
> the only bloodless revolution that gives away corn....

> fiends in our government have invented a cold-
> turkey cure for addiction as obsolete as the
> Defense Early Warning Radar System
> I am the defense early warning radar system
> I see nothing but bombs
> I am not interested in preventing Asia from being
> Asia
> and the governments of Russia and Asia will rise and
> fall but Asia and Russia will not fall
> I doubt if anyone will ever fall anymore except
> governments
> fortunately all the governments will fall
> the only ones which won't fall are the good ones
> and the good ones don't yet exist
> But they have to begin existing they exist in my
> poems....
> Now is the time for prophecy without death as a
> consequence.
> (CP, 175-76)

Here is a condensed, powerful claim for the ability of visionary poetry to catalyze social change that is nonviolent ("without death as a consequence") and that prioritizes food over bombs ("the only bloodless revolution that gives away corn"). Ginsberg's technologically cutting-edge call for a poet to be heard as the true "defense early warning radar system" recalls Shelley's call for poets to be understood as the unacknowledged legislators of society. Certainly, an early warning system via poetry would be a lot cheaper than many of the Pentagon or CIA's billion-dollar setups that have failed to predict such tragic events as the World Trade Center attacks of September 11, 2001. As we saw when more than 10,000 poets sent work to a website (www.poetsagainstthewar.org) to protest the 2003 war in Iraq, the poets had a far better radar sense than the government's most expensive technologies about the array of post-invasion difficulties that would ensue.

And, as I pointed out in the last chapter when I argued against some recent views of Ginsberg as a supporter of postmodernist political theory, I think it is important to note again Ginsberg's utopian belief in the possibility of creating a far better political system that the ones we have thus far seen: "they have to begin existing they exist in my poems." As opposed to postmodern *a priori* suspicion of any and all political systems, this is Ginsberg taking up the Blakean prophetic tradition in which it is believed that what a poet can imagine can one day be made real, a powerful rationale for poets to take up social causes.

In "POEM Rocket," Ginsberg writes a long-lined humorous political poem, also stylistically somewhat reminiscent of "America." Although it may not be as funny or as inventive regarding historical matters as the earlier piece, "POEM Rocket" presents a densely packed, engaging exploration of emerging scientific technology. Like Whitman praising the positive potential of a newly expanding America, in "POEM Rocket" Ginsberg praises the upside potential of new and growing rocket science. I would argue that, for both Whitman and Ginsberg, the praise is not mere naïve celebration—it is the prophetic hope that, despite the deep inherent dangers (like slavery or the slaughter of Native Americans during American expansionism or the use of rocket technology for its destructive military capacity), the poet can at least potentially help push technology in a more positive direction. As he had written in "Death to Van Gogh's Ear," "they have to begin existing they exist in my poems."

In "POEM Rocket," Ginsberg writes about science more than he had in previous poems, expressing the belief that interplanetary exploration may show Earth's citizens that new possibilities of social arrangements are possible: "All is possible so we'll reach another life." (CP, 171) Under this scenario, scientists are seen as artist-like visionaries: "Scientist alone is true poet he gives us the moon / he promises the stars he'll make us a new universe if it comes to that." (CP, 171) As in many a popular science fiction novel, interstellar locations offer utopian retreats, described in dense imagistic language, where "not one star disturbed by screaming madmen from Hollywood / oil tycoons from Romania making secret deals with flabby green Plutonians." (CP, 171)

In this 1957 poem, written four years before humans were first sent into space by Russian or American rockets, Ginsberg acknowledges that there are risks and unknowns about what may await us in space ("Slave camps on Saturn Cuban revolutions on Mars?"), but perhaps a visionary poet can help direct scientific research into beneficial sectors:

> I send up my rocket to land on whatever planet
>   awaits it
> preferably religious sweet planets no money
> fourth dimensional planets where Death shows
>   movies
> plants speak (courteously) of ancient physics and
>   poetry itself is manufactured by the trees
>   (CP, 172)

This sort of poetic urging toward a peaceful conception of space would certainly come in handy in today's culture, when so much of governmental focus on space concerns its potential military-related uses. An image that centers this poem alludes to Ginsberg's earlier "Sunflower Sutra": "Which way will the sunflower turn surrounded by millions of suns?" In other words, why lock ourselves into current social habits and modes of thinking, when there are potentially millions of sources of nourishment, of energy and ideas, in the universe? A decade after the introduction of the atomic bomb, this poem uses poetic language to advocate that scientific thinking and exploration go in a more humane direction. By asking readers to think about what outer space might look like, the poem implicitly urges its audience to take a long-range view of Earth, a distanced perspective that might spur readers into viewing Earth's many social crises in a new light.

"Ignu" is another humorous and memorable poem

Kaddish

with "America"-length oratorical long lines. In the poem's second line, Ginsberg proclaims: "Ignu knows nothing of the world." (CP, 211) Immediately thereafter, he begins to redefine generally accepted characteristics of ignorance and inspiration. Those folks exhibiting traits which society often associates with ignorance are inversely seen by Ginsberg as the inspired. W.C. Fields, Rimbaud, Whitman, Celine, Dickens, Burroughs, and Williams are all ignus. Using Ignu as a symbolic thread, Ginsberg stitches together disparate elements to sew a tradition. Those who are truly inspired perform acts which society may often consider odd or crazy: "he attacks the rose garden with his mystical shears snip snip snip"; "Ignu with his wild mop walks by Colosseum weeping"; "Ignu goofs nights under bridges and laughs at battleships." (CP, 211) Peace is presented in a striking image that is both sensible and absurd: "ignu is a battleship without guns in the North Sea." (CP, 211) Ignu listens to jazz, and recognizes the divine within others—"Ignu has sought you out he's the seeker of God." (CP, 212) Significantly, Ignu moves beyond humanity's all-too-common narrow cultural or nationalist prejudices, and recognizes multi-ethnic connectedness, "reborn a bearded humming Jew of Arabian mournful jokes." (CP, 212)

Ginsberg's poem, "Ignu," redefines ignorance and inspiration using language that is fresh, unpredictable, funny, aware of multiple traditions, densely imaginative, and intellectually challenging. Yet within the poetic spontaneity we might also notice that, more even than the "best minds" of "Howl," ignu seems to be a virtue that is found exclusively in men. Unlike the largely expressionist catalogs of "Howl," "Ignu" names names, and they are all male names. Ignu is "a great cocksman" remembered by "Hollywood dolls or lone Marys of Idaho long-legged publicity women and secret housewives." (CP, 211) One ignu "chases girls down East Broadway into the horror movie." (CP, 212)

In the last chapter of this book, I will try to draw out some conclusions about the legacy of Ginsberg's political poems.

Almost all of those conclusions will focus on Ginsberg's progressive legacy, but I will also note how it was certainly true for much of Ginsberg's career (with the exception, I will argue, of his later years) that his views in the area of gender were often circumscribed by the dominant (i.e. far from progressive) views of his time—that, for much of his career, his poems did not explore or explode traditional conceptions of gender as they explored and exploded almost every other dogma of his era.[8]

In my view, the theoretical need to utilize different criteria for judging aesthetics and politics allows for the possibility that the core progressive energies of an artist might move beyond even that artist's own political or ideological understanding. Thus, even as one can note that there were not many feminist aspects visible in Ginsberg's poems from the 1950s and 1960s, one can still understand how their vast liberatory energies provided key inspiration cited by many important feminist poets to follow.[9] And yet, one can also note how the explicitly male-exclusive thread in "Ignu" significantly hinders the poem's effectiveness at redefining genius and inventive intelligence.

Other pieces in *Kaddish and Other Poems* seem to me quite powerful without reservation. These include: "Europe! Europe!" "The Lion for Real," "To Aunt Rose," "At Appollinaire's Grave," and "The End."

In "Europe! Europe!" Ginsberg uses fast-moving short lines, without punctuation, to span the globe and portray the interconnectedness of international misfortunes. The lack of quality love ("love is not perfect") is seen as related to industrialism and war: "cranks / of war" and cities of "work & brick & iron & / smoke of the furnace." (CP, 179) Juxtapositions that highlight social antagonisms indicate the dehumanizing results of a mechanized society: the "think factory" promotes "tin dreams of Eros" so that "mind eats its flesh" and "man's work is most war." (CP, 180) As a consequence, one can survey the interconnected world and find it loaded with horrifying details of hunger, madness, poverty, racism, and death—as the poem's fourth stanza does forcefully:

> Bony China hungers brain
> wash over power dam and
> America hides mad meat
> in refrigerator Britain
> cooks Jerusalem too long
> France eats oil and dead
> salad arms & legs in Africa
> loudmouth devours Arabia
> negro and white warring
> against the golden nuptial
> Russia manufacture feeds
> millions but no drunk can
> dream Mayakovsky's suicide
> rainbow over machinery
> and backtalk to the sun.
>
> (CP, 180)

    These social criticisms are poetically carried by a rhythm with surprising velocity, by super-condensed images that seem simultaneously real and surreal and that in just a few words ("Bony China hungers brain / wash over power dam") can seem to raise a multitude of issues (poverty, hunger, lack of free speech, ecological problems) as well as a literary invocation of Mayakovsky's radical tradition by invoking the Russian poet's "An Extraordinary Adventure which Befell Vladimir Mayakovky in a Summer Cottage." By utilizing short free-verse lines to carry its elevated imagery and condensed linguistic intensity, this poem expands the stylistic repertoire of this poet who had earned his reputation thus far mainly through the long lines of "Howl," "America," "Sunflower Sutra," and "Kaddish." As a poet who well understood the value of surprise in poetry, one of the ways that Ginsberg consistently attempted to be surprising was to keep experimenting with different forms and different rhythms, including varied looks on the page.

Like "Kaddish," the moving poem "To Aunt Rose" interweaves poignant personal and family moments with international political events. In his hometown of Newark, New Jersey, Ginsberg recalls his family's support of the Abraham Lincoln Brigades, Americans who went to Spain in the 1930s to fight with democratic forces against the fascists during the Spanish Civil War. Ginsberg remembers a day room where "I sang Spanish loyalist songs / in a high squeaky voice" while Aunt Rose "limped around the room / collected the money." (CP, 192) As in the long elegy for his mother, the social content here is imbued with increased emotional intensity by virtue of the candor of his personal memories:

> —the time I stood on the toilet seat naked
>   and you powdered my thighs with Calomine
>   against the poison ivy—my tender
>   and shamed first black curled hairs
>   what were you thinking in secret heart then
>   knowing me a man already—
>   (CP, 192)

Death here is viewed as the great equalizer ("Hitler is with / Tamburlane and Emily Bronte") that ends the life of both tyrants and family, and that opens up space for new social developments to come:

> last time I saw you was the hospital
>   pale skull protruding under ashen skin...
>   the war in Spain has ended long ago
>   Aunt Rose.
>   (CP, 193)

For Ginsberg, political change requires creating new social institutions, but also more than that. It additionally requires a transformation, an opening, of human consciousness: "I think the possible direction of development then, to solve problems created by vast population & centralized network control, is toward increasing the efficiency and area of brain use, i.e. widening the area of consciousness in all directions feasible." (Prose Contribution, 342) It is the resolve to explore strategies for "widening the area of consciousness," a resolve stemming from both personal and political desires, that undergirds the poem, "The Lion for Real," as well as the pieces in *Kaddish and Other Poems* written under the influence of hallucinogenic drugs. By connecting political ideas and observations with an exploration of opening up one's own psyche or consciousness, these poems convey their political material through a strategy of personalization of a different sort than the more family-focused verse of "Kaddish" or "To Aunt Rose."

Written in four-line stanzas, "The Lion for Real" reveals a poet both humored and frightened by the shattering of the psychic armor (or, in Reichian terms, the "character armor") that protects empirical senses from unreal or hallucinatory intrusion. In this poem, the intrusion of an imaginary lion into the poet's living room demands to be accepted as a literal description of events: "I came home and found a lion in my living room / Rushed out of the fire escape screaming Lion! Lion!" (CP, 182) The lion, viewed symbolically as a divine presence, physically leaves the apartment before the end of the poem, and yet it still "eats my mind." (CP, 183) For Ginsberg, "widening the area of consciousness" entails opening the mind freely, which both subjects one to potential personal terror on the one hand, and, on the other hand, to the possibility of a positive psychic transformation.

As part of Ginsberg's exploration of "widening the area of consciousness," this was the era in which he famously experimented with, and wrote poems while under the influence of, various mind-altering drugs, including hallucinogenic drugs. James Breslin describes the drug poems in *Kaddish* as "solipsism of purely private associations." (Origins, 402) And yet, if we think of these attempts to explore possibilities for widening consciousness as, at least in part, a component of a larger strategy for opening readers' minds (and the poet himself) up to the possibility of working toward social change, then I think we can see how these poems might, depending on their actual content, at least partially work as political poems as well as personal poems. Ginsberg had previously experimented with traditional plant-based hallucinogenic substances, including peyote, and in the spring of 1959 he tried the human-made LSD for the first time at the invitation of Stanford University researcher Gregory Bateson. After his first experience, Ginsberg wrote a note to his father, placing his experiment into a long-accepted literary tradition of drug-induced inspiration, including Coleridge's, and even urged his father to find a researcher at Rutgers University who might administer LSD to Louis. "It was astonishing," Allen wrote to his father of the initial LSD experience, "I lay back, listening to music, and went into a sort of trance state (somewhat similar to the high state of Laughing Gas) and in a fantasy much like a Coleridge world of Kubla Khan."[10] "It's a very safe drug," he told Louis, describing an acid trip as "like a cosmic movie."[11]

Later, in 1960, Ginsberg was introduced to Harvard professor Timothy Leary, who expected to be embraced by academic institutions for his scholarly research with psychedelics. When, as part of Leary's experiment, Ginsberg tried psilocybin, it was clear that Ginsberg's instincts in these experiments were political as well as personal. According to biographer Schumacher, "Allen wanted to begin with a call to Khrushchev," but was persuaded by Leary's assistant "to call Kerouac instead."[12] Under the drug's influence, "he was going to start his own peace and love movement; he would help settle the differences between Kennedy and Khrushchev; he would save the world!"[13]

In the early 1960s, Ginsberg testified before the U.S. Congress and urged the possibility of students having the opportunity to experiment with LSD in safe environments. This will be understandable to the many thousands of Ginsberg's readers, including many activists, who have tried hallucinogenic drugs and felt at least some degree of increased curiosity or open-mindedness. But in the early 21st century, after decades of a government-initiated "war on drugs," it may be difficult for some readers to fathom the words "LSD" and "safe" appearing on the same page, let alone with utopian sociopolitical intent. And by the late 1960s, it was clear that LSD could potentially carry at least some risks in that it could have lasting, even immediate, harmful effects upon some people who tried it. But it is important to remember that Ginsberg's early 1960s advocacy of drug experimentation was not meant to encourage drug abuse or addiction—for Ginsberg, controlled experimentation with mind-expanding drugs was part of a deeply felt belief at the time that, in Schumacher's words, "psychedelic drugs offered the potential for personal discovery that could lead to a better society."[14] Indeed, in 2014, LSD was once again being used by psychiatrists in controlled experiments to see whether it might help some patients, including some suffering from terminal cancer, to deal better with personal crises around end-of-life issues.[15]

As for the drug poems themselves—that is, the poems identified by Ginsberg in their titles or in interviews as having been written under the influence of psychedelic drugs—I think the results are mixed. My two favorites are "Magic Psalm" and "The End." The other poems seem to me to be filled with too many trite thoughts and images: "a bottle / that never knew it existed" ("Laughing Gas"); "death death death death death the cat's at rest," ("Mescaline"); and "god god god god god god the Lone Ranger" ("Mescaline")—the latter two examples of juxtapositional streams of consciousness that merely seem to offer weak reminders of the powerful last line of "Kaddish."

At their best, the drug poems in *Kaddish and Other Poems* display, in their stream of consciousness style, an attention to the details of mental process that is often quite engaging. And among the mental-tracings and hallucinogenic perceptions, political subjects and social concerns regularly arise. In

"Magic Psalm," Ginsberg offers a magnificent image-packed prayer for a transformed world:

> Descend O Light Creator & Eater of Mankind,
>   disrupt the world in its madness of bombs and
>   murder,
> Volcanos of flesh over London, on Paris a rain of
>   eyes—truckloads of angelhearts besmearing
>   Kremlin walls—the skullcup of light to New
>   York....
> myriad jewelled feet on the terraces of Peking—veils
>   of electrical gas descending over India—cities
>   of Bacteria invading the brain—the Soul
>   escaping into the rubber waving mouths of
>   Paradise....
> this is the Golden Bell of the Church that has never
>   existed.
>
> (CP, 264)

Obviously, this is not a description of historically specific political wishes, but in its internationalist and peace-desiring sweep and in its surrealist "anticipatory illumination" of a world that "has never existed," it seems to me to express successfully the results of a socially concerned psychic experiment to "widen the area of consciousness." Since the unlocked or unprotected imagination may invite the terrifying as well as the beautiful, Ginsberg prays in this poem to "ride out this wave, not drown forever in the flood of my imagination." (CP, 264)

Because, in these drug poems, the hopeful outlasts the threatening, and because social idealism is only realizable if many others in addition to the poet himself accept the challenge to raise their personal consciousness, Ginsberg triumphantly ends this particular group of poems by diving, in "The End," into an imagined universal divine energy—"I am I, old Father Fisheye that begat the ocean"(CP, 267)—and announcing: "come Poet shut up eat my word, and taste my mouth in your ear." (from "The End") "I am I," the phrase that begins the poem, is both a syllogism and a dispersal of subjective identity: Since the I is both Ginsberg and not Ginsberg, the directive to "eat my word" can function both as a directive from a universal presence telling Ginsberg himself to shut up and open his mind to a higher level of spiritual and social awareness, and also as a plea from Ginsberg himself to readers and other poets to open their own minds, since as Whitman reminded readers at the beginning of "Song of Myself": "every atom belonging to me as good belongs to you."

As mentioned above, by the end of the 1960s, it was apparent that psychedelic drugs, including when they were made poorly or when too much was ingested, could do real harm to some individuals, even while they may have helped others expand consciousness. And it was also apparent by the later part of the 20th century that drugs like heroin and cocaine could become major health problems for those who became addicted. It was also clear that the ensuing "war on drugs" was resulting in some major social injustices, such as harmful pesticide spraying in South America or inordinately high numbers of American young people, especially blacks and Latinos, being sentenced to long prison terms, sometimes for minor crimes like simple possession of small amounts, including small amounts of marijuana, a drug which has recently started to become legal, particularly for medical needs, in numerous states across the country.

Ginsberg himself always distinguished between drugs with the potential to widen consciousness (including marijuana) and addictive narcotics. He was never a proponent of the latter, although he certainly urged their decriminalization, arguing that drug addiction ought to be treated as a medical problem and not a criminal one. In a November 13, 1995 interview in *New York* magazine, for instance, Ginsberg said: "Our interest in psychedelic substances as educational tools, particularly marijuana, mushrooms, and LSD, led to a more realistic approach to drug laws, recognizing that tobacco and alcohol are physically more destructive than all other drugs except cocaine. Thus, the junk problem should be decriminalized and medicalized, and hemp, now a problem, should be transformed into an asset for the failing family farm to help reinhabit the countryside and provide some sustainable product (cloth, rope, et al.) as alternative to plastic consciousness."[16]

By the late 1980s, I often heard Ginsberg publicly cautioning against the overuse or reckless use of psychedelic drugs, on occasion advising meditation practice as a way to ground controlled psychedelic experiments. In a 1987 interview with Steve Silberman, Ginsberg acknowledged, "It seems to me that acid can lead to some kind of breakdowns maybe....So I think in the 60s I wasn't prepared to deal with acid casualties from the point of view of a reliable technique for avoiding those casualties." He proposed "that people should be prepared with meditation, before they take acid....There should be an educational program to cultivate meditative practice and techniques, so that when people get high on acid and get into bum trips they can switch their minds easily—and there are ways of doing it."[17] By 1970, Ginsberg himself preferred meditation as a way to "widen the area of consciousness" and "used drugs rarely: the occasional joint at a party or LSD in special circumstances, such as Big Sur or the Welsh countryside."[18] But he always opposed the "war on drugs" as both morally offensive for the injustices it created, and as medically ineffective, and he continued to point out how often U.S. government policy covertly encouraged, overlooked, or even sometimes participated in the international drug trade as a way to help fund international groups it was openly or secretly backing. Several of Ginsberg's most popular later poems, such as "CIA Dope Calypso" focus squarely on U.S. covert policies that secretly supported the international drug trade.

* * *

In *Kaddish and Other Poems*, self- and family-exploration were integral elements in Ginsberg's literary strategy to turn social ideas and observations into powerful poetry. The major exploration, of course, was related to Ginsberg's grieving process in relation to the death of his mother, Naomi. By the mid-1960s, a different kind of death would come to dominate the focus of his most important work, this time the enormous death toll wrought by the escalating war in Vietnam.

Chapter 4: "Wichita Vortex Sutra" and the Anti-Vietnam War Years

After a 1963 trip to Asia, including India and Japan, Ginsberg decided to pursue Buddhist practice more seriously than he had done previously.[1] During that same trip, Ginsberg stopped for a brief four-night visit to Saigon. There, he learned about South Vietnamese President Diem's religious persecution of Buddhists, and of Buddhist-led protests against Diem that were taking place at the time. The war in Vietnam had not nearly grown to full-scale by 1963, but thousands of American advisers had already been sent into the country to support the Diem regime. By spending time in Saigon with United Press reporter Neal Sheehan, Ginsberg was able during his short stay to acquire an insider's sense of the worrisome war that was developing:

> He was in Saigon for four nights and spent most of his time hanging out at Neal Sheehan's office at United Press, where all the U.S. newsmen socialized.... He wrote Peter that he "got the whole story of Vietnam war gossip from them—EEEK—it's like walking around in a mescaline nightmare—I can arrange to fly inland and see 'model hamlets'—battles, but decided no and am scairt.... The war is a fabulous anxiety bringdown. It's *awful*."
> (Miles, 323)

It should therefore not be surprising that Ginsberg subsequently participated in an early political protest on the issue of Vietnam, in San Francisco, October 28, 1963. The protest was organized against the visit of Madam Nhu, wife of South Vietnam's chief of secret police and sister-in-law of then-President Diem, whose "inflammatory statements in the summer and fall of 1963," according to former Secretary of Defense Robert McNamara's later account, "angered South Vietnamese Buddhists and alienated the United States from the Diem regime." (459)

By the mid-1960s, the war in Vietnam had become the most hotly contested foreign policy issue in decades, and the root cause of a new and fast-growing social protest movement. Vietnam was also America's first televised war. With vivid TV reports about the war (even if the coverage was often toned down or "spun,") and about anti-war protests, it seems in retrospect only natural that the war should have created unprecedented national discussion. Whether television coverage served to increase or lower public opposition to the war is a question that I will look at later in this chapter—and a question that may have shifted after Walter Cronkite began to publicly question the war in 1968 after the Tet offensive. I think it is fair to say here that, for those who had decided that the war was morally wrong, often by "seeing through" pro-war commentary, televised coverage of the war and of demonstrations against the war offered many Americans new ways to think about expressing their opposition.

Looking back from his observer's perch in the 1990s, former Defense Secretary Robert McNamara, one of the war's main architects, describes the damage which the Vietnam War inflicted on American soldiers and American society: "By the time the United States finally left South Vietnam in 1973, we had lost over 58,000 men and women; our economy had been damaged by years of heavy and improperly financed war spending; and the political unity of our society had been shattered, not to be restored for decades." (320) While serving under President Lyndon Johnson, McNamara had helped design the military policy which initially escalated U.S. involvement in the region. In his well-publicized 1996 book, *In Retrospect,* McNamara revealed his considered conclusion about the war: "we were wrong, terribly wrong." (p. xx)

Radical historian Howard Zinn describes the U.S. military intervention in Vietnam from 1964 to 1972 as a "maximum military effort" on the part of "the wealthiest and most powerful nation in the history of the world" to defeat "a nationalist revolutionary movement in a tiny, peasant country." (*Twentieth Century,* 171) According to Zinn, the effort included "everything short of atomic bombs"; it was a case of "organized modern technology versus organized human beings, and the human beings won." (*Twentieth Century,* 171)

The historical background for U.S. involvement in the war can be traced back to 1945, when Ho Chi Minh declared Vietnamese independence from France. At that time and with U.S. financial backing, France attempted militarily to retain control of the country. When French troops were ultimately defeated in 1954, an agreement was reached under which "the French would temporarily withdraw into the southern part of Vietnam, that the Vietminh would remain in the north, and that an election would take place in two years in a unified Vietnam to enable the Vietnamese to choose their own government."[2]

A 1954 Joint Chiefs of Staff memo advised President Eisenhower that Ho Chi Minh would almost certainly win such an election. Zinn describes the American maneuvers which followed:

> The United States moved quickly to prevent the unification and to establish South Vietnam as an American sphere. It set up in Saigon as head of the government a former Vietnamese official named Ngo Dinh Diem, who had recently been living in New Jersey, and encouraged him not to hold the scheduled

> elections.... As the *Pentagon Papers* put it: "South Viet Nam was essentially the creation of the United States."
>
> (*Twentieth Century,* 174)

It was in August, 1964, with American military advisers firmly in place, that President Johnson "used a murky set of events in the Gulf of Tonkin, off the coast of North Vietnam, to launch full-scale war on Vietnam." (*Twentieth Century,* 177) As is now widely acknowledged, according to Zinn, "It later turned out that the Gulf of Tonkin episode was a fake, that the highest American officials had lied to the public." (*Twentieth Century,* 177) Although McNamara himself does not admit to having knowingly deceived the American people, he does admit in his book that he "learned in a meeting with General Giap that the presumed second attack in the Gulf of Tonkin, on August 4, 1964, did not occur." (xvii)

In an updated 1985 preface to her prize-winning study of the Vietnam war, *Winners and Losers,* Gloria Emerson describes the delusion under which many Americans continue to view the war as one that was imminently winnable if only the U.S. military had used all the weapons at its disposal:

> Many Americans still say, "Well, we shouldn't have gone in but once we were there we should have tried to win it." It is as if these civilians cannot grasp how ferociously we tried to have our own way, how the U.S. military bombed and burned and defoliated the south and had howitzers, year in and year out, fire at mountains where no human moved as if the mountains must be humbled too. (p. viii)

According to Emerson, close to two million Vietnamese were killed or wounded in South Vietnam alone between 1965 and 1975, with over 10 million refugees generated. (357) After a visit in the late 1990s to Vietnam, Robert

McNamara estimated a Vietnamese death toll from the war of 3.6 million, an astoundingly horrifying figure that should have affected America's foreign policy and mainstream public consciousness in ensuing decades far more than it did. As Emerson notes, "Some 7-1/2 million tons of bombs were dropped on North Vietnam during the war, more than three times the total dropped during WWII. Over half a million tons of toxic chemicals and 7,000 tons of toxic gas were also dropped." (358) In Zinn's illustrative description, this bomb tonnage amounted to "almost one 500-pound bomb for every human being in Vietnam." (*Twentieth Century*, 180)

By 1967, McNamara had changed his mind about the desirability of the war, although he did not speak up while in office, believing that loyalty to the president required his public silence. (320) Subsequently, in his 1996 book, he pointed to five different occasions between late 1963 and early 1973 when U.S. troops could have been withdrawn and, citing the independent character of Ho Chi Minh, he expressed strenuous disagreement with conservative analysts who remain convinced that heavy war casualties were necessary to prevent the spread of Russian and Chinese communism through southeast Asia. (320-21) McNamara also listed "eleven major causes for our disaster in Vietnam" (321), including: a "profound ignorance of the history, culture, and politics of the people in the area"; a failure to "draw Congress and the American people into a full and frank discussion and debate....before we initiated the action"; and a failure to "retain popular support in part because we did not explain fully what was happening and why we were doing what we did." (322)

Crucially, even in his 1996 role as a semi-apologetic critic of the war, McNamara could not bring himself to go all the way and acknowledge that it was simply, morally wrong to unilaterally invade another country that had done nothing to the United States, and that it was especially reprehensible because one of the major goals of the war had been to prevent the country from being led by a person, Ho Chi Minh, whom the U.S. believed would have been elected to office if a democratic vote had been allowed.

In the mid-1960s, growing opposition to the escalating conflict in Southeast Asia took root all across America. According to Zinn, as the war progressed, "there developed in the United States the greatest antiwar movement the nation had ever experienced, a movement that played a critical part in bringing the war to an end." (*Twentieth Century,* 171) Zinn describes the unprecedented growth of the antiwar movement. In early 1965, "when the bombing of North Vietnam began, a hundred people gathered on the Boston Common to voice their indignation." Four years later, at a rally on October 15, 1969 on the same Boston Common, there were 100,000 people. (*Twentieth Century,* 188) And, as Zinn observes, the antiwar sentiment was in no way limited to America's more traditionally liberal cities: "Perhaps 2 million people across the nation gathered that day in towns and villages that had never seen an antiwar meeting." (*Twentieth Century,* 188)

The growth of antiwar protests was similarly felt in the nation's capital. By 1970, "Washington peace rallies were drawing hundreds of thousands of people," and in 1971, "twenty thousand came to Washington to commit civil disobedience, trying to tie up Washington traffic to express their revulsion against the killing still going on in Vietnam. Fourteen thousand of them were arrested, the largest mass arrest in American history." (Zinn, *Twentieth Century,* 188) As Zinn points out, students "were heavily involved in the early protests against the war." (*Twentieth Century,* 192) A 1969 survey of just 232 campuses revealed that over 200,000 students at those schools had participated in antiwar protests.

The antiwar protests had a noticeable effect on public opinion, as well as a real influence on policy decisions. In 1970, a Gallop poll concluded that 65% of Americans believed it was time for the U.S. to withdraw its military from Vietnam. From the internal writings of the *Pentagon Papers*, Zinn concludes that President Johnson's "decision in the spring of 1968....to slow down for the first time the escalation of the war" was motivated "to a great extent by the actions Americans had taken in demonstrating their opposition to the war." (*Twentieth Century,* 202) And while he announced publicly that the antiwar protests would not influence his military decisions, Nixon in his 1978 memoirs "admitted that the antiwar movement caused him to drop plans for an intensification of the war." (*Twentieth Century,* 203) In those memoirs, Nixon wrote: "Although publicly I continued to ignore the raging antiwar controversy....I knew, however, that after all the protests and the Moratorium, American public opinion would be seriously divided by any military escalation of the war."[3] Significantly, Nixon's admission was a clear case of an American president acknowledging the potential power of mass political protests to alter government policy.

The Vietnam War provided a litany of moral concerns for Ginsberg, as for so many other Americans. In addition to his opposition to war in general, and his rejection of America's Cold War foreign-policy philosophy, Ginsberg was also attracted to this cause initially because of the Diem regime's oppression of Buddhist monks. As a poet, Allen Ginsberg was able to capture much of the spirit of the antiwar movement. He was also one of the poets who provided the movement with ideas and inspiration, both through his antiwar poems and by getting involved in actual planning meetings for movement rallies and events.

In 1965, for instance, Ginsberg attended an antiwar planning meeting in Berkeley where organizers were addressing the potential of violence taking place at an upcoming rally at which the notorious biker's group, the Hell's Angels, was threatening to beat up demonstrators. Ginsberg's suggestions to the organizing committee involved putting the protest together as a nonviolent theatrical spectacle, one which would simultaneously convey the group's opposition to the war and also lower the level of anxiety and tension within both the demonstration and the wider community. Ginsberg began his suggestions, which were published in alternative newspapers as "Demonstration or Spectacle as Example, As Communication or How to Make a March/Spectacle,"[4] by highlighting the likely appeal of an "imaginative, pragmatic, fun, gay, happy" event. (*Deliberate Prose,* 9) He suggested the event be organized as a parade that could "embody an example of peaceable health which is the reverse of fighting back blindly," (*Deliberate Prose,* 10) a demonstration that would include flowers, musical instruments, calisthenics, zenlike signs with slogans such as "Nobody Wants To Get Hurt—Us or Them," and candy bars to offer the Hell's Angels and police. (*Deliberate Prose,* 11) In his essay, Ginsberg also suggested that those with movie cameras bring them, in part to help provide documentary support for later court cases to those who might be arrested. (*Deliberate Prose,* 12) As I mentioned in Chapter One, the sort of theatrical techniques that Ginsberg suggested here in 1965 greatly influenced key portions of the anti-Vietnam War movement—including the Yippies' Abbie Hoffman and Jerry Rubin—and the theatrical ways in which that movement would move forward in the ensuing years. And even though few of today's progressive organizers likely know of Ginsberg's influence on the way that many contemporary social movements have been organizing public rallies, Ginsberg's suggestions for theatrical demonstrations have been clearly visible in recent years, from the anti-corporate globalization movement of the late 1990s and early 2000s to the international protests against the 2003 war in Iraq and the Occupy Wall Street movement of 2011-2012.

Ginsberg's most influential poem of the Vietnam war era, written in February 1966, was "Wichita Vortex Sutra," whose climactic line, "I here declare the end of the war!"(CP, 415) —testing the activist potential of poetry— was adopted and spread further into the mainstream culture through popular songs containing similar lines by John Lennon and Phil Ochs. In this poem, Ginsberg not only addressed the military conflict in Southeast Asia, but also incisively explored the way the war was being portrayed, and even promoted, by America's mainstream media.

In the decades before the Vietnam War, social observers like the Frankfurt School theorists in Europe and the American writers Dwight McDonald and C. Wright Mills had begun to write about the influence of media and culture on political power. The Canadian cultural critic, Marshall McLuhan, published *Understanding Media* in 1964, in which he emphasized the growing, all-encompassing importance of electronic media through the now-famous saying, "the medium is the message." Ginsberg had shown a decade earlier that he understood the role of mass media in shaping political consciousness when he asked in his poem, America, "Are you going to let your emotional life be run by Time Magazine?" And by the mid-1960s, he had become an avid reader of America's alternative press, even when he was traveling outside the country. In 1961, he wrote to his father, Louis: "Do you ever see I.F. Stone Newsletter? That's the best glances political comment & reporting I see from USA—I get it regularly, someone put me on a list." (*Family Business*, 152)

In the weeks preceding his penning of "Wichita Vortex Sutra," as he traveled through Kansas for several weeks performing his poetry, Ginsberg noticed with a new clarity the ways in which America's mainstream press was helping to shape support within America's heartland for the Vietnam War. He decided he would address the war in part by addressing that press coverage. In "Writing War Poetry Like a Woman," Susan Schweik shows how literary critics had traditionally privileged antiwar poetry written from the point of view of front-line combatants, whether the poets themselves were front-line soldiers or not. This critical bias, according to Schweik, meant that praise was largely withheld from women writers writing poems about war, such as H.D.'s "Trilogy," since women had not historically had access to the front lines of wars. Schweik does not devalue the importance of high-quality experiential antiwar poems, but she does consider it a problem if, for literary critics, experience is

Wichita Vortex Sutra

"required as an aesthetic, political, and moral criterion for the proper war poem." (180-81)

As an outspoken gay male poet in a society whose army continued until recently to ban openly gay men from serving, Ginsberg in the 1960s was unlikely to write authentic-sounding verse in the voice of a frontline combatant. And yet, "Wichita Vortex Sutra" does appropriate the notion of privileging direct experience—only after subverting the very notion of experiencing war so that it includes the reality of an antiwar poet and activist experiencing the war through direct reception of mainstream media accounts, through face-to-face dialogues with returning soldiers, and through firsthand involvement in the front lines of antiwar rallies.

During the recent war in Iraq, there was a widespread realization on the left, which many readers of this volume will likely recall more easily than they will recall the Vietnam era, about the important role which the mainstream media played in building public support for the initial U.S. invasion in 2003. For example, many readers will remember the pre-war, front page articles in the *New York Times* that appeared to confirm the Bush administration's claims about a weapons of mass destruction program still run by Saddam Hussein in Iraq. One of the reasons that many of us are highly conscious of contemporary media's influence on political policy is that we now have a wide range of independent news sites, media activist groups, and progressive films that focus considerable attention on the role of the media in politics. A small sample of these would include Fairness and Accuracy in Reporting (FAIR), internet sites like commondreams.org and truthout, the nationally broadcast Democracy Now! hosted by Amy Goodman, and movies like Michael Moore's *Fahrenheit 911* and Danny Schechter's *WMD: Weapons of Mass Deception.* In the mid-1960s, such progressive media criticism was not nearly as ubiquitous and a poem like "Wichita Vortex Sutra" was able to help get readers to look at media war coverage in a more critical way. In this poem, his most popular of the 1960s, Ginsberg demonstrated that the Vietnam War could be effectively opposed, not simply by highlighting the immorality of the war and the tragedy of massive numbers of dead persons, but also by addressing questions of language and media in an effort to help reshape public thinking and thereby decrease public support for the war.

As in "Howl," Ginsberg in "Wichita Vortex Sutra" employs a strategy of entering social madness in order to acquire the strength to prophesize its liberation. In this case, the social madness is clearly defined from the start in political terms: that is, the unwarranted war in Vietnam, and the domestic policy and propaganda which supported that conflict. The redemption being sought is a more specific and tangible one than it had been in "Howl"—the end of the war. That substantive goal is reinforced by a literary strategy of modernist montage—Ginsberg's juxtaposition of sensory perceptions, historical reflections, and personal fantasy—insofar as this juxtaposition creates an "anticipatory illumination" in the way that Ernst Bloch used that phrase, whereby a future can be imagined that does not currently exist. The future being anticipated here is a nonviolent end to the hostilities in Southeast Asia.

Several critics have focused on this poem's strategy of montage to place it within the postmodern tradition,[5] and this is a poem that I have seen several Language poets in personal talks, including Charles Bernstein, cite as an influence on the Language Poetry school. It is certainly easy to see how the non-narrative structure of the poem would appeal to writers in the Language Poetry school, but I would nonetheless argue that Ginsberg's goal in using montage is a different one than the goal of most Language poets, in that he does not seem to me to be using montage to undermine notions of reason and universal values, but to undermine specifically the reason and values that were then being used by those in power to justify the war in order to thereby attain the aim of more reasonable and moral universal values of peace and international cooperation.

In his book, *Allen Ginsberg's Buddhist Poetics*, Tony

Trigilio notes a tension between what he sees as Ginsberg's postmodern tendencies and his yearning for common human values: "Despite my own tendency, too, toward postmodern readings, I find that as I read the 'Buddhist part,'....I see both the groundless ground of 'elements in freefall' (Scalapino) and an effort to combine this freefall and its sacred particularity into an abiding concern for individual and shared human experience that we might call humanism." (193) I would contend that the way to make sense of these different tendencies in Ginsberg's work is to do as I have suggested from the beginning of this volume—to see the aesthetic, the psychological, and the political as different (although often overlapping) categories that require different ways of conceptualizing each. Although Ginsberg's Buddhist spiritual or psychological concerns, which Trigilio examines in ways that yield many deep and important insights, may often contain the attempt to relinquishing the self and accept inner contradictions; and although Ginsberg's poetic process may sometimes, as in "Wichita Vortex Sutra," utilize elements of non-narrative, like juxtaposition, that are common in postmodernist (and also modernist) poetry; I do not believe that his politics, either in his poems or in his life, were postmodernist, in that his politics seem to me to always have humanistic goals based on reason and progressive universal values.

Although I am not sure how familiar Ginsberg was with Muriel Rukeyser's "The Book of the Dead" (1938), "Wichita Vortex Sutra" shares important traits, both in form and substance, with Rukeyser's earlier modernist epic. In her piece, Rukeyser goes to West Virginia in 1936 to investigate a recent Union Carbide industrial tragedy in which 2,000 men have died of silicosis after being given the wrong protective masks by the company. Like Ginsberg in "Wichita Vortex Sutra," Rukeyser takes note of her perceptions and thoughts as they come to her along the road to her destination:

> These are roads to take when you think of your
>   country
> and interested bring down the maps again,
> phoning the statistician, asking the dear friend,
>
> reading the papers with morning inquiry. (10)

In the poem, Rukeyser records and juxtaposes verbatim explanations offered by investigators, recorded testimony of surviving spouses, and her own ideas about the matters at hand. Rukeyser's use of a mix of empirical perception and modernist experimentation structures this long poem, which is clearly written in Rukeyser's humanistic hope of contributing toward lowering the risk of such dire industrial malfeasance continuing to repeat itself into the future.

During the Vietnam War, Ginsberg, like Rukeyser, is also "reading the papers." To record his observations while riding across the middle of the country, as well as his personal responses to those observations, Ginsberg brings a tape recorder (which had been given to him by Bob Dylan) while traveling from Wichita, Kansas to Lincoln, Nebraska in the back of a Volkswagen bus, with his longtime friend and lover Peter Orlovsky doing the driving. In the poem, as Ginsberg notices and records newspaper headlines and radio commentaries, he also presents memories, analyses, and information which his empirical perceptions trigger. This technique of spontaneous recording exhibits a willingness to allow his poem to take its shape from its material, rather than to fit his observations into a predetermined formal package. In this case, the poet's willingness to submit his ego to the flow of the material can be seen as a performative fulfillment of the Buddhist notion of self-relinquishment. Such self-negation contrasts sharply with the boastful, nationalistic strategies of the war-makers, whose calculated phrasings and news spins are self-consciously manipulated to instill support for pre-planned, militaristic goals.

The poem's exquisite title juxtaposes the sutra—a form

of Buddhist wisdom literature which alludes to the Buddha's sermons—with a city commonly thought to symbolize conventional Americana. As in the war itself, East meets West in the title of the poem, producing a vortex which the body of the poem will confront. Buddhism plays a central role in various ways in this poem: Ginsberg's embrace of Buddhist philosophy humanizes the Vietnamese; Buddhist theory of mantra-chanting provides a conceptual foundation for the poem's climactic lines; ideals of self-relinquishment challenge the American ideology of liberal individualism which in this mid-1960s era guides a hawkish foreign policy; and the inclusion of Buddhist perceptions implies a willingness to consider a Vietnamese view of the conflict, asserting an internationalist perspective that challenges the sort of nationalism or blind patriotism that led many Americans toward unquestioned support of their government's military policy.

There have been many studies since the end of the Vietnam War regarding media coverage of the war. In his 2005 book, *War Made Easy: How Presidents and Pundits Keep Spinning Us to Death,* Norman Solomon notes that many people today believe that television coverage of the war was chiefly responsible for turning people against it at the time. Solomon quotes several researchers and studies to debunk that common view, concluding that "during the 1960s and in later decades, TV news has played a much larger role in promoting and accepting wars than in challenging them." (135) Solomon quotes Daniel Hallin who had examined the data from three extensive studies: "All reject the idea...that television was consistently negative toward U.S. policy or led public opinion in turning against the war." (135) Solomon also points to a Harris poll commissioned by Newsweek in which 64 percent said that television had bolstered their belief in the war, while only 26 percent said TV coverage had caused them to increase their opposition. (135) Solomon points out that American media had mostly presented optimistic portrayals about the war, with few alternative viewpoints and almost no interviews with Vietcong representatives, until the Tet offensive in 1968, after which "Walter Cronkite famously decried the war as a 'bloody stalemate'." (140)

According to Chester Pach, in his discussion of TV coverage of the Vietnam war, "And That's the Way It Was," the Johnson administration rejected the possibility of expressly censoring war reporting during the Vietnam War era, realizing that such overt censorship would anger journalists in a nation that prized its First Amendment. Instead, the U.S. military exerted "informal pressures to shape reporting on Vietnam." (92) These informal pressures included warnings that stations showing American casualties might be barred from combat zones, and restrictions on providing exact casualty figures from individual battles. The Pentagon also hoped that its incentives—help with transportation, lodging, and arranging interviews—might garner more favorable articles from reporters. (92-95) In Pach's view, most of the news media bowed to these informal pressures. For example, "editors hardly ever allowed ghostly pictures of the dead or dying into American homes during the dinner hour. Indeed, just 3 percent of news reports from Vietnam showed heavy fighting." (95) Furthermore, the media's "acceptance of the cold war outlook that was responsible for U.S. intervention in Vietnam" (100) contributed to a dearth of historical analysis and debate about the underlying context and morality of the war. Like Norman Solomon, Pach asserts that, until the Tet Offensive, most news reports "suggested that the United States was winning the war." (98)

In filing biased reports that were insufficiently skeptical of Pentagon updates and body-count claims, journalists violated their pretensions of objectivity, pretensions that on other occasions were used to justify a hyper-technical language that deflated the conflict's emotional pitch and physical toll. On those latter occasions, the press would incorporate the Pentagon's Orwellian-sounding code names for military missions in their own news reports—using for example, "Operation Ranch Hand" to describe the saturation spraying of Vietnam with deadly Agent Orange. I. F. Stone had sarcastically written in 1967: "Any time the Pentagon runs out of the glamorous names it gives these operations, we'd suggest a code name suited to this combination of monstrous power with dim intelligence. Why not Operation Dinosaur?"[6]   Noam Chomsky points out that the media's unwillingness to describe fully the scope of American actions in Vietnam continues to this day to result in American misapprehension of the war's enormous casualties. In a study following the 1991 Gulf War, researchers at the University of Massachusetts asked people what they thought were the number of Vietnamese deaths that resulted from that earlier war in Vietnam. As Chomsky notes, "The average response on the part of Americans today is about 100,000. The official figure is about two million. The actual figure is probably three to four million." (*Media Control,* 278)

There were notable exceptions to biased coverage of the Vietnam War in the mainstream press. In mid-1965, Morley Safer, who would later go on to 60 Minutes fame, filed a film report from Vietnam asserting that a U.S. marine company had killed a small group of Vietnamese civilians. The goal, according to Safer's initial and follow-up reports, was to teach Vietnamese villagers that the American military was done "playing with them." (quoted in Pach, 102) According to Pach, Safer's reporting was roundly attacked, the charge led by President Johnson himself. Pach writes: "'Are you trying to fuck me?' Johnson asked caustically in a telephone conversation with CBS president Frank Stanton." (103) While Safer insisted that such criticisms "did not temper his reporting," in Pach's judgment Safer began to describe the atrocities he witnessed, no longer in terms which found the Pentagon at fault, but "as part of the timeless brutality of war." (103) Overall, risk-taking reporting was rare among mainstream television news journalists, so that it seems clear Ginsberg's criticisms of mainstream Vietnam war coverage in his poem, "Wichita Vortex Sutra," were insightfully on the mark.

The Poetry and Politics of Allen Ginsberg

Unlike the long lines of most of his earlier major works, "Wichita Vortex Sutra" uses short lines that cascade across the page, a visual correlative of the poet's unpremeditated and rapidly shifting thoughts and perceptions during his highway journey. In part I, the poet presents sensory observations, and records the provocative musings those perceptions stir. In language condensed to eliminate interpretive moments, Ginsberg begins by describing his eyeing of a mid-western industrial landscape: "Red sun setting flat plains west streaked / with gauzy veils, chimney mist spread / around christmas-tree bulbed refineries." (CP, 402) This is the common Ginsberg poetic strategy of opening a poem by situating himself historically and geographically:

> I come
>   lone man from the void, riding a bus
>   hypnotized by red tail lights on the straight
>   space road ahead—
>   (CP, 402)

The poem's method of responding to the war is presaged by the way Ginsberg responds to the local landscape—through both direct perception and by listening to radio reports: "*In advance of the Cold Wave / Snow is spreading eastward to / the Great Lakes.*" (CP, 402) Ginsberg recalls that "angry telephone calls to the University" have preceded his scenic trip. In an act of Christian-like compassion, Ginsberg turns the tables on those middle-American Christians who would condemn him: "Thy sins are forgiven, Wichita! / Thy lonesomeness annulled, O Kansas dear!" (CP, 403) This is the same sort of humane attitude Ginsberg had urged in his earlier work, "Who Be Kind To" (1965), in which he had advocated a politics based on showing compassion even toward mean-spirited or incompetent political leaders:

> Be kind to the politician weeping in the galleries
>   of Whitehall, Kremlin, White House

Wichita Vortex Sutra
Louvre and Phoenix City
(CP, 367).

In "Wichita Vortex Sutra," whatever political differences may exist, a human need for love and acceptance unites Ginsberg even with his critics in Nebraska and Kansas:

Come, Nebraska, sing & dance with me—
   Come lovers of Lincoln and Omaha,
      hear my soft voice at last
         (CP, 403).

Ginsberg poses emotive expression ("weeping," "ecstasy", "laughter") as a curative for the "staring Idiot mayors / and stony politicians" (CP, 403) who represent the repression of feeling that undergirds war-making. In "Wichita Vortex Sutra," historicizing—or demythologizing the historical and political myths being propagated by the U.S. government and U.S. press—is the poetic strategy used to create a powerful political poem, so that this poem asserts that "Truth breaks through!" the politicians' falsehoods and stone-like lack of empathy. In "Wichita Vortex Sutra," one of Ginsberg's aims was to create a "force field of language which is so solid....that it will contradict—counteract and ultimately overwhelm the force field of language pronounced out of the State Department and out of Johnson's mouth." (quoted in Schumacher, 463)

Throughout part I of "Wichita Vortex Sutra," descriptions of mid-western landscape continue. The commercialism of signs advertising Wrigley's gum and Sinclair gasoline inspires heightened recognition of the importance of "language, language," spurs historical recollections ("William Jennings Bryan sang / *Thou shall not crucify mankind upon a cross of Gold!*"), and urges initial musings about alternative political possibilities: "What if I sang till Students knew I was free / of Vietnam." (CP, 405) Ginsberg's "What if" resonates with the "What if" that Adrienne Rich describes as the question of radical art, the question of considering new possibilities: "Any truly revolutionary art is an alchemy through which waste, greed, brutality, frozen indifference, 'blind sorrow,' and anger are transmuted into some drenching recognition of the *What if?*—the possible. *What if?*....the question the dying forces don't know how to ask." (*Found There*, 241)

Part II of the poem begins by appropriating the title of a mainstream TV talk show, "Face the Nation" and shifts toward a deeper immersion into the political and the historical. While the network TV show may not, according to the poem's implications, have taken its own title seriously, Ginsberg does. Scenic descriptions of his travels are juxtaposed with montages presenting the political distortions and advertising slogans that at the time were being aired to the nation. It is as if these messages were infiltrating American consciousness while U.S. troops were infiltrating Vietnam: "bare trees lining the road / South to Wichita / you're in the Pepsi Generation Signum enroute / Aiken Republican on the radio 60,000 / Northvietnamese troops now infiltrated." (CP, 406) Bits of canned war news are juxtaposed with suppressed or forgotten history: "McNamara made a 'bad guess' .... / '8000 American Troops handle the / Situation'.... / in 1954, 80% of the / Vietnamese people would've voted for Ho Chi Minh / wrote Ike." (398) By juxtaposing commercial slogans with manipulative war reportage and unearthed documentary evidence, part II adopts a strategy to expose and demystify the warmakers' attempts to create public support for the conflict through media spin-doctoring and factual obfuscation. The fact that U.S. leaders understood that Ho Chi Minh would easily have won a popular democratic vote in Vietnam—and that the war was thus at least partially intended to subvert a foreign country's ability to carry out a democratic vote—is one of the ultimate historical truths that should enable audiences to see that the U.S. invasion of Vietnam was both unwarranted and immoral.

In "Wichita Vortex Sutra," Ginsberg records the headlines he observes in local newspapers: "Omaha World

Herald—*Rusk Says Toughness / Essential For Peace*." (CP, 407) Official doublespeak and "television language" serve to objectify human beings, turning human life into quantifiable equations ("the human meat market" [CP, 407]) —thus, the Pentagon can make a "Bad Guess" about the number of American troops that would be needed to win this war, and can attempt to dehumanize casualties by announcing the death toll numerically as "three five zero zero per month." (CP, 407) Along the lines of McLuhan's "the medium is the message," the communication industry's very technology assists in obscuring and abstracting the brutality of the war: TV's "screaming faces" can sometimes appear less lifelike when presented as "electric dots on television." (400) Major corporations with an interest in supporting the power structure own the largest media outlets, and thus Ginsberg names television and print media sources with one long, aggregated label: "N B C B S U P A P I N S L I F E." (CP, 409) In a way, this aggregation may remind readers a little of the aggregation of various social and cultural forces that became Moloch in "Howl," but this time the problem is identified with real-life, current corporate names and not with a mythic name out of a biblical book. This long list of initials provides a corporate label for the "culture industry" theorized by Adorno, the culture industry which Noam Chomsky has claimed "manufactures consent." For Ginsberg, the use of linguistic and visual obscuration aimed at propagandizing in favor of war and against human emotion amounts to a bad magic. Cold war logic has led to irrational "formulas for reality" wherein "Communism" becomes "a 9 letter word / used by inferior magicians." (CP, 409)

To oppose the obfuscation by public officials and the mainstream press, Ginsberg names the war clearly as "the scene of TERROR," whose victims include actual "Pale Indochinese boys." (CP, 406) He poignantly demands the restoration of humanity to the war's victims, those dead Vietnamese whom TV network executives had largely decided not to show during dinnertime: "Has anyone looked in the eyes of the dead?" (CP, 408) It is interesting to think about how sometimes one simple, poignant line can have an enormous effect on people's lives. The outstanding American poet, Andy Clausen, who later became a longtime friend of Ginsberg's and of mine, has often publicly credited that particular line in "Wichita Vortex Sutra," which Clausen saw Ginsberg read on television, for turning his life around—for turning him against the Vietnam War and toward becoming a poet, and for motivating him to leave the Marines in 1966 soon after he had joined up in his early twenties as a young Golden Gloves boxer from Oakland, California.

In "Wichita Vortex Sutra," Ginsberg alludes to literary precursors, like the Civil War nurse Walt Whitman, who have offered more peaceful and cooperative visions for America: "the Prophecy of the Good Gray Poet / Our nation 'of the fabled damned' /or else...." (CP, 408) He alludes to the legend of George Washington chopping down the cherry tree ("Father I cannot tell a lie" [CP, 407]) to highlight the distance between the purported democratic ideals of the nation's founding fathers and the lies currently being handed to the American public as justifications for the war. In a line that I believe is one of the most powerful lines in all of Ginsberg's poetry, he perceives that the mainstream press's overwhelming use of false or obfuscating language to show explicit or implicit support for the war serves to rob language itself of the ability to help create more peaceful alternatives: "almost all our language has been taxed by war." (CP, 414)

A longtime war correspondent for *The New York Times* now turned peace activist, Chris Hedges, has similarly written: "The hijacking of language is fundamental to war."[7] Ginsberg in this poem is presenting alternative information, partially erased history, visions of more cooperative human relations, and humane humor in large part to attempt to return a meaning to language, so that language might once again be enlisted on the side of creating peace.

For Ginsberg, the project of returning meaning to language becomes central to the task of restoring art's potential to alter public views and to help enact social change. In *The Postmodern Turn*, Steven Best and Douglass Kellner describe the role which culture can play in changing public beliefs this way: "It is culture that molds the sensibilities, and thus, a radical cultural politics attempts to undo the enculturation of the dominant culture by providing new ways of seeing, feeling, thinking, talking, and being." (276-77) For Ginsberg, the escalation of the Vietnam War depended on a pro-war ideology and pro-war consciousness taking hold within the American public: If thought and ideology are viewed as potentially productive, then a poetic project aimed at the American consciousness could help speed the war's end by inspiring new, more peaceful ways of seeing and thinking.

Ginsberg's project in "Wichita Vortex Sutra" in large part fulfills one of the political functions of critical art described by Best and Kellner as "a defamiliarization from the dominant mode of *experiencing* reality, what Marcuse has termed an alienation from alienation." (277) As part of Ginsberg's project to subvert the false consciousness of blind patriotism and the media's manufacturing of consent to the Vietnam war, "Wichita Vortex Sutra" alludes to a history of past American adventurism in the service of corporate greed, noting that the U.S. "overthrew the Guatemalan polis in '54 / maintaining United Fruit's banana greed / another thirteen years" and helped pay for "the lost French war in Algeria." (CP, 410)

After Ginsberg quotes a passage from the February 14, 1966 *Kansas City Times*: "Word reached U.S. authorities that Thailand's leaders feared that in Honolulu Johnson might have tried to persuade South Vietnam's rulers," (CP, 408) the poet pronounces that "The last week's paper is Amnesia." (CP, 408) Cultural critics like Myra Jehlen and Sacvan Bercovitch have written persuasively about the ways in which ahistoricism can be seen as a core element of American literature at least through the 19th century. Bercovitch, for example, describes an American "rhetoric of consensus," which, in opposition to European theorists like Hegel or Marx, pretends that important historical contradictions can be encompassed in this large continent rather than resolved through historical struggle. In Bercovitch's terminology, traditional philosophy in the United States, even in dissident philosophers like Emerson, saw this shift from history and historical struggle to a notion of transcendence or moving beyond historical struggle. Against America's tradition of ahistorical nationalism, Ginsberg, in "Wichita Vortex Sutra," offers an historicized view of human interconnectedness: "When a woman's heart bursts in Waterville / a woman screams equal in Hanoi" (CP, 412)—an image similar to Martin Luther King's maxim that injustice anywhere is a threat to justice everywhere

With Vietnam's natural landscape being bombarded by napalm and toxic defoliants, Ginsberg asserts that efforts for peace will require a renewed appreciation for natural beauty ("ponds in the hollows lie frozen, / quietness" [CP, 411]), as well as a renewed focus on the importance of love in social relationships, since "All we do is for this frightened thing / we call Love, want and lack." (CP, 413) As in "Howl," solitude is here seen to further a spiritual alienation which hinders healthy human emotions: "O but how many in their solitude weep aloud like me." (CP, 413) Throughout "Wichita Vortex Sutra," Ginsberg attempts to substitute for a language of polarization a language designed to unify and heal, to create peace between East and West as well as between antiwar poet and skeptical readers: "I search for the language that is also yours." (CP, 414)

If, in much of "Wichita Vortex Sutra," Ginsberg uses historicized observations to give the poem its literary vitality and to counter the Pentagon's pro-war spin, in other parts of the poem, he acknowledges that it will take more than historical perceptiveness to help end this war. Effective opposition to the ill-spirited magic and mythification used by the war industry will require, for Ginsberg, both a restoration of historical memory and a liberatory magic capable of confronting Pentagon lies. While, early in the poem, it may have appeared that Ginsberg was criticizing in a universal way the Pentagon's use of myth-making to shape American consciousness, by the end of the poem it becomes clear that it is only a certain type of mythologization that is criticized—myth-making that is based on false history and that is used by the government to induce public approval of state-sponsored violence.

The critic Myra Jehlen writes that generally "there is some basic opposition in intellectual impulse between those who erect imaginary worlds and those who seek to excavate the foundations of this one." (*Literary Criticism,* 41) Along those lines, the poet Czeslaw Milosz praises imaginative verse while expressing skepticism about the possibility of writing important poetry that revels in journalistic instincts: "documentary poems belong to literature and one may ask, out of respect for those who perished, whether a more perfect poetry would not be a more appropriate monument than poetry on the level of facts." (84) For Ginsberg, who was deeply influenced by the empirical verses of predecessors like William Carlos Williams and Charles Reznikoff, creating an intelligent and progressive mythology does not rest in opposition to empirical perceptiveness, and thus Ginsberg's tonic to war-making propaganda embraces a mix of both humanistic historicism and utopian imagination.

Ginsberg's instincts to combine both the factual and the visionary parallel those of another contemporary political poet, Adrienne Rich, whose literary project is strongly influenced by Muriel Rukeyser. Rich describes Rukeyser's influence in this regard: "Over time, some of the facts circulated by the newsletters enter my poetry. As an image here. A voice there. Muriel Rukeyser spoke of two kinds of poetry: the poetry of 'unverifiable fact'—that which emerges from dreams, sexuality, subjectivity—and the poetry of 'documentary fact'—literally, accounts of strikes, war, geographical and geological details, actions of actual persons in history, scientific invention. Like her, I have tried to combine both kinds of poetry in a single poem, not separating dream from history." (*Found There*, 21) By mixing the imaginative and the factual, "Wichita Vortex Sutra" is able both to deconstruct dominant power-structure myths and falsehoods and to fulfill what Best and Kellner consider the positive function of cultural politics, the "task of 'aesthetic education,' the reshaping of human needs, desires, sense, and imagination through the construction of images, spectacles, and narratives that prefigure different ways of seeing and living." (277)

Approaching the poem's emotional apex, Ginsberg invokes the idealistic promise of widespread happiness from the Declaration of Independence, to "make this nation one body of Prophecy / languaged by Declaration as / Happiness." (CP, 414) As he had expressed as far back as "America," Ginsberg implies that American reality ought at least to live up to its own liberal founding principles. And, as in that earlier work, he simultaneously pushes traditional American liberalism a few steps further, here embracing Buddhism's concept of relinquishing ego to implicitly criticize American nationalism. To fully attempt this prophecy aimed at making a contribution towards helping to creating peace between the U.S. and Vietnam, Ginsberg calls "all Powers of imagination / to my side" (CP, 414), beginning with a litany of Eastern deities, saints, yogis, and swamis, as if to balance out the Western self-absorption chiefly responsible for executing the war. He summons "Shambu Bharti Baba naked covered with ash," symbolizing acceptance of the human form and human mortality. He calls upon "Sitaram Onkar Das Thakur who commands / give up your desire," signifying the need to let go of ego, or self, in the search for peace, compromise and reconciliation.

Inviting "Shivananda who touches the breast and says OM," (CP, 414) Ginsberg asserts the need to connect language with the voice and the body, and alludes to the importance of mantra-theory to his political aims. As Ginsberg notes in *Composed on the Tongue*, the theory of mantra-chanting includes the anticipation of physical transformation: "if you say, AUMMM, AUMMM, for a couple hours, after a while your brain begins vibrating. Or the vibration begins there

Wichita Vortex Sutra

and begins to affect the whole body." (34) In *Buddhism: its essence and development,* Edward Conze writes: "A mantra is an incantation which effects wonders when uttered." (182) By "getting into touch with the unseen forces around us through addressing their personifications," (183) Buddhists have traditionally used mantras as "the chief vehicle of salvation" (182) and used mantra-chanting to protect the spiritual life from material threats: "From the third century A.D. onward, the Buddhists made an ever-increasing use of mantras for the purpose of guarding their spiritual life from interference by malignant deities." (182) Since mantra-chanting is seen theoretically as capable of altering physical reality, the challenge in "Wichita Vortex Sutra" is to invent the right mantra to protect both American and Vietnamese life, both spiritual and material, from the forces of the U.S. war architects.

The litany of Eastern personages called forth in "Wichita Vortex Sutra" is succeeded by an entreaty to William Blake, the "invisible father of English visions." (CP, 415) Ginsberg also summons the three major Western deities, Christ, Allah, and Jaweh, highlighting what he sees as their most positive traits: Christ's non-judgmental acceptance, Allah's compassion, and Jaweh's righteousness. Finally, since along the lines of Saul Alinsky's *Rules for Radicals* effective communication requires speaking "within the experience" of one's audience, and since the aim here is to transform the consciousness of the mainstream American public, Ginsberg must make a "Mantra of American language now." (CP, 415) He is well-equipped for this task, having assembled the powers of poetic imagination, having through the process of poetic juxtaposition reconciled Eastern and Western traditions, and having embraced both accurate historical empiricism and the sort of "anticipatory illuminations" that can be created through modernist poetic techniques. Therefore, from within "this Vortex named Kansas," Ginsberg is ready to utter the poem's historic, climactic lines:

The Poetry and Politics of Allen Ginsberg

>   I lift my voice aloud,
>   make Mantra of American language now,
>   I here declare the end of the War!
>   (CP, 415)

Critic Charles Altieri cites these climactic lines as evidence of a naive tendency on Ginsberg's part to embrace religiosity at the expense of political acumen. According to Altieri, these lines show that Ginsberg "equates abolishing war in one's head with the claim that the Vietnam War has been literally transcended." (*Enlarging*, 131) But, as when Carl Solomon was metaphorically freed from Rockland in part III of "Howl," what is implied here is not any sort of misunderstanding about the dire nature of current events, but another assertion, in the Blakean prophetic tradition, that what can be imagined can be made real, the hope that a poet's strategic attempt to influence public opinion might in the long term bear pacifistic fruit. Culminating in these unforgettable lines, "Wichita Vortex Sutra" puts historical observation, poetic language and elevated imagination to the ultimate test, the test of whether poetry can, in the long run, play at least some positive role in helping to transform reality, under the belief that visionary poetry can have an effect on public consciousness and political debate.

As previously argued, the potential for the real-world success of a poetic experiment like these lines in "Wichita Vortex Sutra" is intimately wrapped up with the work and influence of wider social movements. And, as also mentioned previously, Ginsberg's idea of experimenting to see whether his declaring the end of the Vietnam War in a powerful poem could actually help to speed the war's end was soon taken up by the popular songwriters John Lennon and Phil Ochs, who each wrote and sang songs announcing that the war was over. In November 1967, the anti-war activist group, the Yippies, organized a "War Is Over" demonstration in New York City, which drew about three thousand young people who met in Washington Square Park and then ran through

Wichita Vortex Sutra

downtown Manhattan announcing that the war was over. Although it is usually impossible to say with any level of confidence whether a political poem has had a tangible effect on government policy, these three lines of "Wichita Vortex Sutra"—by first influencing popular songwriters and then antiwar activists—certainly inspired the antiwar movement which in turn helped to shorten the war. Certainly, Ginsberg's pronouncement of the war's end in "Wichita Vortex Sutra" did not have an immediate magical effect, but I would argue that it did make an important cultural contribution toward the anti-war movement's long-term struggle to change the consciousness of many Americans and to force the U.S. government to eventually abandon its disastrous war policy in Vietnam.

* * *

The end of "Wichita Vortex Sutra," beyond its climactic declaration of peace, is, I think, a bit weaker. In the last section of the poem, Ginsberg appears to place a large portion of the blame for the continuation of an escalating social repressiveness that makes war possible on the Kansas-born temperance advocate Carry Nation: "Carry Nation began the war on Vietnam here." (CP, 418) While one can understand Ginsberg's desire (like Wilhelm Reich's) to link the suppression of sensuality with increased militarism, it seems like a poor assertion, in a poem concerned with presenting war's historical context, to blame a woman for this war, when the legacy of American patriarchy is that key military decisions have nearly always been reserved for men.

Critic Paul Carroll persuasively criticizes the poem's last lines ("The war is over now— / Except for the souls / held prisoner in Niggertown / still pining for love of your tender white bodies O children of Wichita!" [CP, 419]) for reducing the problem of racism and black poverty in America to a repressed desire for interracial romance. There is also, I think, the question of why Ginsberg utilizes an insulting slang description of the black section of Wichita in a poem that has been so careful to create a new, more liberatory language. Even if the poem's ending is admittedly weaker than its earlier sections, we can nonetheless see the progressive intent inhabiting these lines. Earlier parts of the poem have made the case that different aspects of social exploitation are interconnected. Here, at the end of "Wichita Vortex Sutra," Ginsberg asserts that domestic racism and social inequality are ingredients within America's wider militaristic culture and will remain problematic even after the Vietnam conflagration has ended. Indeed, long after the war did end, Ginsberg continually addressed issues of racial discrimination in his poetry and in his activism. In his later years, he may have come to realize that the poem's ending was not its strongest suit. In his four-volume CD box set, *Holy Soul Jelly Roll!*, the selection from "Wichita Vortex Sutra," read with musical accompaniment, written by Philip Glass, ends soon after the poem's declaration of peace.

Cultural critic Sacvan Bercovitch writes that early American prophecy was largely a rhetoric of permission-giving, a discourse which offered European settlers a license to expand: "the newness of their New World was prophetic.... The desert land they were reclaiming had its past in Bible promises: America was there so that in due time they could make it blossom as the rose....That was one tenet of their consensus: migration as a function of prophecy, and prophecy as an unlimited license to expand." (32-33) By forcefully promoting goals that were meant to be viewed as common goals for all American settlers, early American prophecy, in Bercovitch's view, had the effect of limiting or marginalizing dissent. In "Wichita Vortex Sutra," Allen Ginsberg offers an alternative prophecy. It is a prophecy that encourages dissent from a war that is seen not only as impractical, but as immoral and even genocidal. And far from encouraging geographical expansionism, Ginsberg's prophecy encourages America's leaders and its people to respect different cultures and to bring American troops back home from a militaristic adventure across the globe.

* * *

Allen Ginsberg's impact on American popular culture was felt dramatically during the Vietnam War years. As record producer Hal Wilner describes in the Liner Notes to *Holy Soul Jelly Roll!*, this was "the highly visible period in Allen's history when posters of a bearded, long-haired Ginsberg dressed in flowing robes and beads adorned the walls of college dormitories, and many of his poems and activities reached the homes of middle America." (7) Although it is usually impossible to quantify exactly how much influence a writer or artist may have had on reshaping a country's political policies, it is fair to say that Allen Ginsberg had more influence during this era than most poets ever have the chance to achieve, by helping to inspire and grow the anti-Vietnam War movement, whose protests and peace-advocacy campaigns eventually helped to force the U.S. government to end the war. In this book's closing chapter, I will look more closely at the question of Ginsberg's political impact, and at his activist participation from the Vietnam years until the end of his life. But to conclude this chapter, I would like to focus briefly on four more poems that I think show different literary tools and strategies that were part of his literary repertoire to turn anti-war views into powerful verse.

In "A Vow" (1966), Ginsberg makes an explicit promise to remain engaged with America's social affairs: "I will haunt these states / with beard bald head / eyes staring out plane window / hair hanging in Greyhound bus midnight." (CP, 467) It is a striking use of the verb "haunt." The image comes out of a Poe tale or a Hollywood horror movie, and the promise is to remain an image that continues to provoke, and sometimes even frighten, the American conscience. These haunting eyes are radical eyes observing American culture with the intent to radicalize—especially, I think, with regard to young people who were by 1966 listening in far greater numbers than previously both to 1960s poets and novelists, including those of the Beat Generation, and to the growing number of songwriters and musical groups, including Bob Dylan and the Beatles, who had been influenced by Ginsberg and other contemporary poets.

Here, once more as he had in "Kaddish," Ginsberg personalizes the political. Interestingly, by "haunting" the states, Ginsberg hopes that he can impart increased sanity to a nation being driven out of control, just as, later in the first stanza, he calms "an angry cursing" taxi driver so that the cabbie can more safely direct "his outraged vehicle." (CP, 468) As he had in the last line of "America," Ginsberg again alludes to Williams' "no one to drive the car" (*Spring and All*), attempting to cure a deranged driver who has momentarily lost control of the symbolic wheel. The key in the poem to redirecting the out-of-control vehicle—"the Green Light of common law. / Common Sense" (CP, 481)—alludes to Thomas Paine's democratic manifesto, with Ginsberg using all capital letters in "Common Sense" to make that allusion clear. In fact, Ginsberg cites a litany of anaphorically connected "common" elements as prerequisites for positive social change: "Common Sense, Common law, common tenderness / & common tranquility / our means in America to control the money munching / war machine." (CP, 468) The repetition of the word "common" urges community-building, and also structurally connects the different qualities listed. Thus, creating cooperative communities in America will require sensible laws steeped in compassion and based on America's best radical traditions as exemplified by the writings of Thomas Paine.

The thematic challenge in the poem, rendered in cascading lines, is to combat a profit-driven war machine, ecocide, and mass media advertising/propaganda:

> to control the money munching
> war machine
> everywhere digesting forests and excreting soft pyramids
> of newsprint, Redwood and Ponderosa patriarchs
> silent in Meditation murdered & regurgitated as smoke,
> sawdust, screaming ceilings of Soap Opera,
> thick dead Lifes, slick Advertisements
> for Gubernatorial big guns
> burping Napalm on palm rice tropic greenery.
> (CP, 468)

These lines powerfully connect the mentality which ransacks redwood trees in America with the war-making spirit dropping napalm on the people and foliage of Vietnam. Through a repetition of the prefix "de-," Ginsberg in this poem reiterates his intention to challenge—to deconstruct, although that word was not yet in popular usage—mass media manipulation of American working-class consciousness: "I'll haunt these states all year.... / decoding radar Provincial editorial paper message, / deciphering Iron Pipe laborers' curses as / clanging hammers they raise steamshovel claws / over Puerto Rican agony lawyers' screams in slums." (CP, 468) As in "America" and "Wichita Vortex Sutra," this poem encourages the demythification of the culture industry's popular mythologies and media spin.

In "America," Ginsberg had challenged the way that typical portrayals of American history too often erase the country's radical past. In "Crossing Nation" (1968), he enters contemporary activists into the literary record, keeping left activism's chronicles concretely available to future readers:

> Jerry Rubin arrested! Beaten, jailed,
> coccyx broken--
> Leary out of action—"a public menace....
> persons of tender years....immature
> judgment....psychiatric examination...."
> i.e. Shut up or Else Loonybin or Slam

LeRoi on bum gun rap, $7,000
	lawyer fees, years' negotiations—
SPOCK GUILTY headlined temporary, Joan Baez'
	paramour husband Dave Harris to Gaol
						(CP, 507).

Although the poem's journalistic directness may alienate some readers who have come to think of poetry as an art form which addresses politics only indirectly through couched metaphors or linguistic subtleties, it seems to me that the condensation and line breaks produce urgencies and reflection-enhancing pauses that make this verse lively, not anything like the kind of "flat prose" that Ginsberg believed poetry should avoid. Earlier in this volume, I cited Yeats' poem, "Easter 1916," and it seems to me that "Crossing Nation" attempts to provide a sense of poetic timelessness in order to immortalize contemporary American activists in the way that Yeats had, in his poem, carved the names of MacDonagh, MacBride, Connolly, and Pearse into our literary memory.

Recording radical history is also one of the aims of "Grant Park: August 28, 1968," which memorializes one of the most consequential moments of the antiwar movement, indeed of the 1960s era—the demonstrations and police riot outside the 1968 Chicago Democratic Convention. The poem opens with an edenic pastoral portrait, "Green air, children sat under trees with the old, / bodies bare." (CP, 515) Under the clean air, the demonstrators are clearly presented as the good guys. Their antagonists, the Chicago police, are described in language which recalls the brownshirts of the Nazi era: "ring of Brown-clothed bodies armed / but silent at ease leaned on their rifles." (CP, 515) Although the poem utilizes empirical observation, it is not "objective" in any traditional journalistic sense: This is a poem which chooses sides.

After a symbolic machine-in-the-landscape image ("helicopter roar") intrudes on the pastoral tranquility, Ginsberg notes that the day has the potential to result in one of two opposing outcomes: either "Police State or Garden of Eden?" (CP, 515) While delegates and elected officials are satirized—"magicians exchange images, Money votes," "naked on the toilet taking a shit weeping" (CP, 515)—the poet sees the police unleash their teargas. He imagines it drifting up to the Vice President, suggesting that the police force's mean-spirited actions will backfire to hurt the authorities themselves, an accurate prediction of doomed Democratic Party fortunes in the upcoming 1968 presidential election in which Richard Nixon defeated Hubert Humphrey. Ginsberg ends the poem asking half-sarcastically: "Who wants to be President of the / Garden of Eden?" (CP, 515), fusing the dual poetic strategies of historicizing and mythologizing, and proposing that the current powers-that-be do not even recognize when their own young citizens enact their ostensibly cherished Judeo-Christian mythologies.

As a poem of witness describing a significant historical event in the antiwar movement, an event in which the poet played a central role which will be described further in Chapter 6, the historicization is rather an impressionistic one. In its broad brush strokes and allegorical allusiveness, "Grant Park: August 28, 1968," unlike "Crossing Nation," shies away from journalistic reportage even while it embraces the poetic possibility of recording for posterity a key historical moment in verse. A similar poetic strategy of commingling history and myth is undertaken in "Anti-Viet Nam War Peace Mobilization" (1970), a poem which makes cartoon-like images out of pro-war symbols, so that the Washington Monument becomes an "Iron Robot" (CP, 549) and Nixon's brain becomes a "Presidential cranium case spying thru binoculars / from the Paranoia Smog Factory's East Wing." (CP, 549) As in the Moloch section of "Howl," Ginsberg incorporates William Blake's technique of creating larger-than-life characters out of actual historic figures to elevate the importance of the subject matter at hand, and to add a sense of moving beyond historical specificity so that these explorations will seem relevant to audiences of the future.

The Poetry and Politics of Allen Ginsberg

In "Anti-Vietnam War Peace Mobilization," the protest movement itself is revealed to have learned to make theatrical use of traditional mythology: one of the activists is a "black man strapped hanging in blue denims from an earth cross." (CP, 549) The insinuation, I think, is that potential military draftees, disproportionately black and Latino, were the innocent, Christ-like martyrs of contemporary America. Throughout this book, I have assumed an underlying idea of art and politics as theoretically distinct spheres that can push against each other or overlap. In discussing many of Ginsberg's poems, I have focused on his attempts to make inventive use of politics and history in order to enhance the aesthetic quality of his poems. In "Anti-Vietnam War Peace Mobilization," we see that the anti-war movement is also willing to see aesthetics and politics overlap, in this case by bringing elements of theater into its public actions. Indeed, in groups like the Yippies, poetry and symbolic theater played key roles in building the antiwar movement. In this poem, as in Blake's "Nurses Song" ("And all the hills ecchoed" [114]) which Ginsberg often sang at his readings, nature expresses its approval of the young protestors: "Soul brightness under blue sky." (CP, 549)

Of course, these Ginsberg poems do not function as a substitute for clear historical writing. "Grant Park: August 28, 1968," does not fulfill the role, say, of David Farber's terrific book, *Chicago '68*, which offers a comprehensive study of the Chicago 1968 demonstrations outside the Democratic Party convention. Farber's study is intricately detailed, offers a broad historical background and context, and moves chronologically through the days' events. In his critical study, Farber describes the demonstrations and the Chicago police department's violent actions in response to those demonstrations from three different perspectives—from those of the Yippies, the Mobe (a large nonviolent anti-war coalition), and the police. It describes, for instance, the following scene in Grant Park:

A small group of uniformed officers, most of them black, handed out leaflets warning the protestors that they would be arrested if they attempted to march. Dozens of plainclothes officers traveled in groups of eight to ten through the crowds, pushing people and threatening them....At approximately 3:30, after a variety of speakers, and just as Carl Oglesby, ex-SDS president, began to speak, a teenage boy climbed the flagpole to the south of the bandshell and began to lower the flag. Police, assuming the young man intended to desecrate the flag, immediately pushed their way through the crowd and arrested the teenager. While beating him with their clubs and fists and struggling to drag him back behind the police line, the officers were pelted with food, rocks, bags of urine, chunks of concrete, and other debris. While the police dragged off the teenager, a group of young men, including at least one undercover police officer, surrounded the flag-pole and took down the flag. In its place, they raised a red t-shirt. A group of approximately eight police officers followed by several others tore into the crowd, once again, in an attempt to arrest the red flag raisers. They beat several bystanders with their clubs while chasing the perpetrators....Under the direction of a sergeant, a group of approximately thirty enthusiastic police, clubs in hand, attacked in "a punitive assault." (195-96)

Farber's account, as Ginsberg's had and as did an official follow-up investigation, places primary responsibility for the Chicago violence on the police—although it also clearly describes some acts by individual antiwar protesters, including throwing rocks and bags of urine, that were far from "edenic." Inside the Democratic Party's convention, Connecticut's Senator Abraham Ribicoff clearly agreed with the assessment that the police were primarily to blame for the violence in the streets when he famously declared over the microphone: "With George McGovern we wouldn't have Gestapo tactics on the streets of Chicago." (quoted in Farber, 201)

Farber's prose descriptions clearly offer an account containing far more historical specificity than one finds in Ginsberg's verse-portrayal of Grant Park, or for that matter in any of Ginsberg's poems describing antiwar protests. This is not to say that poems cannot attempt such detailed historical specificity. For an example of a poet's engaging attempt to write the history of this era in verse, one can read poet-activist Ed Sanders' epic poem, *1968: A History in Verse*, written with information and memories culled from journals and news clippings and published nineteen years after the fact. But Ginsberg's antiwar poems do not purport to offer a complete historical record or to replace his audience's need for other history books; rather they offer a partial history that successfully complements other texts, and that often simultaneously features a strategy of mythification that is intended to give these poems an air of timelessness which most purely historical writings do not achieve.

A poem like "Wichita Vortex Sutra" is both history and not history. It exhibits the dual intellectual tendencies which Myra Jehlen describes as the desire to "erect imaginary worlds" and the commitment "to excavate the foundations of this one." (*Literary Criticism*, 41) Ginsberg's anti-Vietnam War poems embrace these dual impulses simultaneously: deconstructing government and mainstream media myth and spin by providing historical context and analysis; and mythologizing current events, including peace activism, in ways that work to elevate the stakes of choosing peace, since such choices are seen as affecting not merely the present but the long-range future as well. It is also significant that poems like "Grant Park: August 28, 1968" can serve to inspire readers to search for those alternative history books that provide further information about important and often unacknowledged events and movements in the chronicles of American radicalism. It would be interesting, for instance, to find out how many readers of Allen Ginsberg's poems have, like me, gone on, inspired initially by poetry, to devour alternative history books like Howard Zinn's *People's History of the United States*.

Like "Howl," "America," and "Kaddish," Ginsberg's poetry from the Vietnam era continues to locate itself within a roomy arena of wide-ranging left traditions. Opposing a war that was carried on by three American presidents beginning with John F. Kennedy, Ginsberg's antiwar verse exhorts America to live up to its liberal ideals, and simultaneously interrogates those liberal ideals from a more contemporary and more radical stance, opposing the sort of blind nationalism that was evident in too much of America's foreign policy during the Cold War era, and that has remained too evident in recent U.S. foreign policy as well.

Chapter 5: "Plutonian Ode" and Continuing Lifelong Radicalism

Ginsberg's poetry from the mid-1950s to the late 1960s was clearly his most influential work, and it was his verse from those years which reshaped the international literary landscape. But it is important to note that Ginsberg continued to write powerful poems, sometimes underrated, for another three decades. These later poems would surely, I would argue, have had a more noticeable impact on the American literary scene if they had not been competing against Ginsberg's own prior poetic achievements like "Howl" and "Kaddish." Right up until his death in April, 1997, Ginsberg in his poetry continued vigorously to explore a range of intellectual and social concerns, to examine relations between political and spiritual arenas, and to test the ability of a wide variety of poetic forms to express personal and political ideas.

It was also during these later years that I personally met Ginsberg, first briefly after a 1976 reading that he did at Rutgers University, after which the event's organizer, a New Brunswick poet and neighbor of mine, asked me if I could drive Ginsberg back to New York. During that drive, which I undertook with two New Brunswick poet friends—Danny Shot, one of my then-roommates on Guilden Street and my future collaborator on *Long Shot* literary journal, and Kevin Hayes, the event's organizer who lived across the street from us—Ginsberg guided us on an extremely informative automobile tour of the Lower East Side of Manhattan, pointing out buildings where well-known writers and activists like Abbie Hoffman and Emma Goldman had lived or worked. Four years later, in the summer of 1980, I took a one-month apprenticeship with Allen Ginsberg at Naropa Institute in Boulder, Colorado, and also took his course on William Blake. Although my poetry at the time was not yet very developed, he seemed to appreciate that I was a young poet-activist from New Jersey, and that I had studied William Blake at Rutgers University with Alicia Ostriker, whose annotated edition of Blake's *Complete Poems* Ginsberg was himself using to study Blake and to teach Blake to his classes.

When my poetry began to improve in subsequent years, Ginsberg grew supportive of my work, sending letters on my behalf to publishers and taking the time to answer many poetry-related questions. He also agreed to participate in a number of readings that I helped to organize, especially readings trying to help connect poetry with progressive political causes. In the early 1980s, Ginsberg came down to do a benefit reading to help Danny Shot and I start *Long Shot* literary journal, an independent, small-press journal that lasted for over 20 years. Once he came down to read with me and another New Brunswick poet, Cheryl Clarke, to help us draw more young people to a national student activist conference we had organized at Rutgers University in 1988, and whose goal was to create a new national multi-issue student activist group somewhat modeled on SDS. He also participated in an antiwar reading that I put together at the Nuyorican Poets Café in New York City to protest the 1991 Gulf War. When our New Jersey Anti-Apartheid Mobilization Coalition, chaired by a terrific Central Jersey activist Valorie Caffee, organized a public media campaign, endorsed by dozens of artists across the country, to pressure a national arts group to move its national convention out of a New Brunswick hotel owned by the Johnson and Johnson Company, which was then the largest U.S.-based corporation that was refusing to divest from apartheid South Africa, Ginsberg signed onto our campaign and opened up his rolodex for us to look up other key phone numbers and addresses. I often like to say that, long before the invention of the Internet, Allen Ginsberg coordinated his own version of a Worldwide Web of Poets, Activists, and Alternative News Reporters, a web that was incredibly helpful to those of us organizing informational events, readings, and rallies.

Although my friendship with Ginsberg, from 1980 through the end of his life in 1997, admittedly has made it impossible for me to write a traditional "unbiased" volume about his work, I hope that the advantages of this friendship outweigh the disadvantages for the purposes of this book, in that they offered opportunities to see first-hand some of the projects that Ginsberg was working on, and to have personal conversations with him about a wide variety of poetic and political matters.

Mainstream media have for the most part succeeded in spreading a false myth that the vast majority of former 1960s radicals became more conservative as they grew older. A few real, notable examples are used to present this myth as indisputable fact: Jerry Rubin, who converted from radical Yippee to liberal Yuppie in the 1980s, and David Horowitz, a former leftist editor of *Ramparts* magazine who later received extraordinary attention from the mainstream press by virtue of his willingness to repudiate his former world outlook in favor of right-wing zealotry. In a *New York Times* film review, Stephen Holden concisely encapsulated this prevailing mythology: "The conventional wisdom about political ideology and personal growth has always held that as we age we inevitably cast off our youthful dreams of changing the world and become increasingly conservative."[1]

As highlighted earlier, along with thousands of other known and unknown organizers from that era who continued to display long-term progressive commitment, whether through their public activism or their private socially relevant professions, Allen Ginsberg's life and work help put the lie to that conservative myth. He continued publicly and persuasively to show that 1960s radicals did not all take sharp right turns along life's highway, that it was possible not only to stay radical in one's world-view but to evolve and grow sharper in explaining that viewpoint. In a 1995 *New York* magazine article, for instance, Ginsberg offers a lucid and passionate description of his evolving progressive response to contemporary American reality: "Many of these values have entered mainstream thought—e.g., ecology, grass, gay lib, multiculturalism—but haven't seen fruition in government behavior, so that now we have more folk in our prisons or under government surveillance than any country West or East....This 'Beat generation' or 'sixties' tolerant worldview has provoked an intoxicated right-wing 'Denial' (as in AA terminology) of reality, codependency with repressive laws, incipient police state, death-penalty demagoguery, sex demagoguery, art censorship, fundamentalist monotheist televangelist quasi-fascist wrath, racism, and homophobia. This counterreaction seems a by-product of the further gulf between the rich and poor classes, growth of a massive abused underclass, increased power and luxury for the rich who control politics and their minions in the media. Prescription: more art, meditation, lifestyles of relative penury, avoidance of conspicuous consumption that's burning down the planet." (84) During our current era of a still-evolving economic gap and a growing threat of climate change, Ginsberg's concise remarks from 20 years ago still seem quite on the mark.

In the 1970s, throughout the so-called Me Decade of the 1980s, and right up until his death in 1997, Ginsberg remained committed to his radical ideals: challenging American policy in such wide-ranging areas as nuclear proliferation, environmental destruction, skyrocketing homelessness, the increasing disparity of wealth during the Reagan and George H. W. Bush eras, continuing racial discrimination, CIA covert actions, the "drug war," domestic censorship of art and speech, and military adventures in such places as Panama and Iraq. Ginsberg did readings to benefit and publicize countless progressive organizations and projects and served on the advisory boards of numerous organizations, including the progressive media watch group, Fairness & Accuracy in Reporting (FAIR), and a national student activist group that I worked with during the late 1980s and early 1990s, Student Action Union. In the years that I knew Ginsberg, he was constantly writing or calling government offices to advocate for improved social policies and urging younger writers like myself to do the same—whether on the larger political issues like war and peace, or on more targeted cultural issues like the jailing or censorship of writers (an issue around which Ginsberg worked with the PEN Freedom to Write Committee) or the state of New Jersey's intention to close Walt Whitman's final house in Camden, a house which the state was maintaining as a museum and which continued to remain open after the appeals, initiated by Ginsberg, from many New Jersey-associated writers, including myself.

In terms of Ginsberg's literary work, I do not want to claim that Ginsberg's most moving later poems are all politically focused—one of my personal favorites is the unforgettable elegy for his father, "Don't Grow Old." (CP, 659-664) But in this chapter, I would like to talk about some of the political poems that I feel were among his most accomplished after 1970.

My personal favorite among these is "Plutonian Ode," written in 1978. In Robert McNamara's 1996 book, the former Defense Secretary describes the astounding scope of the world's continued proliferation of nuclear weapons: "Today, there are 40,000-50,000 nuclear warheads in the world, with a total destructive power more than one million times greater than that of the bomb that flattened Hiroshima." (337) The majority of those warheads are American, with most of the remaining held by the varied republics of the former Soviet Union. McNamara cites existing treaties which insufficiently call for a reduction down to 12,000 warheads. In McNamara's words, if there is a nuclear war, "I doubt a survivor—if there was one—could perceive much difference between a world in which 12,000 nuclear warheads had been exploded and one subject to attack by 40,000. Can we not go further? Surely the answer must be *yes.*" (337-38)

In the mid-1970s, protest movements against the dangers of both nuclear weapons and nuclear power began to grow considerably in the U.S. and internationally. In the U.S., one of the most prominent anti-nuclear activist groups, the Clamshell Alliance, was formed in 1976 in the Northeast. In 1977, the Clamshell Alliance organized a civil disobedience action at which over 1,400 people were arrested protesting the Seabrook, New Hampshire nuclear power plant. "Plutonian Ode" draws on and attempts to amplify these growing anti-nuclear sentiments taking hold among activists. The poem takes aim at one of the key components of modern nuclear weapons as well as one of the waste products of nuclear energy—the element plutonium. The wordplay of the title (plutonium/plutonian) alludes to the sinister character of the material's creation and existence.

"Plutonian Ode" uses long lines approximating the line-length of William Blake's prophecies or Walt Whitman's "Song of Myself"—that is, shorter lines than those of "Howl," but longer than those of most traditional English-language poetry. Through intense condensation of ideas and imagery, the lines of "Plutonian Ode" achieve a level of surface electricity reminiscent of "Howl." Appropriating Blake once more, as he had in the Moloch section of "Howl," Ginsberg again articulates a poetic vision with the intent to give a body to error, in this case to make visible to readers an invisible but very real and deadly danger, the intense radioactivity from the material plutonium, a human-made element with a radioactive half-life estimated to be 240,000 years. As Ginsberg writes in the endnotes to his *Collected Poems*: "Ten pounds of Plutonium scattered throughout the earth is calculated sufficient to kill 4 billion people." (CP, 805) Even to this day, scientists have yet to discover a safe way to store plutonium waste. An episode of ABC's "Nightline" in the mid-1990s called the plutonium processing plant at Rocky Flats, Colorado the most dangerous building in America. The literary timelessness of this poem is thus made more likely given the subject matter's extraordinary and frighteningly long shelf life, the latest reminder of which has been the nuclear power plant disaster in Fukushima, Japan.

"Plutonian Ode" begins with a query that is also a presentation of scientific data: "What new element before us unborn in nature?" (CP, 710) Unlike most bacterial or viral dangers, plutonium is human-invented. It is the "most / Ignorant matter ever created unnatural to Earth!" (CP, 711) By circulating information about this substance, little understood by the public-at-large in the late 1970s, the poem allows the audience figuratively to "see" this invisible danger, a danger that has been reproduced in absurd quantities by U.S. nuclear weapons manufacturers: "I turn the Wheel of Mind on your three hundred tons," (CP, 711) the "amount produced for American bombs" by 1978 as Ginsberg tells us in his endnotes. What the renowned British historian, E.P. Thompson, concludes about Blake is equally true of Ginsberg: "As always Blake's visionary spiritualism combines with a combative polemic against the 'Beast' of the State." (226)

Here is E.P. Thompson's telling description of Blake's poem, "London": "'London' is a literal poem and it is also an apocalyptic one; or we may say that it is a poem whose moral realism is so searching that it is raised to the intensity of apocalyptic vision." (187) The same combination of literalism and apocalypticism can be found in Ginsberg's "Plutonian Ode." The "Moloch" section of "Howl" gave body to error by creating an imagined amalgam of existing, repressive institutions. Although here again Ginsberg ascribes mythological ingredients to earthly reality, we should note that, unlike Moloch, the element unmasked in "Plutonian Ode" is not a metaphorical assemblage but a real one, isolated in 1940 and named by Dr. Glenn Seaborg in 1942. Since the subject of the poem is a key ingredient of nuclear weapons and a dangerous waste product of nuclear power plants, one might say that the apocalypticism of the poem is interwoven within the very fabric of the literal. While giving a mythic (plutonian) "body" to plutonium, Ginsberg challenges both its public secrecy ("My oratory advances on your vaunted Mystery!" [CP,711]), and its invisible radioactive risk.

Ginsberg gives a body to plutonium by citing the element's origins ("First penned unmindful by Doctor Seaborg with poisonous hand, named for Death's planet through the sea beyond Uranus"), by naming its radioactive danger ("Radioactive Nemesis"), by detailing its manufacturing locations in the U.S. ("silent mills at Hanford, Savannah River, Rocky Flats, Pantex"), and by identifying its corporate maker and manufacturing process ("where nuclear reactors create a new Thing under the Sun, where Rockwell warplants fabricate this death stuff trigger in nitrogen baths" [CP, 710-11]). As Ginsberg writes later in the poem, "I publish your cause and effect!" (CP, 711)

Like Blake's Los, Ginsberg becomes what he beholds: "I carol my spirit inside you, Unapproachable Weight." (CP, 711) And in another strategy reminiscent of Blake, Ginsberg's description of plutonium includes Urizen-like connotations of hyper-rationality: "Manufactured Spectre of human reason!" (CP, 711) As the Moloch figure of "Howl" is the "heavy judger of men," plutonium represents the "Judgment of judgments." (CP, 711) In other words, plutonium is a dangerous element created by instrumental reason without enough concern for moral or ethical values. By exposing the hidden values which undergird the vast nuclear buildup, Ginsberg attempts to restore humane considerations and values to scientific discourse. Regarding plutonium, this project entails exposing the material's massive potential for death and destruction: "ten pounds of heavy metal dust adrift slow motion over gray Alps / the breadth of the planet, how long before your radiance speeds blight and death to sentient beings?" (CP, 711)

If there is a hell, the poem implies, this element must have been born there. Plutonium is thus metaphorically labeled the "magma-teared Lord of Hades....billionaire Hell-King." (CP, 710) Not only is this element born of hell; it is born of an expensive hell that is only possible in a super-wealthy modern nation in which weapons manufacturers are allowed to reap unfathomable profits. If, as E.P. Thompson suggests, Blake's "London" was both literal and apocalyptic, then Ginsberg has penned an extension of Blake that is simultaneously more literal and more apocalyptic.

When Ginsberg builds on the work of poetic predecessors, he inevitably does so only after adding interesting personal twists. This poem adopts Blakean techniques with noteworthy changes. In William Blake's prophecies, his prophetic figure, Los, uses a hammer to give body to error, to bind Urizen in chains of iron:

> And Los formd Anvils of Iron petrific. for his blows
> Petrify with incessant beating many a rock. many a planet
> ....in his hand the thundering
> Hammer of Urthona. forming under his heaving hand the hours
> The days & years. in chains of iron round the limbs of Urizen.[2]

Significantly, Ginsberg as the narrator in "Plutonian Ode" performs a Los-like prophetic act nonviolently, with his tools being simply the poet's meditative breath and voice:

> I begin your chant, openmouthed exhaling into spacious sky over silent mills at Hanford, Savannah River, Rocky Flats, Pantex, Burlington, Albuquerque
> I yell thru Washington, South Carolina, Colorado, Texas, Iowa, New Mexico,
> where nuclear reactors create a new Thing under the Sun, where Rockwell war-plants fabricate this death stuff trigger in nitrogen baths.
> (CP, 710-11)

The poet's breath is seen not only capable of turning the invisible radiation visible, but also of entering nuclear plants

Plutonian Ode

to help dissipate their danger: "I enter with spirit out loud into your fuel rod drums underground on soundless thrones and beds of lead /....to Spell your destiny, I set this verse prophetic on your mausoleum walls to seal you up Eternally with Diamond Truth! O doomed Plutonium." (CP, 712)

The poem performs interesting variations on Whitmanic as well as Blakean themes and techniques. It proclaims that plutonium is more powerful than Whitman's universal self: "Father Whitman I celebrate a matter that renders Self oblivion" (CP, 710) Instead, it proposes the Buddhist belief in self-relinquishment—i.e. "the doctrine of not-self" (Conze, 18)—as the only conception of human selfhood capable of addressing or surviving the vast challenge of plutonium. After all, plutonium cannot devour what refuses to exist. And yet, while turning Whitman's universal self on its head, Ginsberg nonetheless infuses a Whitmanic touch in the poem's very powerful final section III, democratically suggesting like Whitman ("every atom belonging to me as good belongs to you" ["Song of Myself," section 1]) that all human beings have the potential to carry out transformational Blakean prophecy, and offering a Whitmanic ("look for me under your bootsoles," ["Song of Myself," section 52]) suggestion that Ginsberg's radical legacy will remain available to future generations through contact with the poet, in this case with his poetic and meditative breath:

> This ode to you O Poets and Orators to come, you
>   father Whitman as I join your side, you Congress
>   and American people,
> you present meditators, spiritual friends & teachers,
>   you O Master of the Diamond Arts,
> Take this wheel of syllables in hand, these vowels
>   and consonants to breath's end
> take this inhalation of black poison to your heart....
>   enrich this Plutonian Ode to explode its empty
>   thunder through earthen thought-worlds.
>   (CP, 712)

Since plutonium will last a quarter of a million years, it will be up to future generations to remain vigilant in safeguarding the planet from its dangers. In doing so, these future caretakers will be guarding Ginsberg's legacy as well, just as Ginsberg in this poem asserts his own desires to guard prior poetic legacies ("old orators' inspired Immortalities" [CP, 710]) from the potential apocalyptic extinction which plutonium's existence now makes realistically imaginable.

Note once more, as in "Wichita Vortex Sutra," Ginsberg's belief in language as a material force ("this wheel of syllables") seen as at least potentially capable of motivating improved social policies by changing America's public consciousness. The poem has expressed a desire for "a tranquil politic" to oppose "horrific arm'd" nations and "Satanic industries," and it ends with "so Ah" (CP, 713), a two-word phrase that conjoins logical argumentation with supra-rational breath, and that symbolizes a nonviolent poetic and political legacy that future generations can employ. Ginsberg asks future citizens of the world to "Magnetize this howl," and I do think this is a poem of his post-1970 career that can be justifiably compared in quality and transhistorical relevance with his earlier epic work.

Allen Ginsberg did not only write against nuclear weapons and nuclear energy; he also participated in many rallies and demonstrations focused on these issues. In this regard, his most well-known act was undoubtedly, in the summer of 1978 right after completing "Plutonian Ode," joining a sit-in on the train tracks in Rocky Flats, Colorado, to prevent the transport of plutonium across those tracks. (See this book's cover.) Ginsberg's participation in that courageous demonstration, literally putting his body on the line, gave the event far more attention and publicity than it would have garnered without his presence. By the late 1970s, movements against nuclear weapons and nuclear energy were growing, and Hollywood even entered the picture in March, 1979 with the film, "The China Syndrome," starring Jane Fonda and Jack Lemmon. Just 12 days after that film came out, and less than a year after Ginsberg's "Plutonian Ode" was written and published, the Three Mile Island nuclear power plant accident in Pennsylvania occurred, the worst nuclear power plant accident up to that time. In 1986 came the even larger accident at Chernobyl. After these accidents, and after a growing No Nukes movement, of which Allen Ginsberg was a participant, the building of new nuclear power plants around the world was dramatically slowed, including in the U.S. Ginsberg's poetic and activist efforts were certainly at least a small part of the culture that educated the public about the dangers of nuclear power and that turned public opinion against the building of new nuclear power plants and toward treaties that at least somewhat reduced nuclear weapons stockpiles and nuclear waste. The most recent nuclear power plant accident occurred in Fukushima, Japan in 2011, and the dangers of that accident have not yet ceased, as new radioactive leaks continue to be regularly reported as I am completing this book. It is therefore clear that Allen Ginsberg's "Plutonian Ode" was indeed filled with long-term relevance.

* * *

There are many other effective Ginsberg poems, from the 1970s on, that undertake interesting strategies within the genre of political poetry, some of which I would like to briefly discuss. The heartrending "September on Jessore Road" (1971) displays an impressive formal resourcefulness in its ability to combine objectivist perceptions with rhyming ballad form, recording Ginsberg's direct observations of Asian poverty in moving quatrains:

> Millions of babies watching the skies
> Bellies swollen, with big round eyes
> On Jessore Road—long bamboo huts
> Noplace to shit but sand channel ruts.

The Poetry and Politics of Allen Ginsberg

(CP, 579)

In the *Holy Soul Jelly Roll* Liner Notes, Ginsberg writes: "In between Record Plant sessions I wanted to write something worthy of Dylan's attention, a poem long and beautiful like 'Sad-Eyed Lady Of The Lowlands,' but W.C. Williams-like natural reportage, and spiritual—something to astonish Dylan to tears." (35) Ginsberg himself considered the poem a "magnum opus, which I thought as good as anything I'd written since 'Kaddish,' though in a more classic rhymed form." (Liner Notes, 36) The poem's "reportage" is gripping indeed, and Ginsberg adds intralinial spatial-pauses to his formal repertoire, both to effect a blues rhythm and to give his readers a little extra time and space to reflect more deeply on the severity of Asian poverty described:

> Mother squats weeping & points to her sons
> Standing thin legged   like elderly nuns
> small bodied   hands to their mouths in prayer
> Five months small food   since they settled there....
> (CP, 579)

> On Jessore road   Mother wept at my knees
> Bengali tongue   cried mister Please
> Identity card   torn up on the floor
> Husband still waits   at the camp office door.
> (CP, 580)

As in "Wichita Vortex Sutra," "September on Jessore Road" does not limit its journalistic consciousness to empirical perception and observations of, as he describes in his *Collected Poems'* endnotes, millions of Hindu refugees from East Pakistan living at the time on the flooded main road between Calcutta and Bangladesh. When he notes that "One Million aunts are dying for bread," (CP, 579), he has obviously not seen or counted these million aunts first-hand. And yet, given the vast poverty on Jessore Road, the anaphoric repetition of the word "Millions" can be read as both literal and allegorical:

> Millions of daughters walk in the mud
> Millions of children wash in the flood
> A Million girls vomit & groan
> Millions of families hopeless alone.
> (CP, 579)

The poem includes explicit self-reflexivity, wondering aloud how it will be possible to think of his own pleasure after seeing such large-scale pain:

> Is this what I did to myself in the past?
> What shall I do Sunil Poet I asked?
> Move on and leave them without any coins?
> What should I care for the love of my loins?
> (CP, 582)

And, as an American poet, Ginsberg interrogates the U.S. role in Asia by questioning why American foreign policy energies and finances are being used at that moment in 1971 to bomb Vietnamese and Laotian cities rather than to assist Asia's homeless and hungry:

> Where is America's Air Force of Light
> Bombing North Laos all day and all night?
>
> Where are the President's Armies of Gold?
> Billionaire Navies   merciful Bold?
> Bringing us medicine   food and relief?
> Napalming North Vietnam   and causing more grief?
> (CP, 581)

While these are in a sense rhetorical questions, there is nevertheless an actual bewilderment etched in the lines: a serious querying as to the "why" of American policy. With this combination of editorializing and interrogation, the poem moves beyond a simple reportage of Ginsberg's Asian observations. "September on Jessore Road" ends in questions and allegory:

> How many fathers in woe
> How many sons   nowhere to go?
> How many daughters   nothing to eat?
> How many uncles   with swollen sick feet?
>
> Millions of babies in pain
> Millions of mothers in rain
> Millions of brothers in woe
> Millions of children   nowhere to go.
>
> (CP, 583)

In 1971, the implicit question posed is whether Ginsberg's American readers can force their government to end its militaristic adventurism and to assume a more peace-oriented international foreign policy that would help provide these poverty-experiencing children with better lives. In this poem, by utilizing a more traditional rhymed form, Ginsberg shows that he is capable of offering progressive social explorations by using a variety of formal techniques, that his poetic toolbox is not limited to the free verse forms of "Howl," "Kaddish," or "Wichita Vortex Sutra." Using multiple poetic styles, he consistently displays a commitment to challenge America's nationalistic, ahistorical, and denial-filled rhetoric and mythology. "September on Jessore Road," by using a ballad form, makes a moral appeal that will engage readers more accustomed to the long tradition of rhymed quatrains than to jazzed-up long lines, as well as to an audience that has been growing used to listening to Bob Dylan and others on the contemporary blues and folk circuit. From my own conversations with Ginsberg as well as from simply reading his work, I believe that ongoing stylistic exploration and experimentation was essential in his efforts to keep his poetic energies refreshed. Such formal dexterity, I would argue, also adds to his long-term legacy by proving, yet again, that this was a poet who was deeply skilled in the history of poetic forms and traditions.

From my conversations with Ginsberg, through the years that I knew him from 1980-97, it was clear that one issue that was always on his mind was a desire, partly stemming from his progressive Jewish background: to see peace in the Middle East, including between Israelis and Palestinians. Ginsberg's poems had been translated into Hebrew by such well-known Israeli poets as Natan Zach, who was a dedicated peace advocate that I had the pleasure to spend a day with during my one trip to Israel in the mid-1980s. Ginsberg wrote his most memorable poem on the subject of Israel/Palestine in 1974, entitled "Jawah and Allah Battle." A parodic commentary on long-running Israeli-Arab and Israeli-Palestinian conflicts, the poem plays with mythological and historical elements in a slightly different way than in Ginsberg's previous poems. In this piece, mythic imagery is adopted to critique continuing mid-East violence and wars, and as in prior poems, the mythologization adds an element of literary timelessness to a political poem. But in the Middle East, where warring parties often cite biblical justifications for acts of violence and for hard-line negotiating positions, and where third-party onlookers often simply assume that such religious conflicts have always taken place and will always continue, the very idea of mythification carries unique political ramifications. In this poem, Ginsberg's mythification serves simultaneously to highlight the historical issues at stake, and also to parody the way in which the warring parties and purveyors of violence use mythological arguments to support unreasonable and even deadly acts.

The irrational ridiculousness of using biblical citations to attempt to justify contemporary violence is exposed in the poem in upper case lettering: "JAWEH AND ALLAH SENT ME HERE!" (CP, 623) Destructive acts undertaken by religious fundamentalists on either the Jewish or Arab side are inexcusable: "Both Gods Terrible!" (CP, 622) Israel has developed nuclear weapons ("Jaweh with Atom Bomb") and Arab countries stifle dissent ("Allah cuts throat of Infidels"). (CP, 622) Naming actual historic groups, the poem implicitly criticizes the region's all-too-common biblically justified rhetoric of destiny by focusing on both sides' past use of terrorism to achieve desired ends: "What mind directed Stern Gang Irgun Al Fatah / Black September?" (CP, 622)

In "Wichita Vortex Sutra," Ginsberg was clear that one challenge to a U.S. poet was to address media representations and misrepresentations of the Vietnam War in one's home country. A similar case is made in "Jawah and Allah Battle," since mid-East militarism, along with the actual sale of weapons, is endorsed and promoted by journals from other countries, including the United States: "*Commentary* and *Palestine Review* sent me here!"; "Republics Dictatorships Police States Socialisms & Democracies / are all sending Deadly Weapons to our aid!" (CP, 623) Both Jewish and Palestinian rejectionists are indicted by Ginsberg for a fervent nationalism which maintains enemies in order to keep its own side united in separatist-style patriotism: "We shall triumph over the Enemy! Maintain our Separate Identity! Proud / History evermore!" (CP, 623)

But the social and religious traditions of the Middle East also have their peaceful and cooperative traditions and the poem ends by connecting, through juxtaposition, the cooperative spirits that can be found in both Jewish and Islamic traditions: "SHALOM! SHANTIH! SALAAM!" (CP, 624) If there is a language for peace, then there can potentially be a vision of it—and, as we have previously seen, in the poet-prophet tradition, what can be envisioned can be made real. The poem uses mythology in a way that is both serious and parodic to interject a message of peace in a long-running historical conflict. Of course, at the same time, the mythic aspect of the poem cannot answer particular historical questions that will need to be negotiated before actual peace can be accomplished: what the borders of a Palestinian state ought to be, how to guarantee each side's desire for security, how to divide scarce water resources, etc. Like the last line of "Kaddish," the linguistic juxtaposition in this poem's ending, as much as it points to a desire for peace, leaves many concrete earthly questions unanswered. Again, I would say that this is not an inherent weakness in a political poem, which as I have argued throughout this book, should not be seen as requiring the same elements one would usually demand to see in an effective political essay. It is important to note that the poem does not preclude specific and reasoned solutions in these areas; it just does not offer them. In Ginsberg's poem, sympathetic readers are left to fill in the blanks in order to figure out concrete methods of negotiating a more peaceful future in the region. The poem does, however, take both effective mythological and historical aim at the violence on all sides which, along with too many regressive political leaders, has made it nearly impossible, even to this day, for effective solutions in specific policy areas to be developed and implemented in the Middle East.

Ginsberg's 1976 poem "Junk Mail" lists, in montage fashion, the contents of his daily mail. By presenting such a list—a list which includes a wide range of contemporary activist appeals and projects—this poem counters a commonly held perception that little progressive organizing was going on in mid-1970s America. The poem notes letters from both political and literary activist groups: "Boycott Gallo Grapes lettuce United Farmworkers of America   Our struggle is not over   make checks payable   Si Se Puede   Cesar E. Chavez   Union Label /....Give Poets & Writers CODA to a friend   subscribe United Nations Childrens' Fund." (CP, 665) It records for historical purposes the existence of groups such as the Southern Poverty Law Center, Planned Parenthood, the Catholic Peace Fellowship, the National Resources Defense Council, and the War Resisters League, all groups which remain in existence to this day. It also records fleeting activist groups that no longer exist like the Ad Hoc Coalition for a New Foreign Policy. The poem mentions groups that are working on behalf of a range of social-justice causes—from ending racial discrimination in housing to addressing widespread environmental pollution. In an essay in *What Is Found There*, Adrienne Rich performs a similar function of bringing attention to the surprising number of lesser known progressive groups engaged in serious political advocacy work, groups which are not typically discussed in the corporate media:

> Newsletters come in the mail: North Carolinians against Racial and Religious Violence; The Jewish Women's Committee to End the Occupation; The Center for Constitutional Rights; Men of All Colors Together; The United Farm Workers; The National Coalition against Domestic Violence; The Center for Democratic Renewal—facts, appeals for money, responses to crisis. I have written checks to these and other such organizations in the past and continue to do so: this is 'checkbook activism,' money in lieu of or in addition to time, to actual presence. And without checks the fragile movements for justice in this country could not exist beyond the local level....[I]n an interstitial time between selective democracy, shot through with intimidation, and the fever break this country must inevitably undergo as it enters the next century, they provide essential information not available in the mainstream press. (20-21)

"Junk Mail" ends with a splash that is humorous for its condensed syntax and unrealistic idealism, yet it is simultaneously an attempt to offer helpful advice to people who would like to get involved in making the world a better place:

> Dear Citizen of the World: First days explosion
>   bomb radioactivity starve Ozone layer? Isn't it
>   time we did something?
> 1) Send cooperators ten addresses w/ zip codes
>   2) Mail friends endorsement 3) Write your
>   Congressman President Newspaper editor &
>   Presidential Candidate.
> As a final move, the World Authority would destroy
>   all Nuclear Weapons.
>
> (CP, 667)

On one hand, it is easy to imagine that many readers would find this poem to be a kind of throwaway piece that is too focused on minor details about Ginsberg's personal mail. Of course, Ginsberg's decision to title the poem "Junk Mail" shows that he is well aware of this possibility. But I think that it is also possible to see "Junk Mail" as a poem that, through condensation and collage, attaches poetic energy to an historical moment in a way that interestingly reveals a spectrum of American activist life that was not otherwise often portrayed at the time. For Ginsberg, as an unusually well-known public poet receiving more literary and activist letters than most Americans at the time, a poem like "Junk Mail" enables him to help bring needed attention to progressive organizations doing important political advocacy work. From my own experience, I know that Ginsberg would often talk about activist groups like these in private conversations, but publishing a poem like "Junk Mail" allows him to promote these groups to a much wider readership. And in poetic terms, by revealing the contents of his personal mail, Ginsberg helps to subvert commonly established private/public boundaries.

In "Garden State," (1979) Ginsberg returns to some of the themes related to industry's destruction of nature that he had earlier explored in "Sunflower Sutra." Writing about his home state of New Jersey, he notes the way that industrialism has hurt the state's ecology, especially ironic and sad considering its inherited nickname which gives the poem its title. In this poem, Ginsberg uses pastoral images differently than he had in "Sunflower Sutra," here urging readers to research the state's history to discover how New Jersey lost its ecological beauty. New Jersey "used to be, farms" with "green lawns" and a "wooded hill to play Jungle Camp / asphalt roads thru Lincoln Park." (CP, 726) Invading such paradisal surroundings "came the mafia, alcohol / highways, garbage dumped in marshes..../ bulldozers." (CP, 727) In addition to its agriculture, New Jersey gained a reputation for its scientific technology for all of that technology's positive and negative possibilities: "Einstein invented atom bombs / in Princeton, television antennae / sprung over West Orange." (CP, 726)

In "Witchita Vortex Sutra," Ginsberg had attempted to establish a relationship between media reporting and the government's ability to launch and continue the Vietnam War. In "Garden State," he similarly indicts the mainstream media for its silence on ecological issues: "Now turn on your boob tube / They explain away the Harrisburg / hydrogen bubble, the Vietnam war, / They haven't reported the end of Jersey's gardens." (CP, 727) The Culture Industry devalues important local issues and obscures major historical blunders, and the results become concretely apparent in a debilitated landscape.

It is also significant in the poem that ecological destruction is linked to repression of the U.S. left. When New Jersey was maintaining its beautiful gardens, "The communists picnicked / amid spring's yellow forsythia." (CP, 726) But then ecological disintegration begins after progressive activists are treated badly in the state, after Paterson's silk strikers were murdered and after "They threw eggs at Norman Thomas the Socialist speaker / ....the police / stood by & laughed." (CP, 727) As in many romantic pastoral poems, "Garden State" yearns for earlier times ("Let's / go back Sundays & sing old springtime music" [CP, 727]). So this is not merely nostalgia for a pre-industrial environmental landscape when greenery was still in view, but also for an idealized America when it still seemed possible that the left might help create more democratic and economically just times.

As mentioned earlier, although I had met Allen Ginsberg briefly in 1976, after a reading he gave at Rutgers, I think he would have probably remembered meeting me when I studied with him at Naropa Institute in Boulder, Colorado, in the summer of 1980, when I did a one-month poetry apprenticeship with him and also took his class on William Blake. As part of my apprenticeship, in exchange for Ginsberg providing helpful suggestions about my own early work, a few of the things that I did for him included typing up poems he had written by hand in his notebook, and doing some of his errands, among the first of which was to deliver a new poem that he had written, "Verses Written for Student Anti-Draft Registration Rally," to some young Boulder peace activists. Although the U.S. government had not re-introduced the military draft, which had been discontinued after the end of the Vietnam War, it had once again begun to discuss the possibility of reinstating the requirement that young American men register for a potential draft. Since Congress was insisting that military service would remain voluntary, it was difficult to understand why draft registration should be back on the national agenda, except perhaps as a way to keep the public on edge during the Cold War and continue justifying exorbitant military budgets. A group of Boulder students who were organizing a protest against that re-introduction of draft registration had asked Ginsberg if they could use one of his old antiwar poems on the poster that they were going to use to publicize their upcoming rally in town. Ginsberg was glad that young activists wanted to include his poetry in their efforts, and he generously told them he would try to write a new poem especially for their cause, rather than giving them an old poem to reprint.

In that new poem he wrote, "Verses Written for Student Anti-Draft Registration Rally," Ginsberg creates a new mythic figure, the "Warrior," in order to challenge dominant conceptions of bravery and masculinity: "The Warrior is afraid / the warrior has a big trembling heart." (CP, 738) For Ginsberg, the Warrior is a figure who confesses to fear and who "never goes to War," since only "The Conquered go to War, drafted into shadow armies." (CP, 738) Again, pointing to the influence of mainstream media on American policy and on personal subjectivity, the poem notes that the heart of a real Warrior, being a human heart, is "not the heart of most Television." (CP, 738) Years later, the way in which mainstream media could influence public opinion on war-and-peace issues was certainly evident once again in the early part of the 21st century when the media failed to examine deeply enough the Bush administration's claims about weapons of mass destruction in Iraq, claims that later proved to be clearly false but that nonetheless helped garner public support for the 2003 invasion of Iraq.

Ginsberg's anti-draft registration poem ends with a strong condemnation of national leaders, claiming that a real Warrior would not manufacture billion dollar missiles to fight battles from afar, or build hollow mountains, as the U.S. government had, to ready escape routes for themselves:

> This kind of sadness never goes to war, never spends
> $100 Billion on MX Missile systems, never
> fights shadows in Utah,
> never hides inside a hollow mountain near Colorado
> Springs with North American Aerospace
> Defense Command
> waiting orders that he press the Secret button to
> Blow up the Great Cities of Earth.
>   (CP, 738)

Utilizing language that is both mythical and historical, the lines offer a powerful, image-packed and multi-pronged censure of military spending, nuclear weapons, ecological abuse, government secrecy, and the insanity of planning to survive—rather than to prevent—an apocalyptic war. By the summer of 1980, I was certainly familiar with the growing media depiction of 1960s activists becoming less radical in ensuing years, less interested in addressing unjust government policies. It was thus inspiring to see up close Ginsberg's continuing progressive commitment in his desire to write this new, compelling poem, penned especially to be helpful to a new generation of peace activists. During the remaining month of my apprenticeship, I would also see up close his willingness, through letter-writing and phone calls, to help young people working on a range of political issues, including homelessness, freedom of expression, racial discrimination, and the environment.

As Ginsberg grew older, he made it a priority to keep up at least to some degree with youth activism and youth culture, including evolving musical styles. By the time I studied with him in 1980, the most popular new musical style among young Americans disenchanted with the political status quo had become punk rock. During my stay in Boulder in the summer of 1980, I remember taking a few trips to a popular punk-rock club in Denver, one night seeing a band, The Gluons, with whom Ginsberg would later record his poem, "Birdbrain." During one of my trips back from Denver to Boulder, I was riding in a car that was rear-ended on a highway and that fishtailed slowly into a telephone pole on the side of the road. Luckily, no one was hurt, and a poem I wrote about that car accident was, I think, the first poem of mine that Ginsberg really liked.

In his 1980 poem, "Capitol Air," Ginsberg again put his politics into rhymed verse, as he had in "September on Jessore Road," this time with a punk-rock rhythm that would later enable him to record the poem with musical backing by the internationally known British punk-rock group, The Clash. In "Capitol Air," Ginsberg's political philosophy, including his opposition to both existing capitalism and existing communism, is explicitly detailed:

> I don't like Communist Censorship of my books
> I don't like Marxists complaining about my looks

> I don't like Castro insulting members of my sex
> Leftists insisting we got the mystic Fix
>
> I don't like Capitalists selling me gasoline Coke
> Multinationals burning Amazon trees to smoke
> Big Corporation takeover media mind
> I don't like the Top-bananas that're robbing
>   Guatemala banks blind.
>
> (CP, 751)

According to the critic Jonathan Holden, whose view in this regard I think would probably be representative of a large segment of literary critics, "Capitol Air" is an illustration of "bad poetry," (81) because it embraces its own philosophy too quickly, clearly, and easily: "Because the poem discovers nothing, we discover nothing as we read it; nor are we drawn—as we would be by well-made art—to return to this poem. It is expendable." (81) To Holden, who says he agrees with the poem's political views, the poem is nonetheless too didactic and "offers its platitudes too smugly....Nowhere do I feel that the speaker has questioned the assumptions behind his dogma." (84)

I would argue with Holden's negative evaluation of the poem on three counts. First, it seems mistaken to assert that a poem that criticizes political dogmatism, political dogmatism that has led to wide-scale death and destruction in both the East and the West, is merely another form of political dogma. Secondly, I believe that Holden ignores the formal character of the poem—the fact that this poem is written in a humorous punk rock style that seems likely to engage young readers and listeners and that will potentially motivate at least some of those young people to look at politics in some new ways. And thirdly, it seems arbitrary for Holden to assert an aesthetic criteria which denies the potential value of a poem whose politics is known in advance. In her book, *What Is Found There*, Adrienne Rich describes the potential literary merit of just such a poetry:

There is a kind of political poetry that does not surprise the poet, in which the poet foresees and controls the poem's development according to an ideology of theme and even style—the poem as propaganda for revolt, for a specific revolutionary program, for a new kind of consciousness. Bertolt Brecht, Ruben Dario, Pablo Neruda all wrote such poems, and such poems can be very good indeed. (47)

In "Capitol Air," I would argue, Ginsberg demonstrates once again—with wit, lively imagery, rhythmic invention, surprise phrasing, and an infusion of literary tradition—that it is possible to write accomplished poetry that is also politically didactic. Written soon after the arch-conservative Ronald Reagan was elected President, the poem utilizes satiric and condensed vernacular phrasings to describe particularly deplorable aspects of American Cold War-era foreign policy, including recent military aid to the horrendous government-backed paramilitary death squads in El Salvador, and a covert role in Iran in the overthrow of the country's democratically elected Mossadegh and the installment of the dictatorial Shah in the early 1950s:

> Kermit Roosevelt and his U.S. dollars overthrew Mossadegh
> They wanted his oil then they got Ayatollah's dreck
> They put in the Shah and they trained his police the Savak
> All Iran was our hostage quarter-century That's right Jack
>
> Bishop Romero wrote President Carter to stop
> Sending guns to El Salvador's Junta so he got shot
> Ambassador White blew the whistle on the White House lies
> Reagan called him home cause he looked in the dead

nuns' eyes.

(CP, 753)

The assertion of the U.S. holding Iran hostage for twenty-five years after helping to overthrow its popularly elected leader urges Ginsberg's audience to reflect more deeply on the context and background of the 1980 hostage crisis in Iran ("Iranian hostage Media Hysteria sucked" [CP, 753]), during which Iranian terrorists held a group of Americans hostage for months. Ginsberg's poem injects a challenge to the nationalist bluster which viewed these Iranian hostage-takers as irrational zealots. Ginsberg's poem is by no means a defense or justification of the Iranian hostage-takers, but simply a reminder that the U.S. has engaged in unjustifiable acts of its own: "Truth may be hard to find but Falsehood's easy / Read between the lines our Imperialism is sleazy." (CP, 753)

"Capitol Air" explicitly rebukes the Cold War style of government propaganda under which the U.S. labeled Central American right-wing dictatorships in El Salvador and Guatemala "emerging democratic" simply because they were willing to serve as American allies in the fight against Communism: "School's broke down 'cause History changes every night / Half the Free World nations are Dictatorships of the Right." (CP, 753) It also condemns actually existing socialist nations, where "The Communist world's stuck together with prisoner's blood." (CP, 753) Embracing Thomas Paine's notion of world citizenship, "Capitol Air" urges concerned peoples to speak out against injustices East and West: "Arise Arise you citizens of the world use your lungs / Talk back to the Tyrants all they're afraid of is your tongues." (CP, 753)

"Capitol Air" does not promote any single systemic alternative to existing capitalism or existing communism—it merely ends with a call to use awareness and humor to help feed and enlighten humanity: "Aware Aware whereever you are   No Fear / ....Armed with Humor Feed & Help Enlighten

Plutonian Ode

Woe Mankind." (CP, 754) In chapter 6, I will discuss further the question of political alternatives in Ginsberg's work. For now, I would simply like to note that here is an example of a powerful political poem which makes its views known openly and explicitly. There is no mythologization or allegorization of its presentation of Cold War history. And yet, using elevated diction, cutting-edge insight, electrified imagery, and punk-rock-style rhythms and rhymes, Ginsberg is able to express his politics in effective poetry, including the following couplet which concisely rebukes the Cold War reality of the early 1980s: "The bloody iron curtain of American Military Power / Is a mirror image of Russia's red Babel-Tower." (CP, 754)

* * *

Allen Ginsberg's *Collected Poems* was originally published in 1984, and included poems written through 1980. He published two more volumes of verse during his lifetime: *White Shroud: Poems 1980-1985* and *Cosmopolitan Greetings: Poems 1986-1992*. Additionally, one final book of poems was published posthumously: *Death and Fame: Last Poems 1993-1997*. His last three books of poetry were eventually incorporated into a second, nearly 1,200-page edition of his *Collected Poems*, from which I have cited throughout this volume, and which I had the pleasure to help proofread, with the honor of having been thanked by the Ginsberg estate for that proofreading help in a page near the beginning of the volume.

Many of the poems in Ginsberg's last three books explicitly address political themes. I do not want to argue that all of his published poems, including all of the poems in these last three volumes, were of powerful or memorable quality. In *Happening Now?*, for example, he follows an interesting list of nightmarish high-tech weaponry ("Neutron bomb Nerve Bacteria gas, fruit fly recombinant / Germ plasm, Stratospheric X-ray laser") with the recounting of a ten-year old dream of a sky "covered with ink-black cloud / Tanks and bombers moved toward the distant horizon." (CP, 868) Of course, such opinions are largely subjective, but it seems to me that the nostalgic juxtaposition of an youthful bad dream with a nightmarish roster of weapons sounds a bit forced. In "Going to the World of the Dead," Ginsberg writes a song lyric containing flat repetition, and which ineffectively, in my opinion, attempts to add humor by appending "Ho Ho Ho" to the end of lines:

> Millionaires of Detroit
> Millionaires of Chicago
> Millionaires of New York
> Millionaires of Hollywood
> Let go of your money Ho Ho Ho.
>
> (CP, 875)

In this song, Ginsberg does not, it seems to me, succeed in creating an interesting poem out of political materials. The anaphoric repetition of "Millionaires" does not evoke nearly the same level of the poignancy as the repetition of "millions" that we saw in his earlier poem, "September on Jessore Road."

If aesthetics alone were the editorial measure, some of the poems in Ginsberg's final *Collected Poems* could probably have been left out. Ginsberg himself was certainly well aware of this, as he discussed these issues with me while he was putting together his *Selected Poems*, for which I served as one of his credited informal advisors. But as candor had always been one of the beliefs underpinning his poems, Ginsberg believed that it would be interesting to include even some of his weaker poems in his collected volume of poems, which he saw as something very different than a collection of selected poems, out of the sense that the inclusion would provide future readers with an interesting and comprehensive literary biography of a poet's life and times.

In addition, poets have historically been judged by the importance of their best works, not their weakest ones. And as I have previously mentioned, I do think that Ginsberg wrote and published more poems in the 1980s and 1990s that are compelling than he was often given credit for, with the main obstacle again being that he was competing in some ways against himself, with critical readers looking to see whether he would again be capable of writing another earth-shattering poem like "Howl," "Kaddish," "America," or "Sunflower Sutra." In his best poems from the 1980s and 1990s, although we don't find another "Howl," we do find effective extensions of his previous techniques for making political poems effective—through the use of personalization, mythification, demystification, wit, humor, imagery, imagination, surprise phrasing, and an impressive range of formal experimentation.

As we saw in "Kaddish," the interconnection of personal and political content can ascribe a heightened sense of emotional intensity to a poem. In Ginsberg's poems of the eighties and nineties, the personalized elements include a variety of themes—spirituality, death, love, daily experience, and subjective historical reflection—often viewed in the context of aging.

As a poet who often referred to himself as a Buddhist Jew, it is not surprising that many of his poems which connect spirituality with politics explored themes related to one or both of these two religions or philosophies. In several outstanding poems, political questions are discussed in the light of Buddhist meditation. In "Why I Meditate" (1981), Ginsberg uses anaphoric repetition to sew together his literary, personal, Buddhist, and political concerns and desires:

> I sit because the Dadaists screamed on Mirror Street
> I sit because the Surrealists ate angry pillows....
> I sit in America because Buddha saw a Corpse in Lumbini
> I sit because the Yippies whooped up Chicago's teargas skies once....
> I sit because after Lunacharsky got fired & Stalin

> gave Zhdanov a special tennis court I became a
> rootless cosmopolitan
> I sit inside the shell of the old Me
> I sit for world revolution.
>
> (CP, 851)

In this poem, Ginsberg implicitly proposes a community that crosses generational, national, and literary-political boundaries. The act of meditation attempts to ground that community. Whereas the "best minds" of "Howl" were moving around frantically seeking existential meaning, here the process for seeking existential answers is calm, sane, spiritual, and historical. Ginsberg implicitly identifies himself as a poet of the democratic left by highlighting how Stalin's deplorable actions caused him to become a citizen without solidly existing roots.

Both "Do the Meditation Rock" (1981) and "Thoughts Sitting Breathing II" (1982) also explore aspects of meditation in conjunction with social concerns. The former is a song, published alongside musical notation, which gives readers a set of instructions on how to meditate in Ginsberg's particular Buddhist tradition:

> Follow your breath out   open your eyes
> and sit there steady   & sit there wise....
> Follow your breath   when thought forms rise
> whatever your think   it's a big surprise.
>
> (CP, 863)

The poem suggests that meditation will aid the practitioner in learning "a little Patience and Generosity." (CP, 863) According to the poem's spiritual and political logic, after a reader has learned to focus in such a grounded manner, and has acquired the qualities of patience and generosity, then the reader has acquired the tools necessary to make effective demands upon the government: "If you sit for an hour   or a minute every day / you can tell the Superpower   to sit the same way." (CP, 864)

In "Thoughts Sitting Breathing II," he uses the process of meditation as a poetic tool to structure the poem. In theme, the piece follows the thoughts which arise during a meditation session, thoughts which alternate between the personal and political:

> As I breathed between white walls, Front Range
>   cliffs resting in the sky outside south windows
> I remembered last night's television suitcoat tie
>   debate, the neat Jewish right wing
>   student outwitted a nervous Dartmouth pimply
>   liberal editor
> knowing that boy who swears to "get the
>   Government off our backs" would give my tax
>   money to Army brass bands FBI rather than St.
>   Mark's Poetry Project.
>
>   (CP, 878)

In these lines, Ginsberg criticizes a common conservative rhetoric that purports to oppose government spending, but that actually creates a hierarchy of government spending priorities which consistently puts military spending above all else—even second-rate military bands above more important grassroots culture—in this case the St. Mark's Poetry Project in New York City, which Ginsberg was instrumental in helping to create and which he continued energetically to support throughout his life. As if restoring the breath back to the body through inhalation, the poem which has traveled from the self to the outside world then returns. After focusing on questions of international war and peace and humorously fantasizing an American weather-related initiative to end the Cold War ("Maybe get rid of Cold War, give Russian Empire warm weather access" [CP, 879]), the verse returns to focus back on the poet sitting in meditation at his Boulder, Colorado home: "So remembering the old story of Russia's claim to a

Allen Ginsberg at St. Mark's Poetry Project.
Photo by Eliot Katz.

warm weather harbor I came back to myself, blue clouded Colorado sky adrift above the Bluff Street Boulder house." (CP, 879)

In "Improvisation in Beijing" (1984), a poem-preface to his volume *Cosmopolitan Greetings* and one of my favorites among his later poems, Ginsberg links spiritual and political elements while listing his reasons for being a poet: "I write poetry because my mind wanders subject to sex politics Buddhadharma meditation." (CP, 937) The poem succinctly bridges the spiritual with the physical: "I write poetry because the English word Inspiration comes from Latin *Spiritus*, breath, I want to breath freely" (CP, 937) It concisely and beautifully expresses a belief in the potential of poetry to connect a desire for subjective freedom with an urge toward human solidarity: "I write poetry because I want to be alone and want to talk to people." (CP, 938) Within the poem, Ginsberg credits some of his most important literary influences: "I write poetry because Walt Whitman gave world permission to speak with candor....I write poetry because Russian poets Mayakovsky and Yesenin committed suicide, somebody else has to talk." (CP, 937) And citing the importance of Judaism in his work, of writing as a Jewish poet in post-World War II America, Ginsberg notes: "I write poetry because Hitler killed six million Jews, I'm Jewish. / I write poetry because Moscow said Stalin exiled 20 million Jews and intellectuals to Siberia, 15 million never came back to the Stray Dog Cafe, St. Petersburg." (CP, 939) The poem ends with a funny acknowledgement that, despite his attempt to inventory his rationales for writing poetry, ultimately any such list must be incomplete, but must simply be what the artist feels is his or her most desired mode of expression: "I write poetry because no reason no because / I write poetry because it's the best way to say everything in mind within 6 minutes or a lifetime." (CP, 939)

In another poem that uses an anaphoric-based form, Ginsberg's sense of Jewish identity is the explicit subject of "Yiddishe Kopf" (1991), which offers a range of political explorations amid a comic menu describing the reasons the poet considers himself Jewish despite a lack of any institutional religious participation and despite a long-held secular disbelief in the traditional Jewish concept of God:

> I'm Jewish because love my family matzoh ball soup
> I'm Jewish because my fathers mothers uncles
> grandmothers said "Jewish," all the
> way back to Vitebsk & Kaminetz-Podolska via Lvov.
> Jewish because reading Dostoyevsky at 13 I write
> poems at restaurant tables Lower East Side,
> perfect delicatessen intellectual.
> Jewish because violent Zionists make my blood boil,
> Progressive indignation.
> Jewish because Buddhist, my anger's transparent hot
> air, I shrug my shoulders.
> Jewish because monotheist Jews Catholics
> Moslems're intolerable intolerant.
>
> (CP, 1013)

Of course, Ginsberg's Jewish roots were apparent throughout his poetry career, from his inventive adoption of an Old Testament-like prophetic stance in "Howl" to his personalized appropriation of the Jewish Mourner's Prayer in "Kaddish." In those earlier poems, Ginsberg both extended and subverted elements of traditional Judaism, and this later poem is no different. On the one hand, it challenges dominant religious and political Jewish notions of monotheism and Zionism. On the other hand, such social and intellectual challenges to dominant thinking have been at the core of Jewish teaching and literature (Kabbalah, Midrash, etc.) for over a thousand years. The concluding line of "Yiddishe Kopf" expresses his bewilderment at the fate of young people in the contemporary world, with the uncertainty caused by growing economic insecurity exacerbated by the nightmarish ever-present threat of annihilation made possible by the theories of history's most well-known Jewish scientist, Albert Einstein: "How can they stand it, going out in the world with only $10 and a hydrogen bomb?" (CP, 1013)

Using an enticing metaphor to entitle the poem, "Elephant in the Meditation Hall" (1990) entwines spirituality and politics by revealing an underside to the actual practice of supposedly utopian streams operating in both camps. With regard to Buddhist practices in the U.S., the poem surveys a litany of scandals:

> What about San Francisco Roshi & the board
>   director's wife
> What about high living limousine expense accounts
>   in Moscow?
> What about the late Rajneesh & poisoned gefilte fish
>   in Oregon?
> What's hiding under Rajneeshis' Orange skullcaps?
>   Brains?
>   (CP, 985)

Even Ginsberg's own longtime guru, Chogym Trungpa Rinpoche, is not spared in this poem which alludes to a well-publicized 1975 scandal at Naropa Institute in which the poet-couple W.S. Merwin and Dana Naone were forcibly stripped against their wills by Rinpoche's vajra guards at a Halloween party: "Vajracharya Trungpa! Dont mention the naked poet at the Halloween Party!" (CP, 985)[3] After noting these Buddhist scandals Ginsberg is forced to acknowledge that "Marxists were right, religion the people's opium!" (CP, 985) But the Marxist house is not exactly in perfectly scandal-free order either: "They still had pictures of Stalin on truckcab windows in Gori 1985 a scandal! / ....And marvelous atheist Khmer Rouge read Marx Sartre & Erich Fromm, / how many'd they murder with religious good intentions?" (CP, 985) Back to American politics, Ginsberg asks rhetorically:

> What US President hasn't sponsored war,

> Lumumba's assassination, an H-bomb,
> trillion dollar Savings & Loan mistakes? Scandals!
> taxpayers gotta subsidize banks!
> Now we gotta digest Plutonium? how evacuate CIA?
> (CP, 985-86)

Ginsberg notes that he himself has been criticized for his personal behavior—"My own life, scandal! lazy bum!..... / How many boys let me caress their thighs! / How many girls cursed my cold beard? I better commit suicide." (CP, 986) The conclusion: Born into this universe, there is no way to avoid making mistakes: the "whole universe a scandal, illusion, everyone deluded, a cosmic elephant in the meditation planet." (CP, 985) Of course, the realization that mistakes are inevitable is paradoxically no reason to avoid continuing to criticize the most egregious kinds of political injustice, and the poem ends by reciting a panorama of recently alleged outrages, including reports that as a presidential candidate Ronald Reagan's team had secretly negotiated with Iran to delay release of the American hostages until after the 1980 election, and other recent news stories documenting CIA involvement in the Central American drug trade:

> Ronald Reagan delayed hostage release till the
> Elephant party's Inauguration Day
> George Bush peddled coke for the contras in
> streetcorners banks downtown
> > Panama City! ....
> Anyway, the national debt'll approach 4 trillion any
> day say the homeless on
> > Tompkins Square.
> > > (CP, 986)

In Ginsberg's later poems, many of his political explorations are personalized around thoughts of his own aging and physical deterioration and musings on the possibility of approaching mortality. In the emotionally moving "Airplane Blues" (1981), he uses a blues form to express a poignant evaluation of the state of the world in the 1980s, noting pessimistically that the world's violent thoughts and acts will surely outlast his own life now that he is beginning to move further into his middle-age years:

> Mankind's great delusions
>   Scrape sky with red rage
> Build bombs out of Atoms
>   to blast out the words on this page
> Majestical jailhouse
>   our Joy's in the Cage
> Hearts full of hatred
>   will outlast my old age.
>   (CP, 859)

"After Antipater" (1985) is a poem which personalizes a political message by including social themes within a touching love lyric. Ginsberg recalls a wide range of worldly travels, including the time he "Stood in Red Square snow across from the Kremlin wall-tomb of th'assassin of millions." (CP, 921) These abundant international experiences are overwhelmed by the thought of a particular lover naked on his bed: "But when you lay on my bed, white sheet covering your loins, your eyes on mine / I forgot these marvels, my heart breathed open, I saw life's glory look back at me naked." (CP, 921) As the saying goes, love does indeed sometimes seem to conquer all, even the political worries of a world-traveling poet-activist.

    The quantity and quality of world-historical imagery at Ginsberg's fingertips during his late period is striking. After all, perhaps no other poet in history had been translated into foreign languages as much during his or her lifetime, nor invited to travel the globe so extensively, which is largely why Tom Clark could justifiably write in his review of Ginsberg's poems during the 1980s, "If there were elections for the office of World Poet, Ginsberg would certainly be the odds-on favorite." (31) During one mid-1980s visit to Rutgers University for a poetry reading that I helped to organize, Ginsberg stopped off at my apartment before the reading. I remember him phoning his office and talking to his secretary, Bob Rosenthal, in order to discuss upcoming travel plans for the next six months. At one point in their conversation, Ginsberg, without looking at any notes, said something like, "why don't we just pick three," and he named three foreign countries whose invitations to read he would accept for the coming half-year. Although I could, of course, hear only one end of the telephone conversation, I had the sense that, in picking three countries without looking at any notes or written invitations, it was as if Ginsberg, by this time in his career, had standing invitations to visit and perform from poets or organizations in just about every country on the planet.

In some of his most effective political poems of his last two decades, Ginsberg's style of personalizing politics takes the form of connecting his political thoughts with personal experiences that took place during his many trips abroad. For instance, in "Europe, Who Knows?" (1986), he records the strangeness, uncertainty, and health-related fears he encounters in Europe immediately following the Soviet Union's nuclear power plant accident at Chernobyl:

> Woke up in Poland, maple leaves just wilted down
> Not a cloud in the sky inexplicably cold on the
>   ground
> Kids in the yard were playing without any clothes
> All over Europe people are saying, "Who knows?"
>   (CP, 959)

Of course, Ginsberg by this time well understood the dangers of nuclear power as someone who had done extensive research into the subject in order to write his earlier poem, "Plutonian Ode."

In "You Don't Know It" (1986), Ginsberg's personal travels through Eastern Europe are recounted during a trip to Nicaragua, where he cites Communism's disastrous environmental history to the Sandinista government then in power: "Non passaron whispers from the Elbe, intellectual teeth chattering on Danube & Vistula / Village churchbells drowned in Volga waters dammed by Commissar engineers, riverwater evaporating faster than it reaches the sea." (CP, 944) In this piece, Ginsberg shows that he continues to remain interested in using a poetic strategy of historicization or demythification to make some of his political poems poetic. Here, he attempts to subvert idyllic myths about actually existing communism which he feels are still upheld by some in the Sandinista leadership in Nicaragua:

> In Russia the tyrant cockroach mustache ate 20 million souls
> and you don't know it, you don't know it ....
> In Hungary tanks rolled over words of Politician Poets
> and you don't know it ....
>
> (CP, 943)

Clearly, Ginsberg was not a poet who hesitated to criticize government policies whether he was in a country that called itself capitalist or socialist. In Nicaragua, he wanted to make sure that the Sandinista leaders, many of whom were poets themselves, realized that it was not only Western media or history books that spoke of atrocities committed in communism's name, but the bohemian poets whom he has personally met in East European nations: "No you don't know it's not N.Y. Review of Books it's bohemian Krakow Prague Budapest Belgrade E. Berlin." (CP, 944) Ginsberg here is essentially acting as a world citizen-messenger, delivering information to Sandinista poets from their Eastern European poet counterparts. The critiques of "actually existing socialism" are therefore not dismissible as simply the disinformation campaign of America's corporate media propaganda. As one of the few American-left dissidents to tour Eastern Europe extensively, Ginsberg is in a rare position to convey believable truths about those nations. While the poem urges the leftist Sandinistas not to ignore the ills of Eastern Europe, it also urges the poets of Eastern Europe not to ignore the ills of Western capitalism, including a lengthy record of deplorable U.S. interventions in Nicaragua and its neighboring Central American countries:

> And they don't know it, Aksionov Skvorecky
> Romain Rolland Ehrenburg
>   Fedorenko Markov Yevtushenko—
> don't know midnight Death Squad clubs on cobblestone no
> the ears cut off, heads chopped open in Salvador
> don't know the million
> Guatemala Indians in Model Villages—
> Don't know 40,000 bellies ripped open by the
> d'Aubisson hit-men for Born Again
>   neoconservative Texans.
>
>   (CP, 945)

The cautions extended to East European poets would certainly prove prescient in the 1990s, as the fall of communism throughout Eastern Europe was followed in many cases by the painful shattering of illusions about the consumer-paradise promises of shock-capitalist economic reforms. Soon after the fall of communism in Eastern Europe, I remember having a long conversation in New York City with one of Ginsberg's Czech translators, Joseph Rauvolf. When the subject of politics came up, Rauvolf made it clear that most Czech writers he knew wanted to take a complete break from thinking about politics for a while, having spent too many years living up to that point in a society which attempted to force its writers to create socialist-supporting art. Just a few years later, however, during his next visit to New York City, Joseph Rauvolf was asking me lengthy questions about my thoughts on Noam Chomsky's idea of the Latin Americanization of Eastern Europe, the idea that Western Europe and the U.S. would likely, after the fall of communism, begin to look at Eastern Europe as a potential new source for cheap labor and exploitable natural resources. Because Ginsberg was always sensitive to the injustices fostered by political leaders claiming to govern from a variety of ideological frameworks, he was able to remain admired in Eastern Europe, as well as in the West.

Ginsberg's "CIA Dope Calypso" (1972), "NSA Dope Calypso" (1990) and "Just Say Yes Calypso" (1991) were published as a trilogy in *Cosmopolitan Greetings*. Taken together, they tell much about aspects of U.S. foreign policy during the Cold War era. The poems are explicit, unafraid of directness, and told in brilliant, concise, rhyming couplets and quatrains. The year of the trilogy's final section, "Just Say Yes Calypso," was the year of the 1991 Gulf War, the first large-scale American military excursion since the end of the war in Vietnam. The lessons which American leaders drew from the Vietnam War appeared to be far different from those learned by many anti-war protesters, as well as those gleaned by such contrite ex-officials as Robert McNamara. Rather than learning how to avoid undertaking unnecessary foreign interventions, the American military seemed to have learned how to garner greater domestic support for war through such tactics as: demonizing the enemy, in this case a former U.S. ally, Saddam Hussein; keeping photos of the war dead, and of combat in general, off the television screen; minimizing mainstream media coverage of anti-war rallies once the war began; and doing as much fighting from the air as possible to minimize American casualty figures.

As Adrienne Rich writes, the American military with the cooperation of the corporate media presented the Gulf War: "via satellite dazzling images of a clean, nonbloody war." (85) The rationale for going to war was grossly obscured. At various times during the military buildup and following the initial bombardment, policy makers held press conferences essentially trying out different news spins to see how each potential explanation might fly with the American public. For example, the need to preserve American jobs was one rationale proffered for a day or two and then quietly dropped. In 1991, ten years before the atrocity committed by Al Qaeda terrorists at the World Trade Center, the American public was not likely to believe that their own safety was at stake, one of the implied justifications for the later 21st century wars in Iraq and Afghanistan.

According to Noam Chomsky, the main reason for the U.S. determination in 1991 to wage war on Iraq was that Saddam Hussein had violated what Chomsky calls "Axiom 1 of International Affairs": "no indigenous force is permitted to gain substantial influence over the energy resources of the Middle East. That belongs to the United States, its oil companies and loyal clients." (U.S. Gulf Policy, 16) As mentioned above and as Chomsky points out, the Iraqi dictator Saddam Hussein had been considered a friend—and therefore a recipient of considerable military aid by Presidents Reagan and George H. W. Bush—right up until Hussein's invasion of Kuwait on August 2, 1990, despite his well-known record of severe domestic repression and the gassing of Iraq's Kurdish minority. According to Chomsky:

> on August 2, Saddam Hussein became an enemy. On the 1st he was just as much a torturer and a murderer and a gangster as he was on August 2, his crimes were already behind him, but he was an amiable friend, improving. He was a moderate. We had to be nice to him. He was on our side, nothing wrong with him. Gasses Kurds, tortures people, that's great. But on August 2 he violated Axiom 1 of international affairs and suddenly became the latest reincarnation of Genghis Khan and Hitler.
>
> (U.S. Gulf Policy, 17)

George H. W. Bush's comparison of Saddam Hussein to Adolf Hitler was obviously meant to forge a demon that Americans would want to defeat—as well as to recall an older popular war rather than the more recent unpopular war in Vietnam.

The Iraqi invasion of Kuwait was a terrible act, but it was also appalling for President Bush to reject all non-war alternatives—with an end result of at least 100,000 Iraqi deaths resulting from the war itself; more Iraqi civilian deaths, especially among children, resulting from the sanctions which followed the war; plus additional illness and death on both sides of the war related to Gulf War Syndrome, an illness resulting from a never-quite-determined combination of chemical weapons, depleted-uranium-tipped missiles, experimental vaccines and pills, and/or the environmental hazards caused by burning oil wells.

America's corporate media, throughout the 1991 conflict, consistently understated President Bush's intransigence and generally cooperated with Pentagon war-coverage strategies, with the effect (intentional or not) being to help build popular support for the American war effort. Once the war was initiated, popular support was fostered even further. Before the war had begun, a *Washington Post*-ABC poll revealed that two-thirds of Americans were in favor of an agreement to have Iraq withdraw from Kuwait in exchange for U.N. Security Council consideration of Arab-Israeli issues, a strategy that may have avoided the war. (See Chomsky, Media Control, 287) [4]

How do we know that America's mainstream media played a concrete role in developing popular support for the 1991 Gulf War? A study by Professor Michael Morgan at the University of Massachusetts showed that the more that Americans received their news about the 1991 Gulf War from TV, the greater their support for the war and the less they knew about mid-East history. According to Danny Schechter, who drew the title of his book (*The More You Watch The Less You*

Know) from that study, Professor Morgan's data confirmed the following:

> people who relied the most on television coverage for their news knew the least about the war and its origins. Many of them also had the strongest opinions, which not coincidentally echoed precisely what they had been hearing and seeing. Like the media they depended on, they were virtually of one mind in uncritically embracing the U.S. government position. Most insisted they arrived at their opinions independently. (42)

And, obviously, just as the U.S. government had learned skewed lessons from its media successes and failures during the Vietnam War, when it came to the 1991 Gulf War, they also studied the role of media during the 1991 Gulf War before undertaking the early 21st century wars in Afghanistan and Iraq, including striving again to minimize media coverage of war casualties and antiwar movements. Before the 2003 invasion of Iraq, the George W. Bush administration was even able to help garner mainstream media support for its position, later proven false, that Saddam Hussein possessed active weapons-of-mass-destruction programs and therefore posed a real threat to American lives. Clearly, the kinds of criticisms leveled against the mainstream media by Ginsberg and other antiwar writers has not yet changed the way that America's media functions during war times. As Ginsberg wrote in "Wichita Vortex Sutra," "almost all our language has been taxed by war." It likely will not be too many more years before we see whether the mainstream media has begun paying attention to antiwar writers and thus learned any different lessons before the next potential war is waged for unsound reasons.

In the poetic trilogy beginning with "CIA Dope Calypso," the first two pieces present documented history of the American intelligence establishment's cooperation in unsavory international acts, particularly in the narcotics trade, aiding in the import of drugs first from Asia and then from Central America. The drug trade served as a way for U.S. allies, covertly supported by the CIA and NSA, to acquire the finances and weaponry to fight communism on those two continents. Ginsberg's verse is unafraid to disclose names and places, culled mostly from investigations by independent reporters, investigations which sometimes did and sometimes did not later make it into mainstream newspapers:

> Now coke and grass were exchanged for guns
> On a border airfield that John Hull runs
> Or used to run till his Costa Rican bust
> As a CIA spy trading Contra coke dust.[5]

As one can tell from reading Ginsberg's poems, as well as from a quick look at his library during a visit to his apartment, he was a voracious reader of the independent press, subscribing to a range of progressive newspapers and journals like *The Nation, In These Times, The Progressive,* and *Covert Action Quarterly.*

"Just Say Yes Calypso" (1991) uses a form similar to the trilogy's first two sections to address the 1991 Gulf War. As the first two sections historicize American foreign policy in prior international conflicts, this third section historicizes U.S. mid-East policy, including with regard to Iran and Iraq:

> When Schwarzkopf's Father busted Iran's
>   Mossadegh
> They put in the Shah and his police the Savak
> They sucked up his oil, but got Ayatollah's dreck
> So Thirty years later we hadda arm Iraq.
>   (CP, 1002)

American foreign policy, in this case support of the Shah, had backfired in Iran, leading to the reign of Islamic fundamentalist Ayatollah Khomeini, against whom Iraq fought a longstanding battle. In that conflict, the American government supplied weapons to Saddam Hussein—and, hedging their bets, to the other side as well: "Though he used poison gas, Saddam was still our man / But to aid the Contras, hadda also arm Iran." (CP, 1002) American weapons braced both sides in that earlier war—the lack of any moral principles inherent in such a foreign policy seems obvious. Ginsberg tacitly agrees with Noam Chomsky that one of the real issues behind the American decision to wage war against Iraq in 1991 was oil, and that the U.S. was willing to prop up mid-East governments which endorsed U.S. oil interests whatever their internal domestic policies: "Got addicted to Emirs and their fossil fules / Police state Sheiks & Intelligence ghouls." (CP, 1002)

The poem's final couplet offers a dazzling, condensed, and parodic deconstruction of the inextricably linked aspects of blind nationalism, environmental disregard, oil greed, and public intimidation which were used to fuel popular support in America for that 1991 mid-East adventure: "When they wave a yellow ribbon & an oily flag / Just say yes or they'll call you a fag." (CP, 1003) If a poem's literary value is enhanced by economy and precision of language and ideas, then this final couplet offers an appropriately powerful conclusion to Ginsberg's Calypso trilogy.

As a poet who had helped re-introduce humor into serious American poetry in poems like "America" and "Howl," humor, of course, remained one of Ginsberg's most potent poetic tools for creating engaging political poems. Deconstructing national myths and common national boasts in "World Karma" (1984), he uses satire to deflate notions of superiority in both the East and the West:

> Russia had Czars & Stalin, all Yiddish Poets shot
>   August 12, 1952 in Lubyanka basement,
>   everybody got drunk afterward,
> everyone still whispers on streetcorners

> America forever democratic, lawless sheriffs shot
> > Indians, bad men, good
> men, chinks kikes niggers and each other
>
> Spain always killed bulls & loved blood, matadors &
> > crucifixion, reds &
> fascists assassinated anarchists—
>
> The Jews always complained, kvetching about false
> > gods, and erected the
> biggest false God, Jehovah, in middle of western
> > civilization...
>
> British always had sense of superiority, class, stiff
> > upperlip, the Queen
> and fuck you ducky up your bloody 'ole.
> >   (CP, 913)

After offering stinging critiques of contemporary world powers, Ginsberg casts a vote for Australian Aborigines as the only remaining group of humans capable of safeguarding earth's life-sustaining resources: "Let them run the world after Hi Tech's annihilated all other species & genetic strains / from whale to donkey sperm." (CP, 914)

Humor is also evident in his 1993 poem about the politics of food, "C'Mon Pigs of Western Civilization Eat More Grease," published posthumously in *Death and Fame*. Here, Ginsberg mocks Western notions of pre-eminence in dietary habits. While the West would like to think it can "Set an example for developing nations," in reality the Western diet consists of "cuisine rich in protein cancer heart attack hypertension seat bloated liver spleen megaly." (CP, 1071) The speed at which images are sent to the reader in this poem rhetorically mimics the way artificial sugars and unhealthy fats send the human heart into high-blood-pressure mode. A high-fat, high-sugar Western diet is the nutritional equivalent to "carnivorous civilizations / presently murdering Belfast / Bosnia Cypress Ngorno." (CP, 1072) The poem ends with a deliciously ironic invitation to a tasty, but self-destructive dessert: "And this is a plate of black forest chocolate cake, / you deserve it." (CP, 1072)

Formal inventiveness of a more whimsical sort is the stylistic mode of "Hum Bom!," a poem begun in 1971 and appended in 1991, which addresses the wars in Vietnam and Iraq by playing with both the sound and concept of bombing in much the same way that the influential Russian modernist poet Velimir Khlebnikov played with the sound and concept of laughter in his poem "Incantation by Laughter," a poem that was included in a photocopy anthology of international poets that Ginsberg assembled and passed out to his students during my first summer at Naropa. Here are the beginning lines from the translation of Khlebnikov's poem as it appeared in that collection:

> O laugh it round, you laughsters!
> O laugh it up, you laughsters!
> So they laugh with laughters, so they laugherize
> delaughly.
> O laugh it up belaughably!
> O the laughingstock of laughed-upon—the laugh of
> belaughed laughsters.

The Khlebnikov poem has a kind of cubist effect, urging readers to think anew, and from many different angles, about the many uses of laughter, including its potential value to stir rebelliousness in a society with a repressive and overly serious ruling class. Ginsberg's poem "Hum Bom!" utilizes a similar cubist strategy in which apparently simple phraseology is repeated over and over, but with minor twists, in order to highlight from many different angles the absurdity of bombing Vietnam or Iraq:

> Who said bomb?

Plutonian Ode

>Who said you hadda bomb?
>Who said bomb?
>Who said you hadda bomb?
>
>Who wantsa bomb?
>We don't wanna bomb!
>Who wantsa bomb?
>We don't wanna bomb!
>   (CP, 1006)

Of course, when Ginsberg writes "we don't wanna bomb!" he is adding a degree of explicit political editorializing that is absent from Khlebnikov's "Incantation by Laughter." Yet, it is mostly by linguistic playfulness that he sustains his anti-war message here. Because there is no substantive rationale provided, it remains up to a reader to fill in the reasoning behind the poem's anti-war position. Ultimately, "Hum Bom!" is a poem that might seem simplistic almost to the point of embarrassing if it were not understood to be part of an influential tradition of 20th century modernist poetry.

In the 1980s and 1990s, the homeless population across the United States increased dramatically, a social problem that I saw firsthand while working as a housing advocate in Central New Jersey for ten years with an organization called Middlesex Interfaith Partners with the Homeless. The rise in homelessness had a variety of causes, among those being skyrocketing rent prices throughout the country, especially in urban areas, and the fact that the federal housing budget had been slashed by about 75% by the conservative Reagan administration. That rise in homelessness during the 1980s and 1990s was especially visible on the streets of New York City, including in Allen Ginsberg's Lower East Side neighborhood. In *Death and Fame,* several moving poems deal with this crisis in various poetic forms. In "New Stanzas for *Amazing Grace,*" Ginsberg writes in rhymed quatrains to the tune of the well-known spiritual, imagining himself in the place of a homeless person:

> I dreamed I dwelled in a homeless place
> Where I was lost alone
> Folk looked right through me into space
> And passed with eyes of stone.
> (CP, 1080)

In "Homeless Compleynt," Ginsberg writes even more directly in the voice of a homeless veteran: "I'm sorry buddy, I didn't mean to bug you / but it's cold in the alley / & my heart's sick alone." (CP, 1116) And in "The Ballad of the Skeletons," a poem offering a wide-ranging and comprehensive critique of international politics performed as a rock-and-roll tune that was eventually even aired in a music video on MTV, Ginsberg explicitly places the blame for the rising homelessness on neo-conservative politics and free market economics:

> Said the Neo Conservative skeleton
> Homeless off the street!
> Said the Free Market skeleton
> Use 'em up for meat.
> (CP, 1092)

I remember him talking with great excitement about having performed "The Ballad of the Skeletons" in England, with the musical accompaniment of Paul McCartney, who Ginsberg had known from McCartney's years with The Beatles.

In the last 18 months of his life, Ginsberg also came up with one other idea for promoting socially engaged poetry when he talked with *The Nation* magazine editors about putting together a section of contemporary political poems from poet friends across the country for one of the magazine's upcoming late-1990s issues. At the time of his death in 1997, after having called poets to ask whether they had any poems challenging America's rightward drift or otherwise speaking their political minds, Ginsberg had done a significant amount of work on this project, but he had not yet completed it. Ginsberg's longtime assistant, Bob Rosenthal, asked me and Andy Clausen whether we would be willing to finalize the project, using Ginsberg's substantial notes which were in several manila folders and making some last-minute choices that Ginsberg had not had the chance to make before his passing. That collection was eventually published in 2000 by Greg Ruggiero's Open Media Pamphlet Series and Seven Stories Press as *Poems for the Nation*, with Ginsberg as editor and Andy Clausen and I as assistant editors, and with royalties from the collection donated to three activist groups that Ginsberg had supported for many years: Fairness & Accuracy in Reporting, the PEN Freedom to Write Committee, and the War Resisters League.

* * *

As we can see, a desire to expand his stylistic repertoire is evident throughout Ginsberg's career, from his influential mid-fifties poems to the work of his later years. Ginsberg's poems over the last two and a half decades show an effective and powerful ability to poeticize political themes through the strategies of personalization, historicization, mythologization, humor, irony, and the extension of a wide range of verse forms, including long Whitman-influenced lines, blues lyrics, ballads, and modernist experiments. Using these various poetic tools, Ginsberg maintained a consistently radical vision and an unswerving commitment to delve beneath the apparent surface of political matters in order to imagine healthier social alternatives to many of the most crucial issues of our times. Similarly, he maintained an energetic activist life during these years, working with and supporting progressive organizations, and participating in demonstrations around many of the issues he was writing about, including preventing wars and dismantling nuclear weapons. He also consistently inspired young people across the country to get involved in these movements for progressive change.

Chapter 6:
A Progressive Political Poetics

Ginsberg's poems throughout his nearly five-decade career offer principled and radical critiques of existing political systems West and East. What his own political philosophy is—his vision for a replacement political system—is not as easily apparent. It is interesting to note what different literary critics have concluded about his political ideology from reading his poems and other writings. Barry Miles, one of Ginsberg's biographers, states that Ginsberg has a "deep belief in American democracy." (280) Literary critic Eric Mottram places him into an anarchist tradition, not exactly the tradition of American democracy: "Brought up as a communist Jew, Ginsberg is in the major American tradition of anarchism—Thoreau's 'majority of one'." (260) Floyce Alexander contends that Ginsberg promotes a metapolitics, stepping beyond political ideologies as "an imaginative alternative to the contemporary political and spiritual decay." (255)

I would argue that Miles, Mottram, and Alexander are all correct, but all only partially so. In Ginsberg's journals, he acknowledges internal political contradictions:

> Left wing but suspicious of communism and
>   revolutions including American revolution
> Anti-bourgeois, but want a house & garden & car ....
> Democrat but following guru leader
> Anarchist individualist but involved in sangha.[1]

In various places in Ginsberg's poetry, speeches, and interviews, we find support for each of the different tendencies the critics above have observed. In *Composed on the Tongue,* for instance, Ginsberg seems to clearly embrace anarchism: "I....questioned the whole structure of Law and immediately apprehended the basic principles of philosophical anarchism." (74) Yet, when it comes to differentiating between various anarchist and democratic-left traditions and philosophies, he did not always seem certain. In a scene transcribed in *Allen Verbatim*, he tells a group of 1960s young people that activists have not yet developed the political structures needed to create change: "So we haven't apparently, on a political or a social level, among ourselves, literally among ourselves, or among yourselves, among the younger generation, developed common leadership, organization, or dictatorship, or authoritarian forms, whatever, adequate even to keep the stage together." (220) It is the "whatever" in conjunction with "dictatorship" and "authoritarian" which reveals Ginsberg's uncertainty about political systems, at least at that point in his life.

In my discussion of Ginsberg's major poems from the fifties and sixties, I located his philosophical positions within general left traditions, but showed that he rarely limited his explorations to any particular ideology within that broad arena. His post-1970 poems run a similarly wide gamut of political standpoints. "Manifesto" (1974) seems to support both an anarchist and a metapolitical reading. Opposing government structures, he writes: "let's denounce Democracy, Fascism, Communism and heroes" and "dispense with law except Cause & Effect." (CP, 625) Also urging a metapolitics, the poem ends: "There is Awareness—which confounds the Soul, Heart, God, Science Love Governments and Cause & Effects' Nightmare." (CP, 625) Later poems which seem to express anarchistic leanings include: "On the Conduct of the World Seeking Beauty Against Government" and "Cosmopolitan Greetings."

At other times, Ginsberg seems to praise a democratic-left worldview. In "Hadda Be Playing on the Jukebox" (1975), he berates the U.S. government for subverting Chile's "red democracy" (CP, 644), which he describes in the endnotes as follows: "Salvador Allende (1908-1973), first democratically elected Marxist-socialist head of state in the western hemisphere." (CP, 802) (And as mentioned in an earlier chapter's note, Ginsberg was an enthusiastic supporter of democratic-socialist Bernie Sanders in his Vermont campaign for the U.S. Congress.) In several poems in *Cosmopolitan Greetings*, he offers rare self-descriptions adopting the label of communism. In "Velocity of Money" (1986), he writes "I was always a communist, now we'll win" (CP, 949); and in "Not Dead Yet" (1991): "Drink your decaf Ginsberg old communist." (CP, 1012) Of course, one feels enough of a humorous strain in these references to communism to allow perceptive readers to feel confident that Ginsberg is not referring to a communism of the old Soviet Union's variety. Nevertheless, his willingness to assume that label in his later life, even half-jokingly, seems significant—at the very least an acknowledgment of some potential within communism's theoretical tradition or ideals.

At the end of his poems, "World Karma" (1984) and "Poem in the Form of a Snake That Bites Its Tail" (1990), Ginsberg trumpets indigenous traditions, rather than any contemporary theories of governance, rejecting the East-West binary that we saw scorned in "Capitol Air." "Capitol Air" itself ends with a metapolitical assertion of Buddhist awareness:

> Aware Aware wherever you are   No Fear
> Trust your heart Don't ride your Paranoia dear
> Breathe together with an ordinary mind
> Armed with Humor Feed & Help Enlighten   Woe
>   Mankind.
>
> (CP, 754)

Indeed, this poem condemns actually existing anarchists

A Progressive Political Poetics

("I don't like Anarchists screaming Love Is Free." [CP, 751]) as well as existing communism and capitalism ("No hope Communism no hope Capitalism Yeah / Everybody's lying on both sides Nyeah nyeah nyeah" [CP,754]). Yet, while Ginsberg is prone to claim that a new spiritual "awareness" is needed in any just society, it seldom in his poems replaces the need for a new politics—thus, his call for a "fifth International" in "Howl", and his similar call for a new party, with a president "who'll reverse the denial," in his later poem, "Calm Panic Campaign Promise." (CP, 1035)

So, is this all simply philosophical indeterminacy, or even confusion? Or can we draw some coherent theories from Ginsberg's sometimes-wandering ideological expeditions? First, I think we can fairly say that his political philosophy seems to steer between a libertarian anarchism and forms of radical democracy or democratic socialism, usually linked with Buddhist notions of awareness; an environmentalism which embraces indigenous traditions; and, of course, a deeply held belief in gay liberation. In his varied political explorations, he remains always within the larger arena of left or progressive traditions, never shifting rightward nor even centrist. His posthumous collection, *Death and Fame*, includes a "New Democracy Wish List" offering a host of progressive suggestions to newly elected President Clinton on issues ranging from decriminalizing drugs to funding education to acknowledging past historical mistakes in U.S. support for "dictators in Zaire, Somalia, Liberia, Sudan, Angola, Haiti, Iran, Iraq, Salvador" (CP, 1065) —there is no backing away from left politics in Ginsberg's later years.

It is tempting to say that Ginsberg's ideological exploring is partially a sign that—his political upbringing by ideological parents and his subsequent activism notwithstanding— he seems not to have studied different political theories thoroughly enough to have settled on a single one. Indeed, from personal discussions with him during the eighties and early nineties, I feel comfortable saying that Ginsberg was certainly more devoted to helping to create and inspire political change from a practical perspective rather than from any particular ideological one.

And yet, I believe that we can consider another way of interpreting Ginsberg's reluctance to choose a specific political ideology, one that does not view this reluctance as arising from any lack of knowledge or commitment on his part. Certainly, based on the vast intelligence of his poems and the wealth of historical knowledge at his fingertips, as well as his extensive travels through countries with governments from across the ideological spectrum, there is no reason to underestimate Ginsberg's knowledge of different political systems or theories. Even if he was more interested in helping to create political change from a practical than a theoretical standpoint, it would be naive on any writer's part to assume that Ginsberg did not have enough theoretical background, through readings and conversations with writers from around the globe, to have settled on a favored single political ideology if he had so desired.

Instead, in attempting to fulfill the functions of radical literary criticism as drawing out the potential of a poet's emancipatory energies, I would suggest conceptualizing Ginsberg's refusal to choose a single progressive ideology from among the various left philosophies in a way that acknowledges the poetic and political advantages of this strategy—a conceptualization that I would call an "ideological flexibility." Along these lines, we can read Ginsberg's willingness to embrace different kinds of progressive politics at different moments as an attempt to prefigure the sort of democratic society in which diverse political ideologies and opinions are openly explored and tolerated.

We might also consider Ginsberg's ideological flexibility as advocacy of a coalitional style of politics, or a politics of inclusion—a desire to avoid the narrow political dogmatism that he saw as a demoralizing and self-defeating staple of his mother's Old Left, with its heated debates over such issues as how to interpret the "actually existing socialism" of the Soviet Union, and how to evaluate the theories of those like

Trotsky, Bakunin, and Bernstein, who had offered differing alternatives to dominant Leninist and Stalinist models of communism. Well aware by his formative years of the atrocities that had been committed, and the culture of repression that had been created, in the U.S.S.R. and throughout the Eastern Bloc, Ginsberg had also witnessed—in his youth as well as in his later years—the political ineffectiveness and sometimes plain silliness of sectarian activists in America, decades later, still pushing political programs with fixed ideologies taken in whole cloth from the socialist debates of the 1920s and 1930s. In this sense, a desire for ideological flexibility can be seen as a hope for a progressive American politics that might be both more moral and more effective for its more contemporary time and place. This desire to avoid unnecessary ideological divisiveness perhaps explains why, in his early poem "America," Ginsberg writes so fondly of the IWW, also known as the Wobblies: "America I feel sentimental about the Wobblies." (CP, 154) After all, the Wobblies, in historian Howard Zinn's words, were "socialists, anarchists, and radical trade unionists" who wanted "radical change" and "a new kind of labor union" (*Twentieth Century*, 33) that would unite workers of varied progressive stripes.

Ginsberg's brand of inclusionary politics, intended to avoid sectarian dogmatism, can be seen as a prefigurative model for the sixties' New Left, which similarly attempted to avoid or transcend the divisive debates of the Old Left. Like Ginsberg's poems, the sixties' New Left also added cultural and psychological concerns to the more orthodox economic considerations of the Old Left. Significantly, the New Left also placed special emphasis on the value of solidarity among young people, on students as an increasingly recognized force for social change. The vision of youth solidarity was, of course, one of the key ingredients of Ginsberg's "Howl"—the structural assemblage of the "best minds" of "my generation." Indeed, I think it is fair to say that the many ways in which Ginsberg's ideological flexibility prefigured that same quality in the New Left was likely one of the main reasons that key organizers of the New Left, like Abbie Hoffman and Tom Hayden, were so inspired by Ginsberg's poems.

Stephen Bronner inventories some of the social and cultural concerns which the New Left addressed: increased alienation "in a world of affluence and conformism," ideological control by a growing mass media, "unnecessary constraints on the extension of personal freedom," and the persistence of sexism and racism. (*Moments*, 104-105) In response to these new arenas of contention, the New Left felt that "the traditional politics of the 'Old Left' did not seem sufficient to explode the bounds of such newly discovered oppression and constraint." (*Moments*, 105) Bronner's inventory includes many of the varied concerns that Ginsberg intertwined in "Howl" and labeled Moloch.

At its best, the New Left, like Ginsberg, rejected Cold War-influenced dualistic thinking. As mentioned earlier, at its founding conference in Port Huron, Michigan, in 1962, for instance, Students for a Democratic Society refused to adopt either pro-communist or anti-communist rhetoric, despite intense urging from organizing elders like the democratic-socialist Michael Harrington to include explicit anti-Soviet declarations in SDS's founding principles. These New Left students felt that such anti-communist sentiment would not serve their purpose of creating positive change in the U.S., and would merely mimic the dominant American rhetoric of the day. Rather than become mired in antiquated debates about what Marx or Engels had really intended, or about how much Lenin had deviated from original socialist ideals, the New Left student activists instead, in their Port Huron Statement, developed the concept of "participatory democracy," whose non-dogmatic character became a major asset enhancing the movement's organizing capabilities and attractiveness. I believe that Ginsberg's ideological flexibility can be seen as prefiguring—and, after the mid-1960s, reflecting—this New Left model of participatory democracy.

And finally, in thinking about the potential political

advantages of Ginsberg's ideological flexibility, we might recall Marx's notion that freedom cannot be fully known in advance, which is why Marx "was always justifiably wary of attempting to depict the emancipated communist society of the future."[2] Ginsberg's refusal to become too specific in his ideological choices might, in this sense, be seen as an attempt to avoid unnecessarily circumscribing what a utopian freedom might look like down the futuristic road.

What are the most important political legacies of Allen Ginsberg's political poetry? Ginsberg's political legacies seem to me at least fourfold. First, and most obvious, the poems offer sharp and visionary critiques of existing political, religious, economic, and cultural institutions, and comprehend that these various institutions often function in interconnected ways. The poems criticize American policy makers for failing to live up to America's founding liberal ideals, and they further suggest moving beyond those original notions. While Ginsberg's criticisms originate from a variety of progressive viewpoints, there are certain basic principles that consistently appear—a commitment to internationalism, nonviolence, anti-racism, gay liberation, environmentalism, free expression, non-repressed sexuality, intersubjectivity, interpersonal solidarity, and opposition to the poverty and other economic injustices too often caused by unchecked capitalism.

Secondly, the poems raise social consciousness by urging alternative ways of thinking, by offering alternative information, and by insisting that spiritual qualities like compassion, forgiveness, and creativity remain everpresent in progressive politics. The consciousness-raising aspects of his poems are evident in both thematic and formal elements—the latter, for instance, in the way in which Ginsberg's use of the technique of modernist montage allows readers to participate in the creation of poetic meaning and to glimpse "anticipatory illuminations" (in the phrase of Ernst Bloch) of a world that does not yet exist.

Thirdly, his poems support the notion of poet as a

participant in organized activist struggles. In his book, *Repression and Recovery: Modern American Poetry and the Politics of Cultural Memory, 1910-45*, Cary Nelson convincingly unveils the often-arbitrary criteria under which many politically concerned U.S. poets were marginalized in the early 20th century. Nelson asserts that the traditional 20th century American literary canon displays a "resistance to (and fear of) a literariness that is socially engaged, politically critical, and committed to change." (133) I would describe this in a slightly different way: the poets were marginalized for being committed to progressive change, not merely social change, since the poems of traditionally canonized writers like T. S. Eliot and Ezra Pound are often socially critical and committed to change, albeit a more conservative or regressive kind of change than the progressive poets whom Nelson discusses and recovers in his book. In 1975, Denise Levertov wrote of contemporary poet-activists: "A striking characteristic of contemporary political poetry is that, more than in the past, it is written by people who are active participants in the causes they write about, and not simply observers....these in turn inspire others, both to participation and to the writing of poems." (167) Like Ginsberg, many of the earlier poets that Nelson recovers were not simply politically critical, but were also to varying degrees active participants in movements for progressive change. Today, when many Americans express to pollsters a deep skepticism regarding existing political institutions, yet also remain hesitant to get involved in activist groups, it seems important to note how Ginsberg's work endorses the idea of doing both art and activism.

Lastly, Ginsberg's poems present current world reality as mutable, potentially open to change. This certainly has practical implications for the contemporary cultural scene, where many critical artists in the U.S., and many skeptical young Americans in general, seem to hold a deep-seated cynicism about the possibility of progressive social transformation. This pessimism has seemed to be reversing course at least for brief periods several times in recent decades—for example, after the successful anti-World Trade Organization protests in Seattle in 1999 and after the more recent Occupy Wall Street movement—but it is an overarching pessimism that creates deep-seated challenges for progressives trying to organize mass movements in America. That pessimism, I would argue, was largely reinforced after the election of President Barack Obama, an election once seen as incredibly hopeful by many young progressive organizers, but which subsequently turned out to be largely disappointing as Obama has mostly governed as a pro-corporate Democratic Party centrist, supporting policies like drone bombings, massive NSA spying, and large bank bailouts that have demoralized many of his most enthusiastic previous supporters.

The sort of pessimism which sees progressive social change as impossible, or nearly so, holds much in common with Adorno's belief in the capitalist culture industry's ability to absorb, and thereby undermine, all radical cultural energies. This pessimism is almost a mirror image of the now-discredited orthodox Marxist teleology that viewed radical social change as inevitable. I prefer to believe that the future is uncertain and will depend largely on human actions from here on, including the ability to create the kind of effective solidarity prefigured in part III of "Howl." As ensconced as our corporate-dominated social and economic policies may appear at the moment, profound changes like the fall of the Berlin Wall and the once-unthinkable election of Nelson Mandela ought to provide stirring retorts to entrenched political fatalism. Political change is possible, and sometimes comes when we least expect it. As a tonic to confront today's overriding political cynicism, Ginsberg's visionary poems do not reveal social change to be easy, but they do energetically imagine the possibility.

* * *

To lay out key progressive legacies of Ginsberg's political poems is not to say that one can create a comprehensive political program out of them, although there are some poems, such as the later poem "New Democracy Wish List" (1993) (CP, 1063-65), in which he presents a number of fairly clear political policy proposals: "Fossil Fuels retard the planet. Detoxify America"; "Emphasize prevention & Alternative medicine with medical insurance rebates"; "Coordinate National crash program to research inexpensive anti-AIDS medicines"; "Separate Church & State in arts, education & civil law"; "End tobacco farming subsidies, cut use"; "Encourage international trade in Eco-technology"; and "Open CIA & FBI & NSA archives on Cointelpro raids."

As should be clear from prior chapters, I do not want to claim that poetry should attempt to fill the role of creating complete political programs, although I also do not believe we should foreclose the possibility of some poets undertaking such a project. In Ginsberg's case, in addition to some specific public policies recommended in some of his poems, I also think that a progressive reader can draw out—from his poems as well as from his activism in antiwar, gay rights, environmental, and human rights movements—ways in which the adoption of key elements of his political legacy could be useful, even necessary, for creating truly democratic and egalitarian social change in the contemporary world.

As noted above, I believe that Ginsberg's "ideological flexibility" prefigured an SDS-type model of participatory democracy where people holding a diverse range of progressive viewpoints were all welcomed into the movement, as opposed to many of the Old Left groups which often limited membership to people adhering to more narrow ideological positions. As David Farber observes, the more open or flexible concept of participatory democracy was central to the success of the New Left: "At the core of the New Left," according to Farber, was the idea that, "only through massive participation could democracy be made to work for the People." (*The Sixties,* xv) Democracy, in the New Left's view, meant

A Progressive Political Poetics

participating in life's daily decisions, and "not just vot[ing] every few years." (*The Sixties,* xv) Participatory democracy was itself part of a project of "prefigurative politics," which Alice Echols defines as a "commitment to develop counter-institutions that would anticipate the desired society of the future." (159) "Participatory democracy" was successful in the 1960s as an organizing concept partly because it adopted traditional American rhetoric (about democracy) rather than more explicitly socialist rhetoric that was discouraged in schools and in the society-at-large during the Cold War era.

And yet, if the concept of "participatory democracy" was one of the movement's greatest strengths, it also proved ultimately to be a not-quite-adequate organizing principle—with the limitations of the concept discovered through problematic movement-organizing experiences. As mentioned above, as a generalized concept understood by activists in myriad ways, the call for participatory democracy enhanced the ability of the movement to recruit greater numbers by welcoming a more diverse range of activists. But, on the flip side of the coin, the principle proved slightly too indeterminate to sustain long-term organizational coherence. As Stephen Bronner notes, "SDS ultimately stood hapless before factions growing from within—like RYM1, RYM2, and the Weathermen." (*Moments,* 107) Under the rubric of participatory democracy with its wide and often non-specific guidelines, there was simply no way to tell fringe groups on the left—including those advocating violence—that, in their increasingly irrational rhetoric or harmful actions, they were straying from SDS's guidelines or from the principles of the wider antiwar movement. There was also no way to tell the media that such actions did not represent the core ideas of the group, since core ideas were not comprehensively established.

More recently, a similar dilemma faced the organizers of Occupy Wall Street, which was based on a far more vague "horizontalist" set of organizational principles than SDS. Although those horizontalist principles served initially to welcome many activists from diverse ideological backgrounds into the group, they also created the conditions for a massive amount of infighting within the group, one of the reasons why I believe Occupy dissipated more quickly than many had hoped, and why it was impossible for Occupy Wall Street to dissociate itself from wild or regressive political opinions expressed to the media by activists standing on the margins of New York City's Zuccotti Park.

In today's climate, amid an emboldened corporatism and a relatively splintered progressive movement, a coalitional challenge to the current power structure may likely represent the best hope for advancing social change. For such a project to be successful, it seems important for movement organizations, in the tradition of the New Left, to welcome participants with widely ranging views. And yet, for the sake of building more successful political movements in the future, an openness to ideological and strategic flexibility may need to be both embraced and transcended. While maintaining a certain amount of ideological and strategic flexibility, a successful progressive group or coalition may have to cohere around some basic positive principles and programs, and to develop structures that could democratically elect spokespeople with both the authority to speak officially on the group's behalf and the accountability to be removed if they do not well or accurately reflect or represent the group.

The problem with overly vague organizing principles or structures is that there is no way to challenge spokespeople or factions who misrepresent the group's goals other than by dismantling the group and starting all over, or watching it accidentally implode. Thus, there are an untold number of short-lived progressive projects which do not remain in existence long enough to achieve their enormous potential—most recently Occupy Wall Street, and before that, the global justice movement that successfully opposed the World Trade Organization in Seattle in 1999. In an important essay from the early 1970s feminist movement, Jo Freeman referred to the danger of overly informal movement-group

A Progressive Political Poetics

structures with the insightful moniker, "the tyranny of structurelessness." Freeman maintained that "informal elites," based on personality traits or personal friendships, develop in groups that adopt "the myth of 'structurelessness.'" (*Structurelessness*, 157) In these cases, without any clear lines of democratically accountable leadership, "informal structures have no obligation to be responsible to the group at large. Their power was not given to them; it cannot be taken away." (*Structurelessness*, 157) Freeman concludes that informal structures, carrying no mechanisms of democratic accountability, are effective for getting people initially involved, but inadequate to the task of undertaking long-term political work. In a later essay, Freeman describes how some early feminist groups were "racked by several major crises during the early seventies," including a takeover attempt by the Trotskyist-oriented Young Socialist Alliance, because "structurelessness provided no means of resolving political disputes." (*Women's Liberation*, 543)

While a skepticism of political structures may be seen in part to reflect a genuine desire to avoid overly rigidified bureaucracies or undemocratic hierarchies, I believe that a successful progressive movement will need to recognize that some leadership structures, those with democratic decision-making processes, are better than others. In the words of Stephen Bronner, "*Accountability* rather than *participation* or *autonomy* is the primary category for a new politics willing to recognize that the great battles of the future will take place in what are still burgeoning international and regional institutions." (*Critical Theory*, 307) A movement based on principles of democratic accountability would therefore need to develop flexible structures capable of satisfying the requirements of long-term unity while avoiding rigid and exploitative structures of which so many contemporary activists are justifiably wary. These political strategies do not need to be argued or developed in political poems, but a reader or critic can draw helpful lessons—including the merits of ideological flexibility—for such strategies from poems like many of those from throughout Ginsberg's literary career.

* * *

I have earlier outlined ways in which Ginsberg's poems explore interconnections between the personal and the political, ways in which poetic strategies of personalization are used in a poem like "Kaddish" to add emotional weight to political themes. The 1960s New Left and early 1970s feminist movements explored these relationships as well. Like the concept of "participatory democracy," the notion of "the personal is political" provided these 1960s and 1970s movements with a similar dialectical effect—contributing explanatory and initial organizational vitality to help these movements grow, while simultaneously saddling projects and programs with some unanticipated obstacles for long-term organizing.

Alice Echols notes, for instance, that placing the body as a "site of political contestation" (158) attracted great numbers of participants to the 1970s women's movement. Personalizing the political realm was a key to the project of reconceptualizing public-sphere/private-sphere boundaries to address areas of repression, such as domestic violence, that had previously, out of traditional patriarchal notions, far too often been consigned to private realms considered beyond the scope of public responsibility for protection or prosecution. Yet, Echols also concludes that "'the personal is political' was one of those ideas whose rhetorical power seemed to sometimes work against or undermine its explication," (164) since the focus on the personal often deflected focus away from institutional power dynamics. As Echols writes, "the idea led some to confuse personal liberation with political struggle....In the end, both the women's liberation movement and the larger protest Movement suffered, as the idea....was often interpreted in such a way as to make questions of life-style absolutely central." (164-165) And once all boundaries between public and private are shattered, then there goes the widely cherished right to privacy, since no element of personal life can be considered off limits from public scrutiny. Public/private boundaries need to be continually re-thought, not dismantled. The personal can sometimes be political, but it is not always so.

Even if future movement successes may depend on further developments in reconceptualizing public/private boundaries, this once again does not need to be the quest of every political poem which uses the literary technique of personalization. Yet, one can glean some insights about the relationship between the personal and the political from Ginsberg's poems that would be helpful in any successful socially progressive endeavor. In different contexts, such as the 1950s Cold War era described in "Kaddish," the political environment can certainly have a deep impact on personal psyches. And yet, political change is not reducible to the psychological transformation of individuals, just as every citizen's psychological health would not be assured by a utopian, democratic reform of national institutions. It is likely true, however, that more personal awareness of the kind Ginsberg advocates and an increased understanding of various ways in which public policies impact personal lives would surely not hurt prospects for democratic change. As mentioned earlier, when Allen Ginsberg came to do a poetry reading at Rutgers University in 1988 as part of a National Student Convention of activists that a group of Rutgers students had organized in coalition with some student activists from around the country, Ginsberg advised young people in the audience to learn to separate disagreements they had with their parents from disagreements they had with the state. Ginsberg had insightfully recognized that some of the violent or overly aggressive tendencies of certain factions of the 1960s antiwar movement had originated in part because some people were letting their personal anger affect their activist decisions. He rightly believed that activists coming to the organizing table with lighter personal baggage would most likely make saner and more effective strategic decisions.

As it explores the relationship between the personal and the political, Ginsberg's political poetry also gains strength from investigating the complex relations between culture and politics, including through examining the dominant culture industry in the U.S., and through adopting poetic strategies like mythification to add a sense of literary timelessness to topical political issues. Being the child of two politically engaged parents, and having a father who was a widely published lyric poet, Ginsberg seems to have always believed that culture could at least potentially be used to move policies and practices in the political realm. Exploring the relationship between politics and culture was also important to 1960s movements, especially in countercultural groups like the Yippies, whose members attempted to use theatrical tactics and demonstrations to challenge the war in Vietnam and economic policies in the U.S. And, indeed, the counterculture, including various wings of the music world—folk, rock and roll, rhythm and blues—was successful in motivating many thousands of young people to join the anti-war movement.

And yet, some trends of completely conflating culture and politics may over time have also contributed to the 1960s anti-war movement's decline. In this regard, Stephen Bronner observes that "'political' resistance became synonymous with an assault on the culture....The 'political,' however, thereby became robbed of any determinate meaning. Symbolism was confused with programmatic action." (*Moments,* 105) Both David Farber and Stephen Bronner criticize segments of the 1960s movements for aestheticizing politics by rejecting all notions of reason, not just instrumental reason, thereby adding to the already difficult task of debating, and then reaching agreement, on united principles and strategies, organizational goals, and even the social problems which deserved to be addressed. According to authors like Farber and Bronner, this 1960s aestheticization of politics sometimes inspired a belief that social change would descend apocalyptically, rather than by strategic steps that could lead from the present into the future.

Ginsberg himself did not conflate politics and culture. He insisted on the importance of the cultural realm—for him, the cultural arena was not secondary to any other arena of human life—without denying the need for changing institutional politics. His project, like Blake's, was not to sacrifice analytical reason on the altar of culture or psychology, but simply to couple reason with other human traits.

Ginsberg's poems, like the 1960s counterculture, have served as doors of entry into political activism for many American and international youth (and not only youth) from the 1950s until today. The poems urge young people to investigate worldly reality for themselves, rather than merely accepting "official" versions of newsworthy events. They incite youth to participate collectively in the life of their communities and their nations. They impel a pursuit of honest emotion and healthy sexuality. And they seed a desire among readers to envision the possibility that a better world can actually be created by the living.

The late Abbie Hoffman used to say that trying to create social change without a counterculture is like trying to ski without snow. Poetic urgings like Ginsberg's can help create a foundation for building future progressive movements. Ginsberg's cultural insights may provide only partial answers to a broad range of social needs, but they are important parts. Poetry does not need to be the site where the best theories and strategies for creating progressive political change are comprehensively worked out. But Allen Ginsberg's political poetry does offer a wide range of insights and ways of thinking that could be, and has been, incredibly helpful to developing progressive movements.

* * *

Throughout this volume, I have been attempting to show how one can glean from Ginsberg's poetry many key elements that would be needed or helpful for progressive political advancement. I should also acknowledge, as noted earlier, that one key element is largely missing: the struggle for women's equality. The influential literary critic, Catherine Stimpson, who was a one-time professor of mine at Rutgers University, in summarizing the most well-known of the male Beat Generation writers, argues that there is "a cultural boundary they could rarely cross: a traditional construction of the female, and of the feminine." (378) Writing years before the contemporary work of members of the Beat Studies Association to promote previously marginalized women writers of the Beat Generation like Janine Pommy Vega or Hettie Jones, Stimpson notes that, while the main Beat writers are "scornful of most secular authority," (380) their portrayal of women nonetheless usually adheres to dominant or stereotypical prescriptions for female passivity. According to Stimpson, women "are screwed, taken, burrowed into." (380) In Ginsberg's most well-known poems, Stimpson observes a tendency to feminize passive homosexual roles. Often, according to Stimpson, "In his homosexual acts, he masculinizes some male partners....and feminizes himself." In an article that is otherwise overwhelmingly positive, Charles Shively expresses a similar criticism about Ginsberg's work: "No provision is really made for women as *active* lovers—choosing their own love 'objects'." (214) In Stimpson's view, Ginsberg "presents men as primary movers." (390) In "Kaddish," which some critics have tried to read as a feminist poem, Stimpson notes that Naomi, "the woman, is material and muse, not maker." (390)

 Even if one can, I think, point to Naomi's representation in "Kaddish" in part as a woman and an activist with insightful social observations despite her mental illness, it would be difficult to argue with Stimpson's basic critique. In "Howl," men certainly are, in Stimpson's words, the primary movers. Although Ginsberg cites some women in the endnotes to his *Collected Poems*, the "best minds" of "Howl," when they are gender-specified in the poem, they are generally identified as male. Similarly, in an earlier chapter, I discussed Ginsberg's poem "Ignu" which seemed to present a tradition of comic and tragic genius that was solely masculine.

I do therefore think it would be fair to acknowledge that Ginsberg does not explore or challenge dominant conceptions of gender with anything near the energy or insight with which he explores nearly every other key social and political issue of his time. I do not mean to say that Ginsberg was completely blind to gender-related issues. In his 1966 anti-war poem "Iron Horse" (CP, 445), he expresses disapproval of a male soldier's double-standard view of marital fidelity, and in several poems of that era he decries television's manipulation of female beauty standards. Many of his poems allude to important women activists and poets, such as Mother Bloor, Emma Goldman and Emily Dickinson. In his biography of Ginsberg, Barry Miles relates an episode in Ginsberg's life where he gets angry with Kerouac over the latter's demeaning remark about women: "He called up Jack to tell him to come over and meet Rayanne, but Jack said, 'I only fuck girls and learn from men, so why should I come up?' Allen, annoyed by his misogyny, wrote him a poison pen letter and said, 'that's why you're so dumb!'"(131)

In Ginsberg's later poems, of the eighties and nineties, he clearly grew at least somewhat more conscious of gender issues. There are no poems like "Ignu," praising poetic genius as "a great cocksman" remembered by "Hollywood dolls or lone Marys of Idaho long-legged publicity women and secret housewives." (CP, 211) In his later poems, there are more occasions where Ginsberg advocates more equitable treatment of women—"Insult your girlfriend you'll feel hurt!" ("Empire Air," CP, 843) In several later poems, women are included among his inventory of artistic influences: "empowered by Whitman Blake Rimbaud Ma Rainey" ("Personals Ad," CP, 970); and in later interviews, he often took care to make sure to include women poets like Anne Waldman, Jayne Cortez, and Eileen Myles—along with some of his favorite male next-generations poets like Andy Clausen, Antler, and David

Cope—when he was asked to list some of his favorite living American poets, which earlier in his life he sometimes failed to do in interviews. In his later work, poems with homosexual love themes, such as "To Jacob Rabinowitz"(CP, 972), unlike in his earlier poem, "Please Master," no longer feminize passive sexual roles. And perhaps most significantly, there are lines in his later poems in which Ginsberg tacitly expresses realizations and regrets for his earlier poems' portrayals of women: "my poems have done some men good / and a few women ill." ("Reading Bai Juyi," CP, 905)

But these expressed concerns for gender issues in his later career do not, it seems to me, go nearly far enough to allow us to credit Ginsberg as being a poet advancing feminist concerns in any really interesting ways. As a critic looking at the political ideas and observations of a poet like Allen Ginsberg, I think it is important to recognize that even great writers of protest literature may at times be limited in some key ways by the dominant culture in which they lived and which they often opposed.

I should also mention here that I know friends did discuss this issue with Ginsberg in later decades, which I think reached him and helped him to evolve in his thinking. At one point in the early 1990s, I remember personally having a conversation with Ginsberg at the Odessa Restaurant in New York City's Lower East Side about the portrayal of women in his poetry, and the way some progressive critics had written critically about it. I recall him sighing, which I took at the time to be his recognition that there was at least some truth to the criticism. He told me he had thought about the possibility of writing a poem or poems for some of the historic women writers and activists he admired, like Ma Rainey, Emily Dickinson, Emma Goldman, or Rosa Parks. The problem, I recall Ginsberg saying, was that his writing process in those days really depended on feeling a spontaneous inspiration and not on pre-planning a theme to address. He seemed to hope to one day feel that spontaneous inspiration to write some interesting poems that would change the way that future readers would view his evolving understanding of gender issues. But although there is some noticeable improvement in his later poems' depiction of women, I do not think it would be possible to point to strong feminist poems that cover women's issues in the way Ginsberg's poems covered such issues as war and peace, ecology, economic inequality, gay rights, racism, or free speech.

And yet, it also seems possible for generous readers to look at whether literary works, in the words of George Levine, demonstrate a "capacity to resist the simplifications even of its own ideological commitments." (13) In the case of Allen Ginsberg, I believe that his overwhelmingly progressive ideas and energies do resist the sometimes-clear instances of sexism in his poetry. The fact that his poems are so overwhelmingly progressive is what, for example, enables Catherine Stimpson, despite her strong criticisms, to otherwise praise Ginsberg for openly exploring previously repressed realms of sexuality. It is also what makes it possible for some of our most influential contemporary feminist poets, like Adrienne Rich and Marge Piercy, to credit him as an important influence on their work. And, I think, the overwhelmingly progressive energy of his work, along with many other reasons including the desire to explore the works of previously neglected women writers who were part of the Beat Generation, also helps to explain why so many interesting feminist literary critics have been involved in writing about Ginsberg and other Beat Generation writers and in helping to create the Beat Studies Association.

Writing to Adrienne Rich, the terrific contemporary poet Enid Dame writes about Ginsberg in a letter that is quoted in Rich's book, *What Is Found There,* a letter which generously credits Ginsberg for providing one of the core influences for contemporary American women poets: "You locate the roots of the [women's poetry movement] in the Beat rebel poetry of the '50s and '60s. That's certainly true in my case. Allen Ginsberg's poetry, especially 'Kaddish,' the culture of the East Village, the politics of the New Left, and the emerging women's movement and its encouragement of women artists all affected my own growth and work as a poet." (qtd in Rich, *Found There*, 264)

Critic Nan Nowik notes that both Rich and Piercy praised Ginsberg's poetry for helping to show all contemporary American writers that poetry could liberate the personal imagination from repressive institutions and be used to say what one thinks and feels. (212-213) In her own words, Adrienne Rich explains the influence of Ginsberg and other male poets of his era by relating his influence on contemporary women's poetry to the impact of the civil rights movement and the New Left on the growth of the women's liberation movement:

> Just as the women's liberation movement was a new force released from within the African-American struggle for justice and the New Left, this women's poetry movement was a necessary unfolding, both from the earlier poetic revolution and from the politics of the women's movement. That the origins and nature of poetry are not just personal but communal was an important legacy from the poetics that Kenneth Rexroth, Lawrence Ferlinghetti, Allen Ginsberg, among others, had brought to huge audiences in the 1950s and 1960s and from the Black Arts movement. The women's poetry movement had, thus, both social and poetic roots, and the fact is that they cannot be separated.
>
> (*Found There*, 175)

Thus, while feminist poets, like women's liberation activists of the 1970s, were writing, in part, in protest against the sexism and exclusion found in prior male-dominated poetry circles and traditions, it is simultaneously true that Ginsberg's liberatory impulses provided inspiration even in this one area which his own verse admittedly did not energetically explore. Moreover, the fact that Ginsberg's poetry of the 1980s and 1990s—as well as his later interviews in which he increasingly began to recommend contemporary women poets—show that he was a poet with an open and evolving mind, willing to learn and grow.

* * *

Allen Ginsberg's contributions to a progressive political legacy do not, of course, end with his poetry. Ginsberg's rise to become a well-known political dissident during his lifetime was in large part a result of his long-term and very public activist commitment, a commitment that was nurtured by his unique political upbringing, but that cannot be explained by that upbringing alone.

After all, there was much to discourage Allen Ginsberg from undertaking an outspokenly political life. In the literary arena, there was the New Critical pressure for poets, if they wanted to be published, to produce poetry with a certain degree of historical aloofness. And surprisingly, even some of Ginsberg's own Beat Generation friends tried to dissuade him from dissident pursuits. Ginsberg's response to one such attempt by William Burroughs in the late 1940s was blunt: "Trouble with you is you never had to work for a living....As for me, I have nothing better to do than to help those less fortunate than myself."[3] Jack Kerouac at one point advised Ginsberg: "Why don't you ignore war, ignore politics, ignore samsara fuckups, they're endless."[4] As I have shown throughout this book, Ginsberg dismissed such advice, writing about politics from the start and becoming a public activist beginning with his early 1960s participation in protests against the Vietnam War and remaining publicly and politically active throughout his entire life.

In Chapter One, I sketched some of the important inspiration that Ginsberg's poetry and activism provided to some of America's most influential young organizers.

Young activists like SDS-founder Al Haber, Port Huron-author Tom Hayden, Yippie-cofounder Abbie Hoffman, and Redstockings co-creator, Rosalyn Baxandall all cite the influence of Beat literature in general, or Ginsberg's poetry in particular, on their politically formative years. Not only did Ginsberg inspire young organizers, he often helped them think through political strategy for upcoming events. And he often made sure to introduce activists he knew to each other, introductions that would occasionally stir historic results. In the late 1990s, I traveled to Vermont with Johanna Lawrenson, Abbie Hoffman's co-organizer and widow, to interview Dave Dellinger, one of the 20th century's greatest pacifist, antiwar organizers. During our long conversation, Dellinger, who was a passionate reader of contemporary poetry, recalled that it was Allen Ginsberg who had originally introduced him to Abbie Hoffman in New York, telling each of them that, as two of his favorite political activists, he thought they should meet each other. Later, Dellinger and Hoffman would work together against the war, and stand trial together, in the historic Chicago 8 Trial, a trial that continues to be the subject of numerous books and films and which the ACLU has called one of the most important trials of the 20th century for maintaining American civil liberties. As he had figuratively brought young people together through the anaphoric repetition of "who" in the catalogs of part I of "Howl," so Ginsberg literally introduced them to each other and brought them together in real life.

I had earlier quoted from Abbie Hoffman's description of Ginsberg and it seems worth repeating here: "'Howl'…. was inspired by the Gods. Just as they had spoken to Isaiah and Jeremiah, they talked to Ginsberg and Ginsberg took his poetry into the streets. Jews don't have saints, they just have Ginsbergs every once in a while." (123)

Women's movement organizer and Redstockings cofounder Rosalyn Baxandall recalls early Beat-influenced cultural experiences at the University of Wisconsin that helped shape her determination to lead a progressive life. Baxandall's description of the ways in which a local counterculture helped to open doorways to political activism would, I suspect, resonate in the experiences of thousands of young radicals from the 1960s to today:

> There was also an arty set, many of whom were politically "progressive" as well. They drank, smoked dope and chewed peyote, and hung out in the Rat as well as the 602 Club, Lombardy's, or Glen and Ann's late at night. These bohemians—that was their identification then—hid slouching behind dark sunglasses, in black turtlenecks often adorned by Russian or Mexican motifs. The girls, often theater majors, were *zophtic*, full, bra free; they wore long, layered multicolored skirts and heavy, dark eye makeup and looked pale and sickly, quite a contrast to the blonde, spunky midwesterners who dominated campus life. I, being a hot-headed, enthusiastic Manhattanite fit into neither category, but aspired to beatnik cool. (135)

Ginsberg's influence on 1960s antiwar activists stemmed both from his writings about the war's brutality and his willingness to put his voice and his body on the line. He marched in demonstrations, spoke eloquently at public rallies and to the press, and participated in movement strategy meetings. The poet Tom Clark describes the wide range of Ginsberg's activities that went beyond the writing of verse:

> [Ginsberg is] an accomplished artist whose extracurricular power as a cultural spokesman has given his work a range of effect rivaling that of popular political or religious leaders.... Even if poets have always been, as Shelley suggested, society's unacknowledged

> legislators, Ginsberg has gone one step further, attempting not only to edify and enlighten through his verse, but also to create social change through his non-poetic activity—teaching, touring, proselytizing, conducting a nonstop, self-consuming crusade on behalf of kindness, compassion and mellow understanding in human affairs. (30)

At one strategy meeting with anti-war student activists, recorded in *Allen Verbatim,* Ginsberg offered telling advice: "Rather than badmouthing everybody, rather than complaining about this and that, what would be really interesting is for everybody to use their minds and try to work out an actual scenario." (197) Ginsberg incited these students to help the left "get itself together" (203), and remarked that he saw "the role of poetry in terms of a public thing." (209) Typically, when Ginsberg visited a city to perform, "he read its newspapers and asked countless questions about its people and politics" (Schumacher, 482), in order to contribute, while he was in town, to local needs. Perhaps this is what J.Edgar Hoover had foreseen when he declared the Beat Generation in 1960 among the three most threatening groups in the United States. (Schumacher, 321)

Ginsberg, as poet and activist, enhanced movements for change partly by inspiring them and partly by challenging them. At a planning meeting for a 1965 rally in California's bay area, Ginsberg implored the group to alter its plans. While originally "people were supposed to run and march angry," (Schumacher, 453) Ginsberg impelled the group toward political theater with a more peaceful outlook. According to Schumacher, "Allen offered a twenty-one point plan that suggested the use of old-fashioned floats, masses of flowers, music, flags....a safe, nonviolent affair, suitable for all ages and all people." (Schumacher, 453) In his 1965 poem, "Who Be Kind To," Ginsberg had similarly attempted to shift anti-war tactics toward more compassionate and pacifistic directions: "Be kind to the politician weeping in the galleries / of Whitehall, Kremlin, White House." (CP, 367) In Marty Jezer's biography of Abbie Hoffman, Jezer makes it clear that Ginsberg's influence in inspiring young activists toward a creative blending of radical nonviolent politics and countercultural imagination was substantial:

> Ginsberg, asked by [Jerry] Rubin to be a speaker, read his poem "Berkeley Vietnam Days," which, published in *Liberation*, greatly influenced activists in the East Village. Drawing lessons from the confrontation with the Oakland police and his efforts at mediation with the Hell's Angels, Ginsberg suggested ideas for a new kind of hip pacifism that would blend the older activists' nonviolent principles with the new hippie culture: Gandhian flower power or psychedelic nonviolence. Ginsberg's idea was to transform antiwar protests into visual spectacles, with peace marchers in the front lines carrying gentle props like flowers, children's toys, religious symbols, musical instruments, and American flags to undercut the public's fear of demonstrations. (99)

Ginsberg had not only challenged Old Left orthodoxies. He was also willing to challenge 1960s New Left organizers and to offer concrete proposals for implementing creative ideas. As Jezer notes, Ginsberg's poem inspired "peace happenings" in New York soon thereafter, and as I have mentioned earlier in this volume, the theatrical protest techniques that he suggested and inspired during the anti-Vietnam War protests continue to live on in the visual and theatrical rallies that have been key parts of contemporary movements both here in the U.S. and abroad.

In an earlier chapter, I discussed the way in which Ginsberg's poem, "Wichita Vortex Sutra," with its climactic line, "I here declare the end of the War!" inspired both songs (by John Lennon and Phil Ochs) and demonstrations against the Vietnam War. In his book, *Chicago '68*, David Farber describes a November 1967 "War Is Over" demonstration, organized by the Yippies, which "involved about three thousand young people who massed in Washington Square" and then ran through downtown New York announcing the war was over, influenced by Ginsberg's poem. (Farber, 12) According to Farber, one of the event's main organizers, Jerry Rubin, concluded that this was "an exemplary action, exciting and alive and totally participatory; the best kind of guerilla theater." (Farber, 12) Continuing to work with the creative wings of the anti-Vietnam War movement, Ginsberg was a prominent participant in the notorious exorcism of the Pentagon, and in the demonstrations at the 1968 Chicago Democratic Party Convention. In connection with Chicago 1968 events, Ginsberg attended the initial planning meetings, took part in the rallies, and testified at at the precedent-setting conspiracy trial which followed. It seems more than coincidence how many key historic events found Ginsberg near the forefront.

During the preparations for Chicago '68, Ginsberg maintained dual roles as enthusiastic supporter and constructive critic. Farber notes his persistence in trying to discourage destructive aspects of movement groups and to encourage the positive: "much of his participation in Yippie was aimed at neutralizing its violent tendencies and helping to develop its festive, enlightening, and spiritual possibilities." (*Chicago '68*, 26)

During the police riot which ensued outside the 1968 Democratic Party convention in Chicago, Ginsberg famously spent much of his time in Grant Park engaged in Buddhist chanting in an attempt to lower levels of anger and violence. Farber concludes that Ginsberg's mantra-chanting "calmed people," (*Chicago '68*, 174) while some of the protest's other organizers, including Jerry Rubin, secretly hoped that media-covered police violence would motivate an increased level of militancy among antiwar activists and further polarize the American populace. Farber argues persuasively that those antiwar organizers who favored tactics of violent polarization unwittingly served to undermine their own antiwar cause, since tactics that embraced violence alienated many American citizens who might otherwise have favored or spoken out for peace. Indeed, in his later years, I sometimes heard Allen Ginsberg say in public that he believed that violence on the part of some 1960s antiwar activists may have been one of the reasons that the war lasted as long as it did, since by 1969 the majority of American people, as stated in opinion polls, opposed the war. Personally, I believe that some young activists may have made mistakes that hurt their own cause, but nonetheless they do not deserve responsibility for extending the war. That distinction must be reserved for the government, which held the sole power to prolong or to stop the war, and which often executes foreign or domestic policies that a majority of Americans oppose.

During his testimony at the Chicago 8 Trial, Ginsberg described to the court his hopes that the Chicago antiwar rallies would extend "the feeling of humanity and compassion" (Ginsberg, *Chicago Trial Testimony,* 5) that had been evident at a 1967 San Francisco "be-in": "There was what was called a gathering of the tribes of all of the different affinity groups, political groups, spiritual groups, Yoga groups, music groups and poetry groups that all felt the same crisis of identity and crisis of the planet and political crisis in America." (*Chicago Trial Testimony,* 4)

There were many funny moments in Chicago's courtroom. The theatrical maneuvers by defendants Abbie Hoffman and Jerry Rubin are by now legendary and the subject of several documentary and dramatic films. During Ginsberg's testimony, one of the defendants' lawyers, Len Weinglass, challenged a particular judicial ruling by asking the judge whether "the law does not permit this witness to explain his own poetry?" (*Chicago Trial Testimony,* 58) While Ginsberg had written "Kaddish" in part to witness to

Naomi's life, here in Chicago's courthouse Ginsberg had the opportunity to act as a legal witness at one of the century's most important political trials. In addition to describing some of the events which he had observed on the Chicago streets, Ginsberg had the opportunity to emphasize that his involvement in the Chicago demonstrations was part and parcel of his commitment to advancing humanitarian goals:

> My statement was that the planet Earth at the present moment was endangered by violence, over-population, pollution, ecological destruction brought about by our own greed; ....that it was a planetary crisis that had not been recognized by any government of the world; ....that the younger people of America were aware of that and....we were going to invite them there and that the central motive would be a presentation of a desire for the preservation of the planet.
> (*Chicago Trial Testimony*, 10-11)

Among the many progressive causes for which he advocated for many years, as a prominent gay poet, was gay rights. In the words of biographer Barry Miles, Ginsberg "championed the cause in interviews and the media. In the history of the struggle to achieve acceptance for homosexuals in American society, Ginsberg was a central figure." (532) Earlier in this volume, I noted that Charles Kaiser, in his book, *The Gay Metropolis: 1940-1996,* observed that Ginsberg and other Beat writers were influential, initially, because they were the first American writers to present gay themes as hip. In *Making Trouble: Essays on Gay History, Politics, and the University*, John D'Emilio writes similarly of Ginsberg's early impact on gay consciousness:

> The visibility of the Beat subculture in North Beach had a major impact upon gay

> consciousness in San Francisco....Ginsberg's *Howl*, which became a local best-seller after the obscenity trial, openly acknowledged homosexuality. In describing gay male sexuality as joyous, delightful, and even holy, Ginsberg did in fact turn American values "inside out." (80-81)

On June 28, 1969, several nights of demonstrations, even rioting, began in response to a police raid at a gay bar in Manhattan called the Stonewall Inn. The Stonewall uprising would later be seen universally as a landmark event in the modern gay rights movement. In his book, *Stonewall*, author Martin Duberman takes care to note that Ginsberg came to the bar at 1 a.m., after the first night of the rebellions, to express his solidarity:

> Allen Ginsberg strolled by, flashed the peace sign and, after seeing "Gay Power!" scratched on the front of the Stonewall, expressed satisfaction to a *Village Voice* reporter: "We're one of the largest minorities in the country—10 percent, you know. It's about time we did something to assert ourselves." (208)

In *Unspeakable: The Rise of the Gay and Lesbian Press in America*, Rodger Streitmatter describes how Ginsberg's observations of, and ideas about, the Stonewall uprising had a real and positive impact on media accounts of the event:

> The most insightful comments about the uprising came from gay press veterans Jack Nichols and Lige Clarke, who covered Stonewall in their 'Homosexual Citizen' column.... Nichols and Clarke did not rely only on their own analysis but also reported the uprising through the eyes of a leading guru

of the Beat generation. A few days after the riots, the columnists walked through the riot-torn area with poet Allen Ginsberg. Not only did they document his announcement of his own homosexuality, but they also recorded what became the most poignant description of the change the rebellion created. They wrote: "Ginsberg said, 'Gay power! Isn't that great! It's about time we did something to assert ourselves.' He walked in the Stonewall, dancing and bouncing to the music. He said, 'The guys are so beautiful. They've lost that wounded look that fags had 10 years ago.'"

As was often the case during his lifetime, Ginsberg was there as a key shaper of public perception just as history was being made—there both to express his solidarity with movements and to help develop America's historical memory of events.

Among other causes which saw Ginsberg on the front lines was the ecology movement. After already employing strong ecological messages in his poetry, Ginsberg was a participant in the country's first Earth Day rally, on April 22, 1970 in Philadelphia, Pennsylvania. According to Michael Schumacher, "In Philadelphia, thousands of people, including Ginsberg and former vice presidential candidate Edmund Muskie, marched for three miles from the city's art museum to an assembly in a park." (541) There Ginsberg delivered an ominous message about the seriousness of environmental erosion, telling the gathering that the world had the technological intelligence to avert disaster, but that he was not sure whether that intelligence would be utilized. Throughout the rest of Ginsberg's life, in both his poetry and his activism, concern for the Earth's ecological future would remain paramount—this concern looks more prophetic than ever today with the ever-increasing ecological dangers caused by climate change.

Ginsberg was arrested on numerous occasions participating in acts of civil disobedience. Perhaps the most well-known of these occasions was his act of protesting nuclear weapons by sitting on the railroad tracks at Rocky Flats, Colorado, less than twelve hours after he had finished writing his anti-nuclear poem, "Plutonian Ode," thereby adding another layer of meaning to the project of uniting language and the body and of literally putting one's body on the line. According to Schumacher, "As he was writing the poem, he had no inclination that he would be part of a demonstration later that day. (Schumacher, 631) But Ginsberg was awakened only a few hours after going to bed upon finishing the poem, "by a student calling to inform him that a train shipment of nuclear waste would be leaving Rocky Flats that afternoon." (Schumacher, 631) At the tracks, according to Schumacher, "Allen, Peter [Orlovsky], and four young women went to the railroad line and found a spur in the tracks that was out of sight of Jefferson County sheriff's deputies patrolling the area. Allen pulled off his shoes and sat cross-legged on a rail." (Schumacher, 631) Ginsberg told the assembled press: "I want to sit on the tracks and meditate on this problem....and bring mindfulness to the situation here at Rocky Flats, where 150,000 tons of plutonium have been fabricated." (quoted in Schumacher, 631) The train, which soon turned the corner, thankfully stopped upon seeing the protestors, who had literally risked their lives to bring attention to the life-or-death issues of nuclear weapons and nuclear waste. The participants in this courageous action were arrested for criminal trespass and obstructing a passageway. At his arraignment in court, Ginsberg pleaded not guilty, and as part of the explanation for his plea, he read "Plutonian Ode" to the court.

Until the end of his life, Ginsberg was a visible figure in a multitude of issues surrounding peace and human rights issues internationally: speaking up for peace in the Middle East, protesting U.S. support of brutal regimes like those of El Salvador or Guatemala's in the 1980s or brutal counter-

The Poetry and Politics of Allen Ginsberg

insurgencies like the Nicaraguan Contras in Central America, berating American censorship, advocating for increased civil liberties in the Eastern Bloc (which famously got him kicked out of Cuba and Czechoslovakia), and criticizing the full-scale 1991 bombardment of Iraq. He supported such progressive causes with his poetry, his outspoken voice, his courageous body, and his checkbook. And he often traveled to investigate or witness things for himself. In the latest comprehensive biography of Ginsberg, *I Celebrate Myself* (2006), written by his longtime bibliographer, Bill Morgan, Morgan notes that the 1980 election of Ronald Reagan had brought in a more regressive U.S. foreign policy toward Nicaragua, and its Sandinista government run by a poet, Daniel Ortega, with the minister of culture being Ginsberg's old poet friend, Ernesto Cardenal. Morgan writes: "As usual Allen wanted to find out firsthand what the real situation was, and if necessary call attention to the wrong-headed thinking of the Reagan administration."(554) Ginsberg timed his visit to coincide with a visit by the Russian poet Yevgeny Yevtushenko. In the end, as I noted in the last chapter, Ginsberg did not come away from Nicaragua completely uncritical of the Sandinista government, but on the overall political question, he was definitively opposed to U.S. intervention (including the criminal act of mining Nicaraguan harbors), and to U.S. support for the brutal actions of the Contras. As Morgan writes, Ginsberg, Cardenal, and Yevtushenko decided "to sit down together and write a manifesto asking for nonintervention in Nicaragua by the superpowers....They called their statement the 'Declaration of Three,' and it was carried as front-page news by the Managuan press and even made it into The Nation and Washington Tribune back in the States." (555)

Although I have made a case for avoiding the conflation of poetic and political realms, I would argue that the attempt to challenge those conceptual boundaries, to push the envelope as it were, provided some of Ginsberg's most vital poetic energies. Likewise, Allen Ginsberg's activism pushed his poetry further into a sphere of political and cultural influence.

Let us look at one astonishing example of art successfully pushing the envelope to affect the political realm, the case of John Sinclair. Sinclair, who I had the pleasure to meet many years later at a Kerouac Festival in Lowell, Massachusetts, was a renowned Michigan antiwar activist who had spent over two years in jail on a minor marijuana charge by December, 1970. To those on the left who were concerned about Sinclair's case, it seemed clear that the lengthy jail sentence was aimed at punishing Sinclair for his politics more than for the minor pot charge. On December 10, 1970, Allen Ginsberg and others organized a rally to free him. The event included a mix of artists and activists, including such prominent performers and speakers as Dave Dellinger, Bobby Seale, Phil Ochs, Yoko Ono, and John Lennon. Of course, there had been prior activist focus on this issue, so that one cannot solely credit a single event for what ensued, but as Schumacher describes it, "Fifty-five hours after John and Yoko ended their set, John Sinclair was released from prison." (561) Throughout this volume, I have advocated for a conceptual distinction between the poetic and political arenas. But I have also urged seeing these arenas as interacting, as spheres which contest, interplay, overlap, and push against each other in different ways in different historical contexts. In the case of John Sinclair, it took only fifty-five hours to shake down the walls that can separate culture and politics. In this case, and in the case of many of Ginsberg's outstanding literary moments, poetry (along with other art forms including music) and politics made a powerful team indeed.

While Allen Ginsberg's poems do not offer a complete program for progressive social transformation nor a comprehensively detailed description of a desired human future, they do provide visionary assertions of progressive, utopian desires, and glimpses of some of the aspects that would hopefully appear in a more humane and compassionate world. They offer something akin to what Stephen Bronner metaphorically describes as a "sketch," a partial outline for a painting of the future:

> Perhaps that is why 'the best life' is never defined by a system. It is close to a sketch.... Sketches are always incomplete. They are often little more than half-visible outlines of a seemingly indeterminate content.... Sketches, however, retain their inner logic.... The sketch serves as a set of coordinates. It shows the way in which a painting of the future can become visible.
>
> (*Of Critical Theory*, 352)

I have argued that the vision of solidarity presented in "Howl" can be seen to have prefigured the youth-led New Left and counterculture of the 1960s. Today, new forms of solidarity, including intergenerational ones, are needed. And in our recent post-9/11 years, we have been confronted with some war-and-peace questions that seem more complicated than the questions evoked during the Vietnam War, during which for most progressives with a social conscience, it was quite easy to see the lack of moral justification for U.S. military engagement. In some situations, such as the initial post-9/11 invasion of Afghanistan, the long-term disaster in the Sudan, or the 2011 bombing of Qaddafi's Libya, well-meaning progressives have taken different sides of debates that have ranged from humanitarian military intervention on human-rights grounds to non-violent diplomatic initiatives. The 2001 mass murders at New York's World Trade Center were committed by a terrorist group, Al Qaeda, holding fundamentalist values opposed to most of the freedoms for which progressives stand. Would Allen Ginsberg, a consistent pacifist in his adult life, have opposed the war in Afghanistan, partly out of concern for innocent Afghans, as did many prominent social critics like Noam Chomsky and Howard Zinn? (I myself was on that anti-war side and helped organize antiwar events with the national coalition, United

A Progressive Political Poetics

for Peace & Justice, and a local affiliate in Astoria, Queens, where my partner, Vivian Demuth, and I were living at the time.) Or would Ginsberg have supported that war as a rare, justified, and necessary war to lessen the future threat from Al Qaeda and depose the fundamentalist Taliban, as did other leading progressive social critics, like Richard Falk, who called the war in Afghanistan the first just war since World War II? I am certainly tempted to take my educated guess based on Ginsberg's history, but people often surprise us in the way they evolve from past to future, so that on principle, I do not like to pretend to have the psychic skills to speak for those who are no longer with us to speak for themselves. But I do believe that many of Ginsberg's poems and other writings are in contrast with the domestic and foreign policy that was developed by the Bush administration after the 9/11 tragedy, including the policy of pre-emptive war in Iraq, a nation which had nothing to do with 9/11; renewed plans for building a new generation of nuclear weapons; renewed discussion of a Star Wars anti-missile shield; the use of torture and long-term detention without trial; remote control killing by drones; and increased authority for widespread spying by government intelligence agencies like the NSA. Some of these policies have subsequently been reversed by the centrist Obama administration, and some—like the drone bombings and mass spying—have been continued.

Even as complex, new political issues arise, I believe that a healthy reading of Ginsberg's work could provide a beneficial foundation for thinking about a wide range of current social concerns. What Frederic Jameson writes about fantasy could, I think, be fairly applied to Allen Ginsberg's poetry: "fantasy is no longer felt to be a private and compensatory reaction against public situations, but rather a way of reading those situations in its own right, of thinking and mapping them, of intervening in them, albeit in a very different form from the abstract reflections of traditional philosophy or politics." (*On Negt,* 66) In this volume, I have tried to show that Allen Ginsberg's poetry can help us with such public visionary mappings.

* * *

Of course, Allen Ginsberg was not the only important poet of his era to offer significant contributions to our political culture. In political poetry, just as in any other literary or artistic category, there are multiple and multidirectional influences among authors, between writers and readers, and often between writers and social activist groups. In order to gauge the effects, even the indirect effects, of poetry on the overall socio-cultural climate, a critic would ultimately want to look at a wide spectrum of the era's culture and place any single individual author or artist in a larger cultural context. In the case of "Howl," for instance, the reception of that poem was affected, in the years following its publication, by the fact that other Beat Generation books, including *On The Road* and *Naked Lunch,* also drew a wide and growingly curious audience.

In post-1950s eras, the reception of Ginsberg's poetry has been aided by the growth of significant poetry movements that followed. I would like here to offer a brief discussion of some of the larger poetry movements here in the U.S. which followed "Howl," which evolved during the last three decades of Ginsberg's life, and which were similarly linked with social activist efforts and activist groups.

Both the Black Arts and women's poetry movements of the 1960s and 1970s were deeply linked with activist causes, and both added new aesthetic elements to American literary traditions. Poet, translator, and critic Eliot Weinberger inventories some of the Black Arts Movement's poetic contributions:

> besides its political agenda, [it] effectively admitted black speech into poetry (something the Harlem Renaissance poets, with the

> notable exception of Hughes, had refused to do), created a large and genuinely populist audience for poetry, had a close and exciting working relationship with jazz and some rock musicians....offered scathing commentaries on white "verse," and brought in a great deal of African and Afro-American history, mythology and religion which had previously been absent in American poetry. (93)

The poetry of the Black Arts Movement was, of course, enlivened by its relationship to the larger and growing civil rights movement. In a 1980 interview, one of the founders and most influential poets of the Black Arts Movement, Amiri Baraka, who was a longtime New Jersey poet friend, credits racial-justice organizing for inspiration: "a lot of what had moved me to make political statements were things in the real world, including poetry that I had read, but obviously the civil rights movement upsurge, the whole struggle in the South, Doctor King, SNCC, the Cuban revolution—all those things had a great deal of influence on me in the late fifties and early sixties." (*Conversations,* 173) In another piece, Baraka identifies some of the Black Arts Movement's key participants and once again situates its inspirational energies deeply within the political efforts of the day:

> The Black Arts Movement of the sixties basically wanted to reflect the rise of the militancy of the black masses as reflected by Malcolm X. Its political line at its most positive was that literature must be a weapon of revolutionary struggle, that it must serve the black revolution. And its writers, Askia Muhammad Toure, Larry Neal, Clarence Reed, Don Lee, Sonia Sanchez, Carolyn Rodgers, Welton Smith, Marvin X, &c its publications, its community black arts theaters,

its manifestos and activism were meant as real manifestations of black culture/black art as weapons of liberation.

(Revolutionary Tradition, 186)

Adrienne Rich similarly credits much of the energy which inspired her own poetry, and which gave rise to the women's poetry movement of the late 1960s and early 1970s, to the growing feminist activism taking place:

> They came as much from a spirit of the times—the late 1960s—that I absorbed through teaching and activism in an institution where the question of white Western supremacism was already being talked about, where students were occupying buildings and teachers either fled the campus or were in constant meetings and teaching 'liberation' classes; in a city where parents were demanding community control of the schools; through a certain kind of openness and searching for transformed relationships in the New Left, which soon led to thousands of women asking 'the Woman Question' in women's voices; and from reading Malcolm X, Chekhov's *Sakhalin Journals*, Barbara Deming's *Prison Notes*, Frantz Fanon, James Baldwin, and the writings of my students. I could feel around me—in the city, in the country at large—the 'spontaneity of the masses' (later I would find the words in Rosa Luxemburg), and this was powerfully akin to the experience of writing poetry. Politics as expression of the impulse to create, an expanded sense of what's 'humanly possible'—this, in the late 1960s and the early women's movement, was what we tasted.
>
> *(Found There, 24)*

A Progressive Political Poetics

Women's liberation struggles inspired a new poetics, and the poets—both nationally well-known poets and less-well-known poets in communities throughout the country—in turn contributed their work, both in writings and in readings, to feminist organizing efforts. And, as Alicia Ostriker points out, the women's poetry movement significantly reshaped the way American literature would be interpreted thereafter: "the advent of this writing was causing the past history of literature subtly, lightly, irretrievably to change." (*Dancing*, 214) Ostriker compellingly argues for viewing the new poetry by women as canonically transformative: "The women's poetry movement, it seemed to me, was on the order of romanticism or modernism, destined to produce substantial rearrangements." (*Dancing*, 214-215) Ostriker analyzes and outlines some of the formal and stylistic innovations developed by the women's poetry movement that were "designed to subvert and transform the oppressor's language," including an exoskeletal style, women's poetry utilizing black vernacular speech, and poetry describing feminist-communal rituals." (*Dancing*, 215) Ostriker also highlights some of the women's poetry movement's new thematic concerns:

> Some linked motifs announce themselves: self-definition, the body, the eruption of anger, the equal and opposite eruption of eros, the need for revisionist mythmaking. What Adrienne Rich has called "the oppressor's language" comes into perpetual question in this poetry, along with the language's rooted dualism: male vs. female, sacred vs. profane, mind vs. body, public vs. private, logos vs. eros, self vs. other, subject vs. object, art vs. life.
>
> (*Dancing*, 215)

It seems inarguable that the public concerns and activist participation of Black Arts and Women's Movement poets energized their literary contributions. And as I have mentioned earlier in this volume, key poets from both movements cite Allen Ginsberg as a key literary influence.

In his autobiography, Amiri Baraka writes: "I thought the book *Howl* was something special. It was a breakthrough for me." (1984: 150) In a 1979 interview published in *Conversations with Amiri Baraka*, he testifies to Ginsberg's impact as a teacher and stylistic precursor:

> [Ginsberg] was, actually, a good teacher. He had, and has, a really strong grasp of poetry, the history of poetry....And he was of great help to me in terms of learning about poetry in general. And, he was a great publicizer of poets, young poets and the whole Beat thing....One of its strongest moments was redefining what poetry was, redefining what art in general was. Questioning those things that had been put out like traditional values and academic values, trying to put forward a more mass-oriented kind of art, a more people-oriented kind of art. For instance, during the whole Beat period readings became more important....When the Black Poetry Movement picked up after that, readings were its principle form....[I]t moved towards American speech. It continued with William Carlos Williams' teachings and it went back to people like Whitman....Later on, of course, the Black Poetry Movement emerged, taking it a step further and talked about the Afro-American people's experience. (154)

As the Black Arts Movement both learned and diverged from the influence of Ginsberg and other Beat Generation writers, Adrienne Rich (whose citation of Ginsberg was noted earlier) affirms that the women's poetry movement was both an extension and subversion of earlier male-dominated antiestablishment poetics:

> The San Francisco Renaissance of the 1940s and 1950s....and the poetic voices of the Black and anti-war movements of the 1960s had created a strong mix of antiestablishment poetics in the United States. But the poetry of women's liberation in the 1970s was *women's* anti-establishment poetry, challenging not just conventional puritanical mores, but the hip "counterculture" and the male poetry culture itself. From muses and girlfriends of poets, from archetypes of the Feminine, women were transforming themselves into poetic authors.
> (*Found There*, 167)

From the 1980s until today, the tradition of poets committed to using their art in some way to attempt to inspire social change continues. Probably the two most influential schools of poetry in this regard, during the last three decades, have been the "Language poets" and the "spoken word" poets.[5] While each school has produced quality verse and a strong internal sense of a literary community, neither has, in my opinion, yet developed the level of external community-building skills that enabled the work of poets like Ginsberg, Rich, and Baraka to obtain considerable impact on the public consciousness and even occasionally the political policies of America.

Both of these groups, the Language and spoken word poets, have included theorists and practitioners explicitly highlighting public and political motives for their work. As noted in an earlier chapter, postmodern literary critic Jerome McGann theorizes language poetry as "textual activism," and argues in Adorno-like fashion that the non-narrative or anti-narrative form of language poetry engages in a negative dialectic of resistance in relation to the dominant political order—whereas the development of narrative, even purportedly radical narrative, serves merely to legitimate the dominant patterns of power. According to McGann, Language poets like Charles Bernstein view narrativity as "an inherently conservative feature of discourse" and therefore undermine it "at every point." (267)

McGann's argument seems to accurately reflect the theoretical positions of some of the most influential Language poets themselves, like Charles Bernstein, who I have already quoted earlier in this volume, and Ron Silliman. Silliman criticizes "referential fetish" (131), while correlating "the nature of capitalist reality" with "the imposition of narrative"—both of which are described as "imperialistic." (129) McGann, Silliman, and Bernstein all seem to make what I consider to be a philosophical mistake of conflating heuristically separate categories of language and politics: while these categories of language and politics may interact or overlap in complicated ways in different historical contexts, they are not the same. Neither corporate nor state power can be made reducible to the rules of grammar. And, since history is a totality of continuities and discontinuities, these Language poet-theorists make an error in assuming that discontinuity is always desirable and that discourses of continuity are always exploitative. The attempt to urge discontinuity—to break the narrative or the referential act—is not inexorably a progressive act. One can think here of the corporate paper shredder and slick montage-style TV commercials to see how dominant culture uses anti-narrativity for its own ends. In the 1980s, we saw the infamous Iran contra "plausible deniability" defense of John Poindexter, which is a kind of appropriation of non-referentiality. President George W. Bush famously mangled traditional rules of syntax, grammar, and logic as much as any nationally elected public official in recent memory, but his policies were certainly not progressive by any means. And contra McGann, Bernstein, and Silliman, narrative discourses can be used to help create activist solidarity as well as to help solidify Pentagon power. If narrativity and continuity were necessarily exploitative discourse, why do so many Language-poet theorists, including Bernstein and Silliman, pen reason-based defenses of their work? By doing so, the Language poets engage in what Habermas—in his critique of Derrida—calls a "performative contradiction.

Of course, a critique of Language poetry theory is not the same as criticizing the poems themselves. For instance, I have found some work by Language poets, like the historical poems of Susan Howe, quite interesting. Literary critic Eliot Weinberger cogently disputes assertions of Language poetry's avant-garde originality by dating its international modernist roots back to the early 1900s, with French surrealism's "alternate forms of temporality" and "critiques of narrative logic." (90) After dismissing claims of the movement's originality, Weinberger is almost entirely dismissive of the value of continued poetic experiments in this deconstructive vein. While Weinberger finds that other poetic movements have offered a sense of worlds opening up, he asserts that "what 'Language' as a movement has given me is the sense of worlds being closed off." (94-95)

I think Weinberger is reacting to is the theory, more than the poetry, of the Language school. In arguing that narrative and representation are inherently regressive, the Language poets narrow the possibility of creating bases for solidarity with progressive poets writing in differing styles; and, perhaps even more importantly, with readers who are not as solely and thoroughly committed to a non-narrative or anti-narrative verse. For me, this is a self-imposed limit that has prevented the political poets of the Language poetry movement from inspiring the sort of external community-building that earlier political poets like Ginsberg, Baraka, and Rich inspired. As Jennie Skerl notes in her introduction to *Reconstructing the Beats,* "the Beats sought and reached an audience for their art outside mainstream cultural institutions and thus recruited more members of their community, perpetuating a multigenerational movement."(2)

Conversely, Language poetry theory has, I believe, fallen

into a philosophical trap of ideological formalism against which literary scholar Myra Jehlen cautions: "ideological formalism may be in danger of generating its own reductionism. Far from there being any need to argue the unity of form and content, it now seems that critics are in danger of ignoring the more explicit content of a work as superficial or even misleading. The marriage of form and content has made them one, and that one is form." (Literary Criticism, 45) In denying the potential of narrative- and representational-based forms to present radical thematic explorations, the Language-poetry theorists have rejected potential allies in some of the very political projects they believe in. While their theoretical writings may have been partially responsible for motivating the reception their writings have garnered, it may be possible at this point to explain the value of their work in terms which are more open to other poetic styles and in terms that would allow for more successful community-building.

One can, for instance, explain the merit of deconstructing prevailing interpretations of reality, without denying the merit of other, more reconstructive projects. For example, Ernst Bloch's concept of "anticipatory illuminations" might usefully explain the progressive potential of Language poetry without dismissing the progressive elements of alternate schools. The ability of different poetic constellations to work together toward broadly progressive political goals—without any pressure to conform to singular or narrow aesthetic principles—would seem to offer the potential for poetry once again to play an important role in influencing public consciousness and furthering artistic solidarity in the years and decades ahead.

"Spoken word" seemed to me at one point, about a decade ago, to have a greater potential to affect public consciousness and opinion, due in part to its wide popularity with young writers and audiences throughout the country. Spoken word is a label usually applied to the performance-oriented, hip-hop-influenced poets of the 1990s, a style of poetry which continues to this day. The 1990s was a decade which saw poetry's popularity, especially in its oral (live or recorded) form, skyrocket to perhaps unprecedented levels—energized by the inclusion of poetry on MTV and Public Television, and by the surprising attraction of "poetry slams": half-serious, Olympic-style poetry-recitation contests which often filled performance venues throughout the country. Of course, it is difficult to imagine a 1990s renaissance of oral poetry, continuing even today, without Allen Ginsberg's contributions.

In a 1995 *New York Times Sunday Magazine* article, Dinitia Smith described this national resurgence of an oral poetry tradition: "These days, almost every city has its 'open mike' readings in bookstores and coffee shops. Every Friday in New York City at the Nuyorican Poets Café, poetry competitions—or 'slams'—are held before a panel of judges who give numerical scores and a crowd of rowdy onlookers who cheer and shout insults. Today, there is hip-hop poetry. There is a poet on MTV." (36-37) Smith describes the many media outlets that embraced and propelled the world of spoken-word poetry: "The resurgence of poetry is happening in little magazines, at the small presses, on CD, on the Internet, on cable TV. The very technology that is blamed for bringing about the end of literacy has made poetry a mass form. MTV videos popularize the Spoken Word." (37) Furthermore, according to Smith, poetry's revival in the 1990s was "a result of the 'democratization' of American literature," (37) further confirmation of which is evident by the fact that there is no longer any single anthology that is authoritatively considered to represent "the canon of American poetry." (37)

Today, as Smith notes, there is no longer a single, universally accepted anthology of contemporary poetry. There are anthologies devoted to women poets, black poets, gay and lesbian poets, spoken-word poets, Language poets, and poets focused on particular areas of interest ranging from the Holocaust to poets and their pets. One of the ironies noted by Smith at the time of her piece was that the rise and attempted commercialization of spoken word had helped create more robust outlets for the written word: "Never before has poetry seemed to be in such a vital, healthy state. Never before have so many poetry books been published—1,200 volumes in 1993 alone." (37)

Since those days Smith describes in the early and mid-1990s, poetry publishers have come into more difficult times, as the fall of many independent bookstores and small literary distributors has made the publishing of poetry books more difficult. On the other hand, the Internet has created more venues for publishing poetry than ever, and the popularity and ease of print-on-demand publishing has also given poets opportunities to publish their verses in print—even if it is not very easy sometimes to connect with audiences beyond a relatively small group of friends.

In her piece, Smith is careful to admit that not everybody was happy with the spoken word explosion of the 1990s: "not everybody thinks all this is poetry at all. Jonathan Galassi, a poet, editor in chief of Farrar, Straus & Giroux and the new president of the Academy of American Poets, has called this new wave of spoken poetry a kind of 'karaoke of the written word'." (37) I would strongly disagree with Galassi. All poetry styles and movements have had some poets that were more vital than others. The spoken word movement was no different. Some spoken word poets, like Paul Beatty, winner of the Nuyorican Poets Cafe's first annual Grand Slam, have effectively adapted, revised, enhanced, and subverted prior literary traditions in exciting ways in order to speak to and with a new generation. Yes, there are many poets reading in today's cafés and bars who have become skilled at theatrical presentations while upholding little in the way of substantive import—but one can find a shallow formal expertise in all poetic camps. The spoken word movement involved so many young poets around the country that it may still take several more decades to sort out the poets whose literary contributions will be considered significant, and the entire notion of "significance" will no doubt evolve as more orthodox notions of "canon" are continually debated and rethought.

My overall sense of the spoken word movement therefore is more geared to the movement's general dynamics than to the literary quality of particular poets involved. Miguel Algarin—a poet, co-founder of the Nuyorican Poets Café, and a former professor of mine at Rutgers in the late 1970s—asserted in his noteworthy introduction to *Aloud: Voices from the Nuyorican Poets Café* that: "The poet of the nineties is involved in the politics of the movement. There need be no separation between politics and poetry." (10) Emphasizing the multi-cultural composition of the café's core group, Algarin writes further about these poets: "It is clear that we are now entering a new era, where the dialogue is multi-ethnic and necessitates a larger field of verbal action to explain the cultural and political reality of North America." (9) To this day, the Nuyorican Poets Café continues to play a laudable and energetic role in fostering a multiethnic consciousness and environment in the contemporary poetry scene.

There are many ways of discussing the complex mediations that can take place between political realms and cultural spaces like the Nuyorican Poets Café, and so many other public poetry spaces around the country and around the world.[6] One helpful model is the concept of the "public sphere" developed by Jurgen Habermas. Habermas defines the public sphere as "a domain of our social life in which such a thing as public opinion can be formed." (*On Society,* 231) For Habermas, "A portion of the public sphere is constituted in every conversation in which private persons come together to form a public." (*On Society,* 231) In theory, for a democracy to function properly all citizens ought to have unfettered access to the liberal public sphere: "Citizens act as a public when they deal with matters of general interest without being subject to coercion; thus with the guarantee that they may assemble and unite freely, and express and publicize their opinions freely." (*On Society,* 231) In Habermas' conceptualization, the public sphere is the realm which mediates between civic society and the state. (*On Society,* 231) Nancy Fraser describes the Habermasian public sphere as a "theater in modern societies in which political participation is enacted through the medium of talk. It is the space in which citizens deliberate about their common affairs, hence, an institutionalized arena of discursive interaction." (1993: 2) Critics like Fraser, Houston Baker, and Oskar Negt have penned revisions of Habermas' public sphere theory to take into account multiple, alternative, and countercultural public spheres made up largely of groups that have been left out of traditional capitalist centers of public discourse. In many ways, a space like the Nuyorican Poets Cafè and other poetry centers around the country may be serving in part as countercultural public spheres exposing audiences, especially young audiences, to ideas rarely aired in mainstream media and providing opportunities for discussion and debate. Of course, many of these debates today are taking place online on a multitude of Internet forums, but there is still something valuable and worth highlighting about an actual, rather than a virtual, gathering place. It is important to remember here that it was Ginsberg and other poet friends of his era, including the famous first reading of "Howl" in San Francisco's Six Gallery, who were largely responsible for developing the idea of the modern poetry reading space. As Clinton Starr notes in an excellent essay subtitled " Individual Resistance and Collective Action," "The focal points of social life in the Beat counterculture were coffeehouses, bars, restaurants, jazz clubs, and parks in urban bohemian enclaves....These public spaces formed the sites wherein beatniks engaged in a quotidian politics of resistance." (45)

Many of the exciting young poets who read regularly in venues like the Nuyorican Poets Café and who compete in the National Poetry Slams, have for the past several decades insightfully engaged in political critique and have been quite inventive, witty, and sharp in perceiving social hypocrisies which too often confront them. And yet, in my own experiences witnessing the spoken word scene, I would also argue that many of the young spoken word poets in these arenas have also remained skeptical about the potential of organized, progressive movement activism. When Miguel Algarin wrote in the early 1990s of the support of most young spoken word artists for the "politics of the movement," he was perhaps attempting to make a prediction, perhaps even to channel more young poets' positive energies toward activist groups, something which would occasionally materialize in small doses, such as in the anti-Iraq war movement or the Occupy Wall Street movement which included an Occupy Wall Street Poetry Collective, but which never reached a consistency in my opinion that would have provided the spoken word movement with more of an influence in our national political affairs or discussions.

The generalized cynicism of young poets in recent decades toward participating in the organizing of activist groups may be partially explained by the relatively weak state of contemporary movement organizing and the lack of prominently identifiable progressive groups which young people could easily find and join. (As this book goes to press, a recently created national Black Lives Matter movement has been created that may end up having significant potential in the years ahead.)

In addition, I believe the community-building aspects of the spoken word scene were somewhat hindered by the competitive aspect of the "slams"—it could be difficult to take seriously a poet's stated desires for community building or political protest against capitalist-economic competition while that poet was actively engaged in a judged competition of his or her own against a group of other poets. Several emcees that I saw made a habit of trying to downplay the seriousness of poetry slam judging and competition, but there was always nonetheless an underlying understanding that victory in these slams could often help a young poet gain wider public recognition and exposure, like an appearance on MTV or HBO.

Because there are at least some young spoken word poets who have performed at anti-war, anti-racism, and global justice protests in recent decades, I have felt for years that this poetry constellation still has at least some fair amount of potential to one day help shift the nation's cultural landscape in a more humane direction. In order to see this kind of cultural influence grow, I believe there is the need for less competition among poets themselves (including for book publication deals), and for far more interactions between contemporary socially concerned poets (spoken word and otherwise) and progressive movement groups—more sharing stages, mixed publishing, and co-organizing events, taking the exemplary examples of poets like Allen Ginsberg, Adrienne Rich, and Amiri Baraka. There is no need to urge any sort of narrow set of aesthetic or stylistic values—in fact, from the experiences of writers and artists during the old Soviet era, we know that any such attempts to force aesthetic conformity must be vigilantly opposed. But aesthetic conformity is not necessary to build new democratically structured, civil-liberties-respecting solidarities, the kind of solidarities that seem especially important in a U.S. system in which the Republican Party has continued to move ever-rightward in recent decades and the mainstream of the Democratic Party, influenced in part by election-finance considerations, seems to have at least temporarily abandoned many of its best liberal traditions. (For reasons of political potential and hope, it is important to note that there are a fair number of progressive Democrats in the Progressive Congressional Caucus and the Congressional Black Caucus, perhaps 60 or 70, so that one possibility for creating positive change in the U.S. would be to help build those numbers so that progressives in Congress would have a much better chance of getting legislative bills through. Although I believe strongly In building grassroots progressive movements, I think that activists ought also to stay involved in the electoral arena.) Through creating new poet-activist interactions, it is possible that new audiences and participants will be created for both poetry and activism—and that new long-lasting coalitions might be built or strengthened. This again is a lesson that can be gleaned from the poetic energies and strategies of writers like Allen

A Progressive Political Poetics

Ginsberg, Adrienne Rich, and Amiri Baraka. Another is the utopian belief that, if such solidarities are envisioned, social change in more humanitarian directions is possible.

* * *

It is not often that the death of an American poet is considered front-page news by the national media. Allen Ginsberg's death on April 5, 1997, was especially tragic for its suddenness. Although he had experienced numerous health problems in his last few years, none were known to be life-threatening. Only months before, after several years of finding it difficult to walk up the steps to his fourth-floor apartment on East 12th Street in New York City—I remember taking that walk with him several times and noting sadly how he would sometimes have to stop at each floor for several minutes to catch his breath and regain his strength—Ginsberg had moved into a loft with an elevator on East 13th Street—a move that was expected to add more years to his life. It was only one week before his death that he was diagnosed with terminal liver cancer.

The articles which followed his death in the nation's major press were mostly complimentary, acknowledging the rarity of a poet who had shifted the landscape of American culture. Henry Allen of *The Washington Post,* who had met Ginsberg on several occasions, called him "A great poet" and tenderly beseeched: "Earth, receive an honored guest." Yet, apparently *The Washington Post* could not publish an article about Ginsberg which did not offer a commonly held conception of journalistic "balance." Henry Allen therefore confessed, "He could bore the hell out of me with his political hustling and poetic droning," (*Washington Post*, 4/6/97) and he used a tone of condescension to describe Ginsberg as an activist logically moving out from under an approaching police car : "He ducked out of the way—he was a poet, not a martyr." Henry Allen professed that Ginsberg "hung around with Abbie Hoffman for the jean-jacket anarchism that tried and finally failed to make politics fun," and he criticized Ginsberg's "later-life doggerel, political and otherwise." Furthermore, Henry Allen describes Ginsberg as a "lonely" and "solitary" poet, somehow failing to observe Ginsberg's striking talent for bringing people together and his amazing number of friends in the U.S. and throughout the globe.[7] It is as if *The Washington Post* is willing to praise Ginsberg for being a great poet, but only despite the political engagement that was inextricably a part of his life and his verse.

Wilborn Hampton of the *New York Times*—which placed Ginsberg's obituary on a two-page spread beginning at the bottom half of its Sunday paper's front page—thankfully acknowledged that "Howl" had earned "its author a place in America's literary pantheon." (4/6/97, p. 1) Hampton's obituary presented in some detail Ginsberg's biography, careful to include subtly insulting descriptions of his literary and political significance through such phrases as "As much through the strength of his own irrepressible personality as through his poetry," (1) and "He was in the forefront of whatever movement was in fashion." (42)

The rock and roll magazine, *Rolling Stone,* carried more fitting tributes. In the feature article, Mikal Gilmore wrote: "More than anything, however, Ginsberg was someone who summoned the bravery to speak hidden truths about unspeakable things, and many people took consolation and courage from his example." (5/29/97, p. 36) *Rolling Stone* also gave space to over a dozen writers who knew Ginsberg to present their own tributes and interpretations of his legacy. Poet Anne Waldman recalled Ginsberg reading a short poem during Bob Dylan's Rolling Thunder Revue: "And I thought more power at times in that lone naked human hungry voice than all the electrified amps in the world." (45) Fellow Beat poet Gregory Corso wrote: "I think of him as the captain of a ship who brought in a great cargo and deposited it here. He was the Beat Generation. He was a great, spirited man." (42) Former SDS activist and later a California congressman,

Tom Hayden, observed Ginsberg's progressive persistence, recalling that Ginsberg's recent poem "The Ballad of the Skeletons" was a "witty denunciation of the official and universal hypocrisy to which Allen never succumbed." (44) In Hayden's summation, Ginsberg "led an exemplary public life, blending Old Testament prophecy with Buddhist centering, creating a monumental body of creative work while still finding time to teach the next generations (like my kid Vanessa, a writing student of his)." (44) Among those citing Ginsberg's influence, Kurt Vonnegut praised him as "a saint and the only politically effective poet of my lifetime." (42) Although I do think there have been other politically effective poets in contemporary times, this is nonetheless high praise coming from Kurt Vonnegut.

One of our era's most perceptive social critics, Cornel West, notes that in the future Americans will either learn a new language of compassion or our shared experience will be bleak:

> [The] challenge will be to help Americans determine whether a genuine multiracial democracy can be created and sustained in an era of global economy and a moment of xenophobic frenzy. Let us hope and pray that the vast intelligence, imagination, humor, and courage of Americans will not fail us. Either we learn a new language of empathy and compassion, or the fire this time will consume us all.
>
> (*Race Matters*, 13)

West's prophetic remarks from 1994 seem especially cogent in our post-9/11 era, where the nation's leaders remain faced with the challenge of keeping Americans safe from external dangers, while preventing American foreign policy from becoming overly and permanently militaristic in a way that would likely make us less safe and less democratic.

Quality political poetry, like that of Ginsberg's, can serve as a lantern illuminating potential paths toward the balance of compassion and protection that the remaining years of the 21st century will require—breaking the bonds of denial, ahistoricism, selfishness, nationalism, callousness, exploitation, violence, ecological destruction, cynicism, and apathy that have found their ways into, not all, but too many of the recorded chronicles of American history. Poetry is no substitute for political movements, but it can and has enhanced public consciousness and political transformation. In the words of Adrienne Rich: "A poem can't free us from the struggle for existence, but it can uncover desires and appetites buried under the accumulating emergencies of our lives, the fabricated wants and needs we have had urged on us, have accepted as our own." (12-13) Another of our time's influential political poets, Denise Levertov, in a statement quoted partially earlier in this volume, made a convincing case for poetry's real, even if immeasurable, public effects:

> I don't think one can accurately measure the historical effectiveness of a poem; but one does know, of course, that books influence individuals; and individuals, although they are part of large economic and social processes, influence history. Every mass is after all made up of millions of individuals....Many forces combine to push now one individual, now another, into prominence at certain crucial moments. (169)

Levertov concludes: "Poetry can indirectly have an effect upon the course of events by awakening pity, terror, compassion and the conscience of leaders; and by strengthening the morale of persons working for a common cause." (174)

* * *

Of course, if one is to have a positive impact as a political poet, it helps to have written powerful verse that would inspire large numbers of readers. And in Allen Ginsberg's best works, we find strengths seldom equaled in American poetry: a dazzling and comprehensive poetic imagination, a unique mixture of humor and information, a principled and radical historical engagement, an inventive prophetic voice and singular ear, a sophisticated extension of wide-ranging poetic traditions, and energetic yearnings for healthier human possibilities.

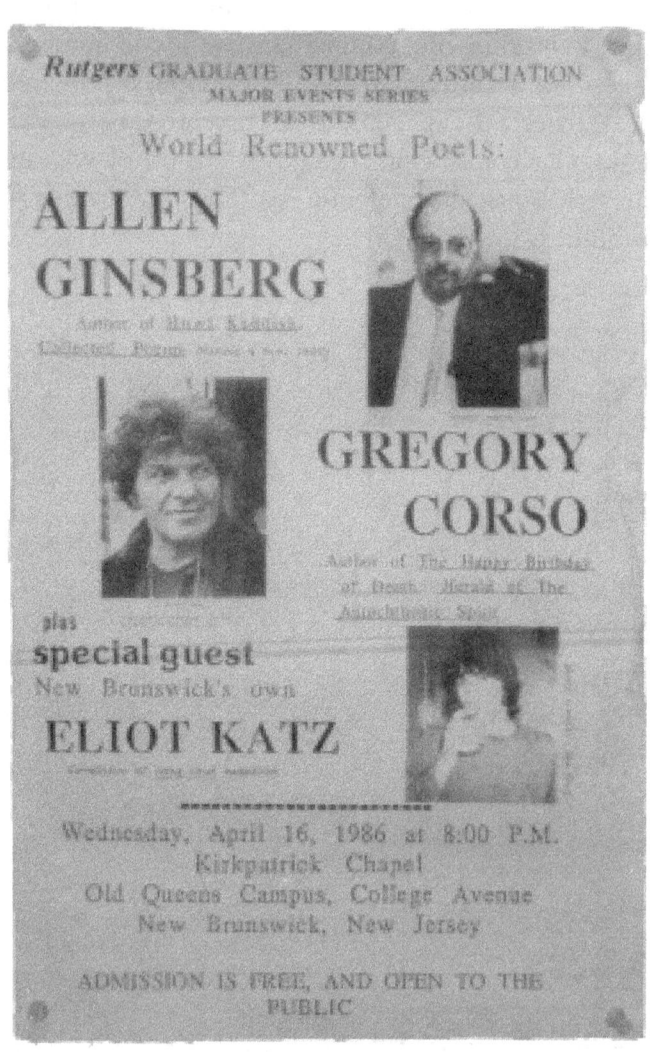

Afterword[1]

Elegy for Allen

Ah, Allen, you gave America a new shape & now you've lost yours.
What a long accomplished road it was from the bridge o'er Paterson Falls
through San Francisco's Six Gallery, Prague's May King, Pentagon exorcisms, mid-America's Iron Horse, Chicago '68, Jessore Road, Rolling Thunder, Rocky Flats, cosmopolitan greetings from NYC's East 12th street,
to heaven, the bardo, a grasshopper, a gray void, the place where all things wise and fair descend, the end of suffering—wherever you are, the most curious place in the universe.
Yesterday in your new Lower East Side loft, I held a clear plastic bag with your ashes inside, fine off-white powder, only a few small bone fragments visible, boxed inside last Buddhist shrine.
O those armor-piercing eyes will look out tender photogenic skull no more!
What happens to us? When did we begin taking this trip from energetic body-souled beings traveling the world for democratic freedoms and dream-forged poetries
to old-age liver cancer bodies lying softly on hospital cots near busy city windows, searching one last glimpse of old friends & sidewalk lovers, devoting life's last energies to finding new ways to breathe?

Why the hell did we accept this ancient bargain? When did we sign this horrific contract for a few mere decades of joy?

Well, you were always discovering a new breath, a new spiritus, a no-money-down person-to-person compassion.
Now millions across the globe are chanting "OM" in your honor,
now you've joined Shelley's children of light, become a portion of the loveliness which once your presence made more so.
But, Allen, how you hung in there! How you gave them hell over four decades!
How you bowled over Howl's critics piercing thy innocent breast!
How you practiced sanity, candor, intelligence, kindness and boundless imagination as your weapons!
How you mixed humor and information, utopian yearnings and minute particulars!
How you extended and subverted literary traditions in the most interesting ways and never tired of formal inventiveness!
How you revealed the academy's shower-curtain'd secret: poetry could be relevant to our lives!
How you taught all nations' youth to dig through the deadwood of exploitation and hypocrisy!
How you were expelled from Prague & erased off primetime radio!
How you showed that a lone human voice well-honed and courageous could challenge a multinational corporate bureaucracy!
How you became the Unacknowledged Democratic Conscience of Cold War America!

Allen, you made me laugh a New Aware Laughter for 20 years I knew your work and you.
I don't think you would have remembered where we met.

Afterword

Danny Shot & I were sitting, 57 Guilden Street, New Brunswick porch, one fall afternoon 1976, awaiting your night's event.

A cab pulled up to Kevin Hayes' apartment across street, you hurried out, unloading cardboard boxes from trunk—

your father's manuscripts stored years at Rutgers' Alexander Library.

We went to help—your friendliness astonished, I'd just read "Song of Myself" & "Howl" first time & decided try poetry—

in one of your last poems you asked for remembrances like this.

With Danny & Kevin, I drove you back to Manhattan that night—you threw out empty food wrappers & newspapers from my lemon orange Vega,

then took us on a radical automobile tour of historic East Village.

Months later, you answered letters Danny & I sent, took ten lines of my manuscript—using cross-outs, exclamation points, a few words, a reading list, taught my first poetry lesson—

the postcard Danny'd received weeks earlier still implanted in memory—each line shd have wit, humor, imagery, perception, double-meaning, a new way of seeing or Poesy in it.

In 1980, I apprenticed with you July at Naropa—in '82, you gave poems & funds to help Danny & I launch *Long Shot* magazine,

you encouraged my poems the next fifteen years—

even after that 1986 early morning Naropa panel where, hungover & nervous, I called some of your famous poetfriends crazy.

These last two weeks, thousands of poets in dozens of countries have told tales of your meetings,

Allen, you were loyal & generous to friends & future generations.

Lucky for the planet your words live on—
Lucky for those not yet born *Holy Soul Jelly Roll!* still carries your baritone voice,
your blues & holy celebrations grab onto mind's lining and refuse to let go,
your meditative consciousness sits a crosslegged raven on our shoulders while we scribble odes & design activist modes,
urging us to write what we saw & rally out of kindness.

What a beautiful new loft you bought, how sad death arrived just a few months after you moved in: high ceilings, room for your office and your stepmother, clean kitchen for macrobiotic scrapings, wall space to frame all yr futuristic portraits—
two bathrooms, bookcases galore, prophetic volumes lining shelves from polished hardwood floor how many hundreds of feet up to the soul's exit door?
Oh Allen, you've finally joined Walt's side amid the enduring dead, how can that be all bad?
now you can forget daily terrors, quit worrying which nation's elected leader the CIA will topple during new terms of presidential denial,
which activist friends will be jailed, which youthful heads will bleed from Tompkins Square Chicago L.A. Moscow Peking police nightstick, where landlords' eviction armies will helicopter next.
Like Blake's Los you gave form to Human Error, Moloch the heavy judge, Plutonium's devouring ghost lingering a quarter million years, Unchecked Capital's skeleton sweeping homeless off the street.
Now it's up to those with flesh on bones to tame our monsters, inside and out, to carry your sexy wheel of syllables into peaceful battle for the next millennium.
Death's phantom steeds have taken one more wondrous singer—one more sweetest wisest soul of all our days and lands—to who knows where?

Afterword

Praised be the cosmic mystery.
Extoled the enlightened fire which outlives the initial spark.
Exalted the echo which rebounds through the universe.
Blessed be these tears, the tears on cheeks of millions who
    touched your soft hands, your glowing aura, your living
    voice, your ink'd page, your Shambhala coffin.
Allen, you tired your heart lungs liver running years up a
    zillion flights of creaky lower Manhattan stairs—
I don't know what happens after death—just that whatever's
    been written is wrong—
wherever you are now, I hope it has an elevator.

                                          Eliot Katz 1997

NOTES

Preface

1. Introduction, *On the Poetry of Allen Ginsberg* (Ann Arbor: University of Michigan Press, 1984), edited by Lewis Hyde, p. 5.
2. For just a few of the terrific anthologies published in recent years rethinking the substance and importance of a wide range of Beat Generation writers—anthologies largely written and edited by members of the Beat Studies Association—please see: *Reconstructing the Beats,* edited by Jennie Skerl; *Girls Who Wore Black: Women Writing the Beat Generation,* edited by Ronna C. Johnson and Nancy M. Grace; and *The Transnational Beat Generation,* edited by Nancy M. Grace and Jennie Skerl.
3. See, for instance, David R. Jarroway's "Standing By His Word: The Politics of Allen Ginsberg's Vietnam 'Vortex'," in *Journal of American Culture 16 (Fall 1993), 81-88;* and Ben Lee's *"Howl and Other Poems:* Is There Old Left in These New Beats?" in *American Literature 76.2 (June 2004), 367-89.*

Notes

Chapter One

1. Quoted in the *Liverpool Daily Post*, "And the Beat goes on," by Mike Chapple, Dec. 1, 2005.
2. Quoted in *Best Minds: A Tribute to Allen Ginsberg*, edited by Bill Morgan and Bob Rosenthal (N.Y., Lospecchio Press, 1986), p. 93.
3. Quoted in James Miller, *Democracy Is in the Streets* (N.Y.: Simon and Schuster, 1987), p. 39.
4. Quoted in *The Rolling Stone Book of the Beats*, p. 280.
5. Personal telephone conversation with Bob Ross, February 2005.
6. Quoted in *Best Minds*, p. 242.
7. As this book is going into its final proofing stages, there is a fascinating sign that some of the previous narrow understandings, or misunderstandings, in much of the U.S. about democratic socialism may be at least somewhat changing, especially among younger generations. The sole member of the U.S. Senate who has for years described himself as a democratic socialist, Bernie Sanders of Vermont, is doing far better than most mainstream pundits had expected as a presidential candidate in the early polling stages of the Democratic Party primary process. In 1992, a few years after Abbie Hoffman's death, I had the pleasure of introducing Allen Ginsberg to Bernie Sanders at an event that I had helped organize with Hoffman's wife and co-organizer, Johanna Lawrenson, and the Abbie Hoffman Activist Foundation. The event was organized by the foundation at Nadine's Restaurant in New York City as a fundraiser for one of Sanders' congressional re-election campaigns. I drove Ginsberg, who had enthusiastically agreed to be one of the featured speakers, to Nadine's, and met Sanders myself before introducing the two to each other.
8. J. D. McClatchy, *New York Times Book Review*, December 24, 1995.
9. Ibid.

10. Ibid.
11. Qtd. in Constance Coiner, *Better Red: The Writing and Resistance of Tillie Olsen and Meridel Le Sueur* (N.Y.: Oxford University Press, 1995), p. 24.
12. Note that my critique of Language poetry theory is not meant to be completely dismissive of the poetry itself. I have enjoyed some of the poetry that has come out of this movement and have included several Language poets in some literary journals that I have edited. But I believe a better explanation for what the Language poets have done would need to utilize a theory (along the lines of my discussion of Ernst Bloch below) that does not reject more representational literary projects, and would focus on the Language poets as carrying on the anti-narrative traditions of writers like Gertrude Stein and Velimir Khlebnikov.
13. See for instance Georg Lukacs, "Realism in the Balance," in *Aesthetics and Politics*, edited by Theodor Adorno, et. al. (N.Y.: Verso, 1977), pp. 28-59.
14. See Levertov's "On the Edge of Darkness: What Is Political Poetry?"
15. Willam Carlos Williams, "Spring and All," in *Imaginations* (N.Y.: New Directions Paperback, 1971), p. 138.
16. Unless otherwise noted, all quotes from Ginsberg's poems are cited from the most recent, posthumously published edition of his collected poems, *Collected Poems: 1947-1997* (N.Y.: HarperCollins, 2006).
17. Quoted from the online translation (2011) by A. S. Kline of Andre Breton's "Free Union."
18. Quoted from "An Extraordinary Adventure which Befell Vladimir Mayakovky in a Summer Cottage," in *The Bedbug and Selected Poetry*, pp. 137-144.
19. Quoted from the Liner Notes to Ginsberg's *Holy Soul Jelly Roll!, Poems And Songs 1949-1993* (Los Angeles: Rhino Records, 1994), p. 15.
20. Quoted from "Easter 1916" in *Selected Poems and Four Plays of William Butler Yeats* (N.Y.: Scribner, 1996),

Notes

     pp. 83-85.
21. Quoted from Amiri Baraka and Amina Baraka's *The Music*, p. 113.
22. Quoted from Adrienne Rich's "North American Time," in *Changer L'Amérique: Anthologie de la Poésie Protestaire des USA 1980-1995*, bilingual edition Edited by Eliot Katz and Christian Haye (Pantin, France: Le Temps des CeRises, 1997), p. 262. Originally appeared in Adrienne Rich's book, *The Fact of a Doorframe* (W. W. Norton).
23. Quoted from Katz and Haye's *Changer L"Amérique, p. 224.*
24. A postcard by Ginsberg from the private collection of Danny Shot.
25. Pablo Neruda from Nathaniel Tarn's translation of "I'm Explaining a Few Things," in *Pablo Neruda: Selected Poems* (Delta Book, 1969).
26. This poem appears in Rich's book, *Time's Power*, p. 35.
27. Quoted from Katz and Haye's *Changer L"Amérique, p. 62.*
28. Quoted from Katz and Haye's *Changer L"Amérique, p. 48.* This poem originally appeared in Andy Clausen's book, *Without Doubt* (S.F.: Zeitgeist Press, 1991).
29. This song later appeared on an album by Michael Franti and Spearhead entitled *Everyone Deserves Music*.

Chapter Two

1. Reprinted in Allen Ginsberg, *Howl: Original Draft Facsimile*, p. 156.
2. See Isserman's *If I Had a Hammer*, p. 145.
3. Quoted in Breslin, *From Modern to Contemporary*, p.

255.
4. From Thomas Campion's "My Sweetest Lesbia"
5. From Andrew Marvell's "A Dialogue Between the Soul and Body"
6. From Thomas Gray's "Elegy Written in a Country Churchyard"
7. See Schumacher, *Dharma Lion*, pp. 123-24.
8. While in the early 1950s, the use of rhymed verse was considered old-fashioned, following the influence of hip-hop, young poets once again began using rhymed verse in the 1980s and 1990s, often with radical political intentions. Thus, in recent years, I have heard free verse poets described as "old school" in youth-oriented "spoken word" venues like The Nuyorican Poets Café in New York City.
9. See Ginsberg's *Deliberate Prose*.
10. Kenneth Fearing, "No Credit," in *Proletarian Literature in the United States*, p. 153.
11. Richard Wright, in *Proletarian Literature in the United States*, p. 203.
12. Mike Gold, in *Proletarian Literature in the United States*, p. 158.
13. Margaret Walker's "For My People" was originally published in *Poetry* magazine, November, 1937.
14. See Ginsberg's *Composed on the Tongue*, p. 43.
15. Note that one of the ways Ginsberg amplifies Williams' efforts to introduce American diction into poetry is by adding street slang and explicit sexual discourse mostly absent in Williams.
16. See Whitman's "Song of Myself," Section 24.
17. Reprinted in Ginsberg's *Spontaneous Mind*, p. 26.
18. Port Huron Statement of the Students for a Democratic Society 1962. Posted online courtesy office of Tom Hayden at http://coursesa.matrix.msu.edu/~hst306/documents/huron.html. All subsequent references to the text of The Port Huron Statement refer to this version.

19. Ibid.
20. See Perloff's "A Lion in Our Living Room," p. 228.
21. In addition to Trigilio's older book cited above on Blake, H. D., Ginsberg, and prophecy, see also his excellent newer volume, *Allen Ginsberg's Buddhist Poetics*, which I would highly recommend for its numerous insightful readings, even if my own theoretical approach throughout this book comes from a different (i.e. non-postmodernist) framework. But it is clear that Trigilio is himself steeped in Buddhist study and practice in a way that leads to some especially perceptive takes on many of Ginsberg's poems with themes related to Buddhist ideas and practices.
22. See William Blake's "The Book of Urizen," in *The Complete Poems*, p. 242.
23. Isserman's book is subtitled: *The Death of the Old Left and the Birth of the New Left*.
24. Qtd in Isserman, *If I Had a Hammer,* p. 99.
25. Qtd in Isserman, *If I Had a Hammer,* p. 100.
26. See Blake's *Complete Poems*, p. 340.
27. See Ginsberg's Liner Notes to *Holy Soul Jelly Roll!,* p. 15.
28. From Tom Hayden's previously cited online posting of the Port Huron Statement.
29. Although Rockland is a real hospital, it should be noted that it is not the real hospital where Ginsberg and Solomon met. That was the New York State Psychiatric Institute. In *Howl: Original Draft Facsimile* (p. 130), Ginsberg notes that he had changed the hospital in "Howl" to Rockland for "rhythmic euphony." One might also note that it carries the rock-sterility association found in T. S. Eliot's Prufrock.
30. See Thomas Frank, "Why Johnny Can't Dissent," p. 34. A version of Frank's essay also appeared in America's largest left weekly, *The Nation,* which underscores the desirability of addressing its key arguments here.
31. The influential American activist, Abbie Hoffman, used

to describe Zinn's *People's History* as the one book he recommended to all young U.S. activists.
32. See Bob Rosenthal's essay, "A Witness," in *The Poem That Changed America,* where he compellingly describes his work for many years as Ginsberg's assistant.
33. See Leo Marx's, "Pastoralism in America," pp. 36-39.

Chapter Three

1. See Ginsberg, Liner Notes to *Holy Soul Jelly Roll!*, p. 17.
2. Quoted in Kolatch's *The Jewish Mourner's Book of Why,* pp. 333-334.
3. I would like to credit Rutgers University professor Harriet Davidson as the person whom I first heard talk about Felman and Laub's book in relation to poetry of witness, including "Kaddish." Note that the coauthors of this book have penned individual chapters, which is why I refer only to Felman as the author of the quotes I am citing from this book.
4. See Emily Dickinson's poem, "#712
5. Quoted in Kolatch, p. 334.
6. See Daniel C. Matt, *The Essential Kabbalah* (S.F.: Harper, San Francisco, 1996), p. 163.
7. See Percy Bysshe Shelley's "Adonais," public domain, originally published in 1821.
8. For a persuasive critique of Ginsberg and other male Beat Generation writers on the issue of gender, see Catherine R. Stimpson, "The Beat Generation and the Trials of Homosexual Liberation," in *Salmagundi v58-59* (1982-83), pp. 373-392.
9. Among the contemporary women poets who have I read citing Ginsberg as an important influence or inspiration are: Adrienne Rich, Marge Piercy, Alicia

Notes

    Ostriker, Jayne Cortez, Anne Waldman, Sapphire, and Enid Dame.
10. Quoted in Schumacher, *Dharma Lion*, p. 311.
11. Schumacher, 311.
12. Schumacher, p. 345.
13. Schumacher, p. 346.
14. Schumacher, p. 472.
15. See New York Times, March 3, 2014.
16. *New York* magazine, November 13, 1995, p. 84.
17. Originally published in the Whole Earth Review. Now available online at www.stevesilberman.com.
18. See Miles, *Ginsberg: A Biography*, p. 433.

Chapter Four

1. See Tony Trigilio's *Allen Ginsberg's Buddhist Poetics* (2007) for more about the history and evolution of Ginsberg's Buddhist practices.
2. See Zinn's *The Twentieth Century: A People's History*, p. 174.
3. Quoted in Zinn, *Twentieth Century*, p. 203.
4. For a reprint of the original piece, see pp. 9-13 in Ginsberg's *Deliberate Prose*.
5. See, for examples, Tony Trigilio's *Allen Ginsberg's Buddhist Poetics* and David Jarroway's "Standing By His Word."
6. Quoted in Solomon, p. 134.
7. Quoted in Solomon, p. 143.

Chapter 5

1. New York Times, January 7, 1998, p. E5.
2. Willam Blake, *The Complete Poems*, pp. 338-39.
3. See Schumacher, pp. 612-619, for a detailed account of this notorious event and its widely reported aftermath.
4. Locally, as an antiwar activist living in Central New Jersey at the time, it was quite easy to discern the difference in the public response to our antiwar rallies once the war had begun. While most onlookers openly expressed support for our work before the war, that changed quickly soon after the initial invasion. Personally, I was hit in the heel by a car (thankfully driving slowly) whose driver obviously opposed our antiwar march after the war was underway.
5. From Ginsberg's "NSA Dope Calypso," p. 1000.

Chapter 6

1. Quoted in Barry Miles' *Ginsberg: A Biography*, p. 483.
2. Quoted in Stephen Eric Bronner's *Of Critical Theory and Its Theorists*, p. 350.
3. Quoted in Miles' biography, p. 123.
4. Quoted in Schumacher's biography, p. 276.
5: See Jim Cohn's excellent online essay at www.poetspath.com/Scholarship_Project/wiki.html , which makes a case for considering the work of yet another group of next-generations poets who were even more directly influenced by Allen Ginsberg and other Beat Generation

Notes

writers, a group which Cohn calls "post-Beat poets." This essay is part of Cohn's comprehensive Museum of American Poetics website.

6. In recent years, Manhattan alone has had at least six regular public poetry spaces, including the Nuyorican Poets Café, the Bowery Poetry Club, the St. Mark's Poetry Project, the 92nd St. Y, Poets House, and the Cornelia St. Café.

7. In his book, *American Scream: Allen Ginsberg's* Howl *and the Making of the Beat Generation,* Jonah Raskin similarly writes of Ginsberg's later years, "I had the feeling that he was an increasingly lonely figure." It is difficult to imagine where these writers got such an idea about a poet with so many friends at home and around the globe.

Afterword

1. This poem originally appeared in my book, *Unlocking the Exits*: *Poems by Eliot Katz* (Minneapolis: Coffee House Press, 1999), pp. 93-97.

Works Cited

Adorno, Theodor, Walter Benjamin, Ernst Bloch, Bertolt Brecht, and Georg Lukacs. *Aesthetics and Politics*. Afterward by Frederic Jameson. N.Y.: Verso, 1977.

Adorno, Theodor. "The Culture Industry Reconsidered," "Lyric Poetry and Society." In Stephen Eric Bronner and Douglass Kellner, eds. *Critical Theory and Society: A Reader* N.Y.: Routledge, 1989.

Alexander, Floyce. "Metapolitics." In Lewis Hyde, ed., *On the Poetry of Allen Ginsberg*. Ann Arbor: University of Michigan Press, 1984, pp. 254-255.

Algarin, Miguel, and Bob Holman, eds. *Aloud: Voices from the Nuyorican Poets Café*. NY: Henry Holt and Company, 1994.

Alinsky, Saul D. *Rules for Radicals: A Practical Primer for Realistic Radicals.* N.Y.: Vintage Books, 1972.

Altieri, Charles. *Enlarging the Temple: New Directions in American Poetry during the 1960s.* Lewisburg: Bucknell University Press, 1979.

------------------. *Self and Sensibility in Contemporary American Poetry*. N.Y.:Cambridge University Press, 1984.

Amichai, Yehuda. *The Selected Poetry of Yehuda Amichai.* Translated by Chana Bloch and Stephen Mitchell. Berkeley: University of California Press, 1996.

Andrews, Bruce. "Writing Social Work & Political Practice." In Bruce Andrews and Charles Bernstein, eds., *The L=A=N=G=U=A=G=E Book*. Carbondale, IL: Southern Illinois University Press, 1984. 133-36

Baker, Jr., Houston A. "Critical Memory and the Black Public

Sphere." In The Black Public Sphere Collective, ed., *The Black Public Sphere: A Public Culture Book.* Chicago: University of Chicago Press, 1995. 5-38.

Baraka, Amiri. *The Autobiography of LeRoi Jones/Amiri Baraka.* N.Y.: Freundlich Books, 1984.

------------------. *Conversations with Amiri Baraka.* Edited by Charlie Reilly. Jackson: University of Mississippi Press, 1994.

------------------. "The Revolutionary Tradition in Afro-American Literature." In Richard Jones, ed., *Poetry and Politics.* N.Y.: Quill, 1985. 175-187.

Baraka, Amiri and Amina Baraka. *The Music: Reflections on Jazz and Blues.* N.Y.: William Morrow, 1987.

Bercovitch, Sacvan. *The Rites of Assent: Transformation in the Symbolic Construction of America.* N.Y.: Routledge, 1993.

Bernstein, Charles. "The Dollar Value of Poetry." In Bruce Andrews and Charles Bernstein, eds., *The L=A=N=G=U=A=G=E Book.* Carbondale, IL: Southern Illinois University Press, 1984. 138-140.

Best, Steven and Douglas Kellner. *The Postmodern Turn.* N.Y.: The Guilford Press, 1997.

Blake, William. *The Complete Poems.* Edited by Alicia Ostriker. NY: Penguin Books,1977.

Bloch, Ernst. "Marxism and Poetry." In *The Utopian Function of Art and Literature: Selected Essays.* Translated by Jack Zipes and Frank Mecklenburg. Cambridge, MA: The MIT Press, 1989. 156-162.

Bloom, Harold, ed. *Contemporary Poets.* N.Y.: Chelsea House Publishers, 1986.

Brecht, Bertold. "Against Georg Lukacs." In Theodor Adorno, et. al., *Aesthetics and Politics.* N.Y.: Verso, 1977. 68-85.

Breslin, James E.B. *From Modern to Contemporary: American Poetry, 1945-1965.* Chicago: University of Chicago Press, 1984.

------------------. "The Origins of 'Howl' and 'Kaddish'." In

Lewis Hyde, ed., *On the Poetry of Allen Ginsberg*. Ann Arbor: University of Michigan Press, 1984. 401-433.

Bronner, Stephen Eric. "Expressionism and Marxism: Towards an Aesthetic of Emancipation." In Stephen Eric Bronner and Douglas Kellner, eds., *Passion and Rebellion: The Expressionist Heritage*. N.Y.: Universe Books, 1983.

------------------. *Moments of Decision: Political History and the Crises of Radicalism*. N.Y.: Routledge, 1992.

------------------. *Of Critical Theory and its Theorists*. Oxford: Blackwell, 1994.

------------------. *Socialism Unbound*. N.Y.: Routledge, 1990.

Brooks, Cleanth. "The Language of Paradox." In David Lodge, ed., *20th Century Literary Criticism: A Reader*. London: Longman, 1972. 292-304.

Carroll, Paul. "The Pentecostal Poems of *Kaddish*," " 'I Lift My Voice Aloud, / Make Mantra of American Language Now.... / I Here Declare the End of the War'." In Lewis Hyde, ed., *On the Poetry of Allen Ginsberg*. Ann Arbor: University of Michigan Press, 1984. 94-95, 292-313.

Chomsky, Noam. "On U.S. Gulf Policy," "Media Control." In Greg Ruggiero and Stuart Sahulka, eds., *Open Fire: The Open Magazine Pamphlet Series Anthology*. N.Y.: The New Press, 1993. 3-22, 267-290.

------------------. "Rollback." In Greg Ruggiero and Stuart Sahulka, eds. *The New American Crisis*. NY: The New Press, 1995. 11-30.

Chomsky, Noam and Edward Herman. *Manufacturing Consent*. N.Y.: Pantheon, 1988.

Clark, Tom. "One Big Movie." In *The Poetry Beat: Reviewing the Eighties*. Ann Arbor: University of Michigan Press, 1990. 30-34, 35-38.

Coiner, Contance. *Better Red: The Writing and Resistance of Tillie Olsen and Meridel Le Sueur*. N.Y.: Oxford University Press, 1995.

Works Cited

Corso, Gregory. *Mindfield: New and Selected Poems.* N.Y.: Thunders Mouth Press, 2nd ed., 1998.

Conze, Edward. *Buddhism: Its Essence and Development.* N.Y.: Harper & Row, 1975.

Damon, Maria. *Dark End of the Street: Margins in American Vanguard Poetry.* Minneapolis, MN: University of Minnesota Press, 1993.

Dawson, Michael C. "A Black Counterpublic?: Economic Earthquakes, Racial Agenda(s), and Black Politics." In The Black Public Sphere Collective, ed., *The Black Public Sphere: A Public Culture Book.* Chicago: University of Chicago Press, 1995. 199-228.

Dellinger, David. "Hope for the Nineties." In Greg Ruggiero and Stuart Sahulka, eds., *The New American Crisis.* N.Y.: The New Press, 1995. 2-10.

Dickinson, Emily. *The Complete Poems of Emily Dickinson.* Back Bay Books, 1976.

D'Emilio, John. *Making Trouble: Essays on Gay History, Politics, and the University.* N.Y.: Routledge, 1992.

Duberman, Martin. *Stonewall.* N.Y.: Dutton, 1993.

Dylan, Bob. *Chronicles: Volume One.* N.Y.: Simon & Schuster, 2004.

Eagleton, Terry. *The Ideology of the Aesthetic.* Oxford: Basil Blackwell, 1990.

----------------. *The Illusions of Postmodernism.* Oxford: Basil Blackwell, 1996.

Echols, Alice. "Nothing Distant About It: Women's Liberation and Sixties Radicalism." In David Farber, ed., *The Sixties: From Memory to History.* Chapel Hill: The University of North Carolina Press, 1994. 149-174.

Eliot, T.S. *The Sacred Wood.* London: Methuen, 1966.

----------------. *The Waste Land and Other Poems. N.Y.: Harcourt, Brace & World, 1934.*

Emerson, Gloria. *Winners and Losers: Battles, Retreats, Gains, Losses, and Ruins from the Vietnam War.* N.Y.: Penguin, 1985.

Farber, David. *Chicago '68.* Chicago: University of Chicago

Press, 1988.
Farber, David, ed. *The Sixties: From Memory to History.* University of North Carolina Press, 1994.
Felman, Shoshana and Dori Laub. *Testimony: Crises of Witnessing in Literature, Psychoanalysis, and History.* N.Y.: Routledge, 1992.
Frank, Thomas. "Why Johnny Can't Dissent." In Thomas Frank and Matt Weiland, eds., *Commodify Your Dissent: The Business of Culture in the New Gilded Age.* N.Y.: W.W. Norton & Company, 1997. 31-45.
Frankl, Viktor E. *Man's Search for Meaning.* N.Y.: Washington Square Press, 1984.
Fraser, Nancy. "Rethinking the Public Sphere: A Contribution to the Critique of Actually Existing Democracy." In Bruce Robbins, ed., *The Phantom Public Sphere.* Minneapolis: University of Minnesota Press, 1993. 1-32.
-----------------. *Unruly Practices: Power, Discourse and Gender in Contemporary Social Theory.* Minneapolis: University of Minnesota Press, 1989.
Freeman, Jo. "The Tyranny of Structurelessness." In *Berkeley Journal of Sociology*, v17, 1972-73. 151-64.
-----------------. "The women's liberation movement: Its origins, structure, activities, and ideas." In *Women: A Feminist Perspective.* Palo Alto, CA: Mayfield Publishing, 1984. 543-556.
Fromm, Erich. *Escape from Freedom.* N.Y.: Henry Holt, 1941.
Fussell, Jr., Paul. *Poetic Meter and Poetic Form.* N.Y.: Random House, 1965.
Garwood, Darrell. *Under Cover: Thirty-Five Years of CIA Deception.* N.Y.: Grove Press, 1985.
Ginsberg, Allen. *Allen Verbatim: Lectures on Poetry, Politics, Consciousness.* Edited by Gordon Ball. N.Y.: McGraw-Hill, 1974.
-----------------. *Chicago Trial Testimony.* S.F.: City Lights, 1975.

Works Cited

----------------. *Collected Poems: 1947-1997*. N.Y.: HarperCollins, 2006.

----------------. *Composed on the Tongue*. Bolinas, CA: Grey Fox Press, 1980.

----------------. *Cosmopolitan Greetings: Poems 1986-1992*. N.Y.: Harper & Row, 1994.

----------------. *Death and Fame: Last Poems 1993-1997*. N.Y.: HarperCollins, 1997.

----------------. *Deliberate Prose: Selected Essays 1952-1995*. Edited by Bill Morgan. N.Y. : Harper Perennial, 2001.

----------------. *Holy Soul Jelly Roll! Poems And Songs 1949-1993*. L.A.: Rhino Records 1994. Includes Liner Note Booklet.

----------------. "How *Kaddish* Happened." In Donald Allen and Warren Tallman, eds., *Politics of the New American Poetry*. N.Y.: Grove Press, 1973. 344-347.

----------------. *Howl: Original Draft Facsimile*. Edited by Barry Miles. Harper & Row, 1986.

----------------. Interview with Jean Nathan, In *New York*, Nov. 13 issue, 1995.

----------------. Interview with Steve Silberman, posted online, originally published in *Whole Earth Review*, 1987.

----------------. *Journals: Mid-Fifties 1954-1958*. Edited by Gordon Ball. N.Y.: HarperCollins, 1995.

----------------. *The Letters of Allen Ginsberg*. Edited by Bill Morgan. Philadelphia, P.A.: Da Capo, 2008.

----------------. "Prose Contribution to Cuban Revolution." In Donald Allen and Warren Tallman, eds., *Politics of the New American Poetry*. N.Y.: Grove Press, 1973. 334-343.

----------------. *Selected Poems: 1947-1995*. N.Y.: HarperCollins, 1996.

----------------. *Spontaneous Mind: Selected Interviews, 1958-1996*. Edited by David Carter. N.Y.: HarperCollins, 2001.

Ginsberg, Allen and Louis Ginsberg. *Family Business: Selected Letters Between a Father and Son*, edited by Michael Schumacher (N.Y.: Bloomsbury, 2001).

Grace, Nancy M., and Jennie Skerl, eds. *The Transnational Beat Generation.* N.Y. Palgrave Macmillan, 2012.

Grahn, Judy. *The Work of a Common Woman: The Collected Poetry of Judy Grahn 1964-1977.* The Crossing Press, 1978.

Grossman, Richard, ed. *The God That Failed.* N.Y.: Harper Colophon Books, 1949.

Habermas, Jurgen. *On Society and Politics: A Reader*. Edited by Steven Seidman. Boston: Beacon, 1989.

------------------. *The Philosophical Discourse of Modernity: Twelve Lectures.* Cambridge, MA: MIT Press, 1992.

Hammad, Suheir. *Zatar Diva*. N.Y.: Cypher Press, 2005.

Harrington, Michael. *The Other America: Poverty in the United States.* N.Y.: Scribner, Reprint edition, 1997, originally published 1962.

Hayden, Tom, *Rebel: A Personal History of the 1960s. L.A.: Red Hen Press, 2003.*

Hemmer, Kurt. *Encyclopedia of Beat Literature.* Facts on File, 2007.

Herring, Scott. "'Her Brothers Dead in Riverside or Russia': 'Kaddish' and the Holocaust." In *Contemporary Literature XLII, 3* (2001).

Hicks, Granville, and Michael Gold, eds. *Proletarian Literature in the United States: An Anthology.* N.Y.: International Publishers, 1935.

Hoffman, Abbie. *The Autobiography of Abbie Hoffman.* N.Y. Da Capo Press, 2000.

Holden, Jonathan. *Style and Authenticity in Postmodern Poetry.* Columbia: University of Missouri Press, 1986.

Hollander, John. "Review of *Howl and Other Poems*." In Lewis Hyde, ed., *On the Poetry of Allen Ginsberg*. Ann Arbor: University of Michigan Press, 1984. 26-28.

Works Cited

Holt, Thomas. "Afterward: Mapping the Black Public Sphere." In The Black Public Sphere Collective, ed., *The Black Public Sphere: A Public Culture Book.* Chicago: University of Chicago Press, 1995. 325-28.

Horkheimer, Max, and Theodor Adorno. *Dialectic of Enlightenment.* N.Y.: Seabury, 1972.

Horowitz, David. *Radical Son: A Generational Odyssey.* N.Y.: Touchstone Books, 1998.

Hughes, Langston. *The Collected Poems of Langston Hughes.* N.Y.: Vintage Classics, 1995.

Hyde, Lewis, ed. *On the Poetry of Allen Ginsberg.* Ann Arbor: University of Michigan Press, 1984.

Isserman, Maurice. *If I Had a Hammer: The Death of the Old Left and the Birth of the New Left.* N.Y.: Basic Books, 1987.

Isserman, Maurice and Michael Kazin, *America Divided: The Civil War of the 1960s.* N.Y.: Oxford University Press, 2000.

Jameson, Frederic. "On Negt and Kluge." In Bruce Robbins, ed., *The Phantom Public Sphere.* Minneapolis: University of Minnesota Press, 1993. 42-74.

Jarroway, David R. "Standing By His Word: The Politics of Allen Ginsberg's Vietnam 'Vortex'." In *Journal of American Culture 16 (Fall 1993), 81-88.*

Jehlen, Myra. *American Incarnation.* Cambridge: Harvard University Press, 1986.

------. "Literary Criticism at the Edge of the Millenium; or, From Here to History." In George Levine, ed., *Aesthetics & Ideology.* New Brunswick, NJ: Rutgers University Press, 1994. 40-53.

Jezer, Marty. *Abbie Hoffman: American Rebel.* New Brunswick, NJ: Rutgers University Press, 1992. .

Johnson, Joyce. *Minor Characters.* Boston: Houghton Mifflin Company, 1983.

Johnson, Ronna C. and Nancy M. Grace, eds. *Girls Who Wore Black: Women Writing the Beat Generation.* New Brunswick, N.J.: Rutgers University Press,

2002.

Kaiser, Charles. *The Gay Metropolis: 1940-1996*. Boston: Houghton Mifflin, 1997.

Katz, Eliot and Christian Haye. *Changer L'Amérique: Anthologie de la Poésie Protestaire des USA 1980-1995*, bilingual edition. Pantin, France: Le Temps des CeRises, 1997.

Kellner, Douglas. *Critical Theory, Marxism and Modernity.* Baltimore: The Johns Hopkins University Press, 1989.

Kolatch, Alfred J. *The Jewish Mourner's Book of Why*. Middle Village, N.Y.: Jonathan David Publishers, 1993.

Lee, Ben. "*Howl and Other Poems:* Is There Old Left in These New Beats?" in *American Literature 76.2 (June 2004), 367-89.*

Lentricchia, Frank. *Modernist Quartet*. N.Y.: Cambridge University Press, 1994.

Levertov, Denise. "On the Edge of Darkness: What Is Political Poetry?" In Richard Jones, ed., *Poetry and Politics*. N.Y.: Quill, 1985. 162-174.

Levine, George. "Introduction: Reclaiming the Aesthetic." In George Levine, ed., *Aesthetics & Ideology*. New Brunswick, NJ: Rutgers University Press, 1994. 1-28.

Lukacs, Georg. "Realism in the Balance." In Theodor Adorno, et. al., *Aesthetics and Politics*. N.Y.: Verso, 1977. 28-59.

Luxemburg, Rosa. *"The Russian Revolution" and "Leninism or Marxism?"* Ann Arbor: University of Michigan Press, 1961.

Lyotard, Jean-Francois. *The Postmodern Condition*. Minneapolis: University of Minnesota Press, 1984.

Marcuse, Herbert. *The Aesthetic Dimension: Toward a Critique of Marxist Aesthetics*. Boston: Beacon, 1978.

Marx, Karl. "Economic and Philosophic Manscripts of 1844," "Manifesto of the Communist Party," in Robert C.

Works Cited

Tucker, ed., *The Marx-Engels Reader*. N.Y.: Norton, 1978. 66-125, 469-500.

Marx, Leo. "Pastoralism in America." In Sacvan Bercovitch and Myra Jehlen, eds., *Ideology and Classic American Literature*. N.Y.: Cambridge University Press, 1986. 36-69.

Matt, Daniel C. *The Essential Kabbalah*. S.F.: HarperSanFrancisco, 1996.

Mayakovsky, Vladimir. *The Bedbug and Selected Poetry*. Translated by Max Hayward and George Reavey. Indiana University Press, 1975.

McClatchy, J.D. "Minds Beyond Themselves," In *New York Times Book Review,* Dec. 24, 1995. 15.

McGann, Jerome. "Contemporary Poetry, Alternate Routes." In Robert von Hallberg, ed., *Politics and Poetic Value*. Chicago: University of Chicago Press, 1987. 253-276.

McLuhan, Marshall. *Understanding Media: The Extensions of Man.* N.Y.: Mentor, 1964.

McNamara, Robert S., with Brian Van De Mark. *In Retrospect: The Tragedy and Lessons of Vietnam*. N.Y.: Vintage, 1996.

Miles, Barry. *Ginsberg: A Biography*. N.Y.: Simon and Schuster, 1989.

Miller, James. *Democracy Is in the Streets*. N.Y.: Simon and Schuster, 1987.

Mills, C. Wright. *The Power Elite*. N.Y.: Oxford University Press, 1957.

----------------. *White Collar.* N.Y.: Oxford University Press, 1951.

Milosz, Czeslaw. *The Witness of Poetry,* Cambridge: Harvard University Press, 1983.

Morgan, Bill. *I Celebrate Myself: The Somewhat Private Life of Allen Ginsberg.* N.Y.: Penguin Books, 2007.

Morgan, Bill and Bob Rosenthal, eds. *Best Minds: A Tribute to Allen Ginsberg.* N.Y.: Lospecchio Press, 1986.

Mottram, Eric. "Anarchic Power." In Lewis Hyde, ed., *On*

the *Poetry of Allen Ginsberg*. Ann Arbor: University of Michigan Press, 1984, pp. 260-267.

Nelson, Cary. "Poetry Chorus: Dialogic Politics in 1930s Poetry." In Bill Mullen and Sherry Linkon, eds., *Radical Revisions: Rereading 1930s Culture*. Urbana: University of Illinois Press, 1996. 29-59.

-----------------. *Repression and Recovery: Modern American Poetry and the Politics of Cultural Memory, 1910-1945*. Madison: University of Wisconsin Press, 1989.

Newberry, Mike. "Remarks from Reviews of 'Kaddish'." In Lewis Hyde, ed., *On the Poetry of Allen Ginsberg*. Ann Arbor: University of Michigan Press, 1984, p. 101.

Nowik, Nan. "Mixing Art and Politics: The Writings of Adrienne Rich, Marge Piercy, and Alice Walker." In *The Centennial Review*, v30(2), 1986. 208-218.

Ostriker, Alicia. "Blake, Ginsberg, Madness and the Prophet as Shaman." In Robert J. Bertholf and Annette S. Levitt, eds., *William Blake and the Moderns*. Albany, N.Y.: State University of New York, 1982.

-----------------. "Dancing at the Devil's Party: Some Notes on Politics and Poetry," in Robert von Hallberg, ed., *Politics and Poetic Value*. Chicago: University of Chicago Press, 1987. 207-224.

-----------------. " 'Howl' Revisited: The Poet as Jew," in *American Poetry Review*, Jul/Aug. 1997, Volume 26, Issue 4.

-----------------. *Stealing the Language: The Emergence of Women's Poetry in America*. Boston: Beacon Press, 1986.

-----------------. *The Volcano Sequence*. Pittsburgh: University of Pittsburgh Press, 2002.

Pach, Chester J., Jr. "And That's the Way It Was: The Vietnam War on the Network Nightly News." In *The Sixties: From Memory to History*. Edited by David Farber. University of North Carolina Press, 1994, pp. 90-

Works Cited

118.

Parra, Nicanor. *Emergency Poems*. Translated by Miller Williams. N.Y.: New Directions, 1972).

Perelman, Bob. *The Marginalization of Poetry: Language Writing and Literary History*. Princeton: Princeton University Press, 1996.

Perloff, Marjorie. "A Lion in Our Living Room: Reading Allen Ginsberg in the Eighties." In *Poetic License: Essays on Modernist and Postmodernist Lyric* (Northwestern Univ. Press, 1990).

Podhoretz, Norman. *Ex-Friends: Falling Out with Allen Ginsberg, Lionel and Diana Trilling, Lillian Hellman, Hannah Arendt, and Norman Mailer*. N.Y.: Free Press, 1999.

Port Huron Statement of the Students for a Democratic Society, 1962. Posted online courtesy of Tom Hayden at http://coursesa.matrix.msu.edu/~hst306/documents/huron.html.

Quinn, Richard. "The Poetics of Beat Improvisation." In *Reconstructing the Beats*, edited by Jennie Skerl (N.Y: Palgrave Macmillan, 2004).

Ransom, John Crowe. "Criticism, Inc." In David Lodge, ed., *20th Century Literary Criticism: A Reader*. London: Longman, 1972. 228-239.

Raskin, Jonah. *American Scream: Allen Ginsberg's* Howl *and the Making of the Beat Generation*. Berkeley, CA: University of California Press, 2004.

Reich, Wilhelm. *The Function of the Orgasm*. N.Y.: Farrar, Straus and Giroux, 1961.

----------------. *The Mass Psychology of Fascism*. N.Y.: Farrar, Straus and Giroux, 1970.

Rexroth, Kenneth. "San Francisco Letter." In Lewis Hyde, ed., *On the Poetry of Allen Ginsberg*. Ann Arbor: University of Michigan Press, 1984, 32-33.

Reznikoff, Charles. *Holocaust*. Black Sparrow Press, 1975.

Rich, Adrienne. *Time's Power: Poems 1985-1988*. N.Y.: W.W. Norton, 1989.

------------------. *An Atlas of the Difficult World: Poems 1988-1991*. N.Y.: W.W. Norton, 1991.

------------------. *What Is Found There: Notebooks on Poetry and Politics*. N.Y.: W.W. Norton, 1993.

Rosenthal, Bob. "A Witness." In *The Poem That Changed America: "Howl" Fifty Years Later.* Edited by Jason Shinder. N.Y.: Farrar, Straus, & Giroux, 2006, pp. 44-46.

Rosenthal, M.L. "Poet of the New Violence." In Lewis Hyde, ed., *On the Poetry of Allen Ginsberg*. Ann Arbor: University of Michigan Press, 1984. 29-31.

Rukeyser, Muriel. *Out of Silence: Selected Poems*. Evanston, I.L.: Triquarterly Books, 1992.

Sanders, Edward. *1968: A History in Verse*. Santa Rosa, C.A.: Black Sparrow, 1997.

Schechter, Danny. *The More You Watch the Less You Know*. N.Y.: Seven Stories Press, 1997.

Schumacher, Michael. *Dharma Lion: A Critical Biography of Allen Ginsberg*. St. Martins Press, 1992.

Schweik, Susan. "Writing War Poetry Like a Woman," in Robert von Hallberg, ed., *Politics and Poetic Value*. Chicago: University of Chicago Press, 1987, 159-183.

Shapiro, Harvey. "Exalted Lament." In Lewis Hyde, ed., *On the Poetry of Allen Ginsberg*. Ann Arbor: University of Michigan Press, 1984. 86-91.

Shively, Charles. "Allen Ginsberg: A Prophet on the Electric Networks." In Lewis Hyde, ed., *On the Poetry of Allen Ginsberg*. Ann Arbor: University of Michigan Press, 1984, pp. 210-215.

Silliman, Ron. "Disappearance of the Word, Appearance of the World." In Bruce Andrews and Charles Bernstein, eds., *The L=A=N=G=U=A=G=E Book*. Carbondale, IL: Southern Illinois University Press, 1984. 120-32.

Skerl, Jennie, ed. *Reconstructing the Beats*. N.Y. Palgrave Macmillan, 2004.

Smith, Dinitia. "The Poet Kings and the Versifying Rabble."

In *The New York Times Magazine*, Dec. 19, 1995. 36-38.

Solomon, Norman. *War Made Easy: How Presidents and Pundits Keep Spinning Us to Death.* Hoboken, N.J.: Wiley, 2005.

Stein, Gertrude. *Selections.* Edited by Joan Retallack. Berkeley and L.A. : University of California Press, 2008.

Starr, Clinton R. "'I Want to Be with My Own Kind': Individual Resistance and Collective Action in the Beat Counterculture." In *Reconstructing the Beats,* edited by Jennie Skerl. N.Y.: Palgrave Macmillan, 2004, pp. 41-54.

Stimpson, Catharine R. "The Beat Generation and the Trials of Homosexual Liberation." In *Salmagundi*, v58-59, 1982-83. 373-392.

Stone, I.F. *The Haunted Fifties: 1953-1963.* Boston: Little, Brown and Company, 1963.

Streitmatter, Rodger. *Unspeakable: The Rise of the Gay and Lesbian Press in America.* Boston: Faber and Faber, 1995.

Thompson, E.P. *Witness Against the Beast: William Blake and the Moral Law.* N.Y.: The New Press, 1993.

Trachtenberg, Alan. "The Social and Cultural Context." In *The New Pelican Guide to English Literature, Vol. 9: American Literature.* London: Penguin Books, 1988. 281-306.

Trigilio, Tony. *"Strange Prophecies Anew": Rereading Apocalypse in Blake, H.D. and Ginsberg.* Madison, N.J.: Farleigh Dickinson University Press, 2000.

----------------. *Allen Ginsberg's Buddhist Poetics.* Carbondale, I.L.: University of Southern Illinois University Press, 2007.

Tytell, John. *Naked Angels: The Lives and Literature of the Beat Generation.* N.Y.: Grove Press, 1976.

Vendler, Helen. *Part of Nature, Part of Us: Modern American Poets.* Cambridge: Harvard University Press, 1980.

------------------. "American X-Rays: Forty years of Allen Ginsberg's poetry," In *The New Yorker 4*, 1996.

----------------*Soul Says: On Recent Poetry* (Cambridge: M.A.: Harvard University Press, 1995).

von Hallberg, Robert, ed. *Politics and Poetic Value*. Chicago: University of Chicago Press, 1987.

Weinberger, Eliot. *Written Reaction: Poetics Politics Polemics*. N.Y.: Marsilio, 1996.

West, Cornel. *The American Evasion of Philosophy: A Genealogy of Pragmatism*. Madison: University of Wisconsin Press, 1989.

------------------. *Race Matters*. N.Y.: Vintage Books, 1994.

Whitman, Walt. *Leaves of Grass, and Selected Prose*. N.Y.: Holt, Rinehart and Winston, Inc., 1949.

Williams, William Carlos. *Selected Poems*, N.Y.: New Directions, 1969.

------------------. "Spring and All." In *Imaginations*. N.Y.: New Directions Paperback, 1971. 88-151.

Williams, Raymond. *Marxism and Literature*. Oxford: Oxford University Press, 1977.

------------------. *The Politics of Modernism: Against the New Conformists*. London: Verso, 1989.

Wolfson, Susan J. " 'Romantic Ideology' and the Values of Aesthetic Form." In George Levine, ed., *Aesthetics & Ideology*. New Brunswick, NJ: Rutgers University Press, 1994. 188-218.

Yeats, William Butler. *Selected Poems and Four Plays of William Butler Yeats*. N.Y.: Scribner, 1996.

Zinn, Howard. *A People's History of the United States: 1492-Present*. N.Y. HarperCollins, 2005. Originally published in 1980.

------------------. "Power, History, & Warfare." In Greg Ruggiero and Stuart Sahulka, eds., *The New American Crisis*. N.Y.: The New Press, 1995. 91-104.

------------------. *The Twentieth Century: A People's History*. N.Y.: Harper & Row, 1984

Index

Locators in *italics* are pictures

1960's rock and roll music, inspiration for the, 1
9/11, 73, 86, 120, 261

A History in Verse (Sanders), 170
"A Mad Gleam", 48
A People's History of the United States (Zinn), 93
"A Strange Funeral in Braddock", 53
"A Synopsis of Metrical/nlSystems", 20
"A Vow" (Ginsberg), 163–164
Abraham Lincoln Brigades, 126
Abu Ghraib, 13
"Adonais" (Shelley), 116, 117, 119
Adorno, Theodor, 108–109
"After Antipater" (Ginsberg), analysis of, 209
"Ah Sun-Flower" (Blake), 98, 99
"Airplane Blues" (Ginsberg), 209
Alexander, Floyce, 224
Algarin, Miguel, 275
Alinsky, Saul
   Rules for Radical, 93
   Rules for Radicals, 159
Allen, Henry, 277–278
Allen Ginsberg's Buddhist Poetics (Trigilio), 144

Allen Verbatim, 250
alliteration, use of, 56
alternative news sources, 93
Altieri, Charles, 160
America
   in the mid-1950s, 37
   social and cultural landscape of, 41
"America" (Ginsberg), 119, 121, 165
America Divided (Isserman & Kazin), 4
American culture, 85
American poetical voice, influence on, 2
American poetry, influence of, 43
American Tea Party, 86
Amter, Israel, 46
"An Extraordinary Adventure which Befell Vladimir Mayakovky in a Summer Cottage" (Mayakovsky), 125
anaphora, use of, 56
Annotated Howl (Ginsberg), 51, 54, 64, 89
anti-censorship trials, 4
anticipatory illuminations, 15, 24, 66, 100, 130, 144
anti-communist hysteria, Cold War, 103
anti-draft registration poem, 194
"Anti-Viet Nam War Peace Mobilization" (Ginsberg),

167–168
anti-war protests and Ginsberg, 173
Antler, 243
Apocalyptic and Violent school, the, 36
assonance, use of, 56
atomic bombs, 39
Australian Aborigines, 219
authority
   inhibiting, 68
   rational, 68
"Axiom 1 of International Affairs", 214

Baraka, Amiri, 266
Bateson, Gregory, 128
Baxandall, Rosalyn, 248–249
Baxandall, Roz, 2
Beat Generation, 1, 2, 46, 47, 175
   and the social revolution, 3
   subculture of, 4
Beat poets, 4
Beat Studies Association, 68, 242
bebop jazz, 55, 66–67. *see also* jazz
Bercovitch, Sacvan, 162
Bernstein, Charles, 12
Best, Steven, *The Postmodern Turn*, 12, 155
"best minds, Ginsberg's, 62–65, 67
Best Minds (Krassner), 3
"Between the World and Me", 53
"Birdbrain" (Ginsberg), 195
Black Arts Movement, 263, 266–267
black youths, police shooting and, 85
Blackmur, R. P., 36
Blake, William, 45, 52, 69, 159
   "Ah Sun-Flower", 98, 99
   "London", 180
      analysis of, 178
   "Marriage of Heaven and Hell", 88
   "Nurses Song", 168
   prophetic poems of, 58
   "The Mental Traveller", 76
Blakean prophetic tradition, 121, 160. *see also* poet, as prophet
Bloch, Ernst, 15–16, 66, 100, 144
"Book of the Dead" (Rukeyser), 91
Brecht, Bertold, 15
Breslin, James, 60, 94, 127
   views on American poetry, 43
   views on modernism, 42–43
Bronner, Stephen, 16–17, 38, 66, 230, 235, 237
Brooks, Eugene, 44
Brown v. Board of Education, 39
Buddhism, 147
Buddhism: its essence and development (Conze), 159
Buddhist, scandals, 207
Buddhists, persecution of, 134, 159
Bunting, Basil, 36
Burroughs, William, 46, 59, 60, 247
bus boycott, 41
Bush, George W., 268
   administration of, 13, 73, 86, 216
   and the Iraq War, 214–215

"Calm Panic Campaign Promise" (Ginsberg), 227
Camp Nicht-Gedeigat, 102
Campion, Thomas, 48
"Canto General" (Neruda), 91
"Capitol Air" (Ginsberg)
   analysis of, 195–199, 226–227
   and Cold war government, 198
   Holden's critique of, 196
   Rich's critique of, 196–197
Carr, Lucien, 46
Carroll, Paul, 161

Index

Cassady, Neal, 47
Cervantes Fraternal Society, the, 38
Charles, Ray, 103
Chernobyl, 183, 210
Chicago '68 (Farber), 168, 252
Chicago 8 Trial, 248, 253–254
Chicago Democratic Convention, 166
Chicago demonstrations, 168–170
Chomsky, Noam, 149, 214, 218
Chopin Cultural Center, the, 38
Chronicles: Volume One (Dylan), 2
"CIA Dope Calypso" (Ginsberg), 132, 213, 216–217
Civil Defense drill, 41
civil disobedience, acts of, 41
civil rights/movement, 38–39, 41
Clamshell Alliance, the, 177
Clarke, Cheryl, 172
Clarke, Tom, review of Ginsberg poetry, 209–210
Clausen, Andy, 154, 223
"C'Mon Pigs of Western Civilization Eat More Grease" (Ginsberg), 219
Cohn, Jim, 296-297
Cold War, 37
  U.S. foreign policy and, 213–214
  history, and "Capitol Air" (Ginsberg), 199
Collected Poems (Ginsberg), 177, 199-200
  endnotes, 184
Columbia University, 46, 47
Committee for the Negro in the Arts, the, 38
Committee for the Protection of the Bill of Rights, the, 38
Communist-front organizations, 38
Complete Poems, Blake's (Ostriker), 172

Composed on the Tongue (Ginsberg), 158, 225
consciousness, 129
  explorations of, 127–128, 132
"Contemporary Poetry, Alternate Routes" (McGann), 12
Conversations with Amiri Baraka, 266
Conze, Edward, *Buddhism: its essence and development*, 159
Corso, Gregory, 29, 47, 278
  Gasoline, 2
Cosmopolitan Greetings: Poems 1986-1992 (Ginsberg), 199, 205, 213, 225-226
Cortez, Jayne, 6, 33, 243
countercultural ideas, 86–87
Crane, Hart, 108
Criticism, Inc. (Ransom), 43
Cronkite, Walter, 135, 148
"Crossing Nation" (Ginsberg), 165–166, 167

Day, Dorothy, 41, 64
Death and Fame: Last Poems 1993-1997 (Ginsberg), 199, 219, 221, 227
"Death to Van Gogh's Ear!" (Ginsberg), 68, 76, 119-120
'Declaration of Three', 258
Deliberate Prose, 52
Dellinger, Dave, 41, 248
D'Emilio, John, *In Making Trouble: Essays on Gay History, Politics, and the University*, 254
"Democracy Now!" (Goodman), 93, 143
Democratic Party, 96
Democratic Socialists of America, 41
"Demonstration or Spectacle as Example, As Communication or How to Make a March/Spectacle" (Ginsberg), 140

315

demythologization, 73, 150
Denitch, Betty, 4
Dickinson, Emily, 30, 44, 105–106
Diem, Ngo Dinh, 134, 136
DiGia, Ralph, 41
discrimination, institutional, 85
dissent, 37–38
    government action and, 85
Dissent magazine, 41, 70, 90
Dixie Chicks, 85
"Donahue", 85
"Don't Grow Old" (Ginsberg), 176
drug poems, 129–131
    "Magic Psalm", 129, 130
    "The End", 129
drug use, and Ginsberg, 128–132
Duberman, Martin, *Stonewall*, 255
Dylan, Bob, 1–2
    Chronicles: Volume One, 2

Eagleton, Terry, 13, 84, 86
"Easter 1916" (Yeats), 166
Eastern Europe
    fall of communism in, 212–213
    Latin Americanization of, 213
Echols, Alice, 238
Economic and Philosophic Manuscripts of 1844 (Marx), 41
Einstein, Albert, 40
Eisenhower, Dwight David, 38, 136
"Elegy for Mama" (Ginsberg), 117
"Elephant in the Meditation Hall" (Ginsberg), 207
Eliot, T. S., 1, 43, 58, 80
    The Sacred Wood, 43
    "The Love Song of J. Alfred Prufrock", 75
    "The Wasteland", 75, 82
    thoughts about poetry, 43
Emerson, Gloria, 137–138
Empty Mirror, 48
Engels, Friedrich, *The Communist Manifesto*, 95
Escape from Freedom (Fromm), 41, 68
"Europe, Who Knows?" (Ginsberg), 210
existential fulfilment, search for, 61–62
existential vacuum, 61

Fahrenheit 911, 143
Fairness and Accuracy in Reporting (FAIR), 143, 223
Farber, David, 168–170, 235
    Chicago '68, 252–253
Fearing, Kenneth, 53, 54
federal watch lists, 38
Felman, Shoshana, 104, 109, 119
Final Solution, the, 118
First International, The, 89
"Footnote to Howl" (Ginsberg), 87, 99
"For My People", 53
Fourth International, 80
Frank, Thomas, 86
    analysis of Ginsberg's work, 83–84
    What's the Matter with Kansas, 83
    "Why Johnny Can't Dissent", 83
Frankl, Viktor, 60–61
Fraser, Nancy, 273
Freud, 59
"From Protest to Radicalism: An Appraisal of the Student Movement 1960" (Haber), 3
Fromm, Erich, 41, 65, 68, 70
    Escape from Freedom, 41
Frontain, Raymond-Jean, 57

"Garden State" (Ginsberg), analysis of, 191–192

Index

Gasoline (Corso), 2
Gates of Wrath, 48
gay rights movement, effect of *Howl and Other Poems* (Ginsberg) on, 97–98
Gilmore, Mikal, 278
Ginsberg, Allen, 1, 2, *29*, 72, *204*
   and 1960's rock and roll music, 1
   "A Vow", 163–164
   "After Antipater", analysis of, 209
   "Airplane Blues", 209
   "America", 119, 121, 165
   Annotated Howl, 89
   "Anti-Viet Nam War Peace Mobilization", 167–168
   anti-war protests and activistisms, 249–250
   "Birdbrain", 195
   and Blakean prophetic tradition, 121
   "Calm Panic Campaign Promise", 227
   "Capitol Air", 226–227
      analysis of, 195–199
   challenge to American policies, 175–176, 185–187
   "CIA Dope Calypso", 132
   civil disobedience and, 257
   "C'Mon Pigs of Western Civilization Eat More Grease", 219
   Collected Poems, 177, 199-200
   Collected Poems endnotes, 184
   Composed on the Tongue, 158, 225
   the conservative myth and, 174–175
   Cosmopolitan Greetings: Poems 1986-1992, 199, 205, 225, 226
   criticism of, 208
   criticism of governments, 211–212
   criticism of Moloch, 74
   "Crossing Nation", 165–166, 167
   Death and Fame, 219
   death of, 277
   "Death to Van Gogh's Ear!", 69, 76, 119-120
   "Demonstration or Spectacle as Example, As Communication or How to Make a March/Spectacle", 140
   "Don't Grow Old", 176
   drug poems of, 129
   drug use and, 127–129
   early life and works of, 45–48
   "Elegy for Mama", 117
   "Elephant in the Meditation Hall", 207
   and the environment, 256
   "Europe, Who Knows?", 210
   explorations of consciousness, 127–128
   family and, 102
   "Footnote to Howl", 87, 99
   gender, 241–247, 242–243
   "Going to the World of the Dead", 200
   government spending and, 203
   "Grant Park: August 28, 1968", 167, 168
   "Hadda Be Playing on the Jukebox", 226
   Happening Now?, 199–200
   Holy Soul Jelly Roll!, 93, 162, 184
   "Homeless Compleynt", 222
   "How Kaddish Happened", 104, 115
   Howl and Other Poems (Ginsberg), 1, 2, 3, 4, 35, 51–52
   Huckleberry Finn, 36
   "Hum Bom!", 220–221
   humor of, 93
   "Ignu", 122–123, 243

analysis of, 122–123
"Improvisation in Beijing", 205
influence of jazz on, 55–56
influences on, 44–45, 54, 55–56
influences on *Howl and Other Poems*, 54
"Jawah and Allah Battle", 187
  analysis of, 187–189
"JAWEH AND ALLAH SENT ME HERE!", 187–189
Jewish roots and, 206–207
"Junk Mail", analysis of, 189
"Kaddish" (Ginsberg), political references and, 101–102
Kaddish and Other Poems, 127
  analysis of, 133
  political references in, 119
line-lengthening techniques of, 52–55
"Magic Psalm", 129, 130
meeting with Katz, 172
and Middle East peace, 187
"Millionaires", 200
"New Democracy Wish List", 234–235
"New Stanzas or *Amazing Grace*", 221–222
"Not Dead Yet", 226
"On the Conduct of the World Seeking Beauty Against Government", 225
and "Paterson", 49–50
"Please Master", 244
"Plutonian Ode", 210
  analysis of, 176–183
"Poem in the Form of a Snake That Bites Its Tail", 226
"POEM Rocket", 121–122
  analysis of, 121–122
poetic techniques and, 19–34
poetry
  analysis of his, 227–230
  anti-Vietnam war poems, 170–171
  criticism of, 83
  discussions of, 200–202
  drug-induced inspiration, 128–129
  explorations of gender and, 124
  humor in, 93, 94, 119, 122–123, 200, 218
  influence of, 1–2, 36–37, 92–93
  legacy of, 123–124
  political references in, 94–95, 199–200, 222–223
  shock value of, 94
  social criticisms and, 124–126
political contradictions of, 224–231
as a political dissident, 247
and political poetry, 44, 183-199
political references, 80–81
and postmodernist tendencies, 144–145
psychological dynamics of "Howl", 58–59
reasons for being a poet, 205
relationship with his mother, 59–60
Selected Poems, 200
"September on Jessore Road", 186, 200
  analysis of, 183–185
Song of Myself, 36, 39
"Sunflower Sutra", 98, 98–99, 191–192
"The Ballad of the Skeletons", 222
"The End", 129
"The Lion for Real", 127
  analysis of, 127
"Thoughts Sitting Breathing II", 203
"To Aunt Rose", 126, 127
"To Jacob Rabinowitz", 244
travels of, 209–211

Index

tributes, 277–280
"Velocity of Money" (Ginsberg), 226
and the Vietnam war, 140–141, 143–144
and the war on drugs, **132**
war poetry, 170–171
White Shroud: Poems 1980-1985, 199
"Who Be Kind To", 150, 250–251
"Why I Meditate", analysis of, 201–203
"Wichita Vortex Sutra", 141–142, 142–143, 149–150, 150, 192
    analysis of, 188
"World Karma", 218–219, 226
writing styles and, 47–51
"Yiddishe Kopf", 205–206
"You Don't Know It", 211
Ginsberg, Louis, 20, 46, 128
Ginsberg, Naomi, 46, 59–60, 101–103, 108–109, 133
Glass, Philip, 162
global justice movement, 76–78
global justice rally, 77
"Going to the World of the Dead" (Ginsberg), 200
Gold, Mike, 53
Goodman, Amy
    Democracy Now!, 93, 143
"Grant Park: August 28, 1968" (Ginsberg), 167, 168
Grapes of Wrath (Steinbeck), 98
Gray, Thomas, 49
Gulf of Tonkin, 137
Gulf War, 173, 213
    role of the media in, 215
Gulf War Syndrome, 215

Haber, Al, 2, 3
    "From Protest to Radicalism: An Appraisal of the Student Movement 1960", 3
Habermas, Jurgen, 16, 73, 87
"Hadda Be Playing on the Jukebox" (Ginsberg), 226
Hampton, Wilborn, 278
Happening Now? (Ginsberg), 199–200
Harrington, Michael, 90, 230
    The Other America, 40–41
Harry, Bill, 1
Hayden, Tom, 2, 3, 63, 230, 279
    Rebel: A Personal History of the 1960s (Hayden), 3
Hayes, Kevin, 172
healthy sexuality, suppression of, 74
Hebrew socialist revolution, the, 80
Hell's Angels, 140
Herring, Scott, 105, 110
    analysis of "Kaddish", 118
Hiroshima, 39
historicization, 96, 150
Hoffman, Abbie, 2, 141, 230, 241, 248, 253
    The Autobiography of Abbie Hoffman, 2
    Soon to Be a Major Motion Picture, 2
Holden, Jonathan, 196
Holden, Stephen, 174
Hollander, John, 35
Holocaust, 118
Holy Soul Jelly Roll! (Ginsberg), 66, 93, 162
    liner note for, 184
"Homeless Compleynt" (Ginsberg), 222
homosexuality
    discrimination against, 255–256
    Ginsberg and, 112
homosexuals, discrimination against, 38
Horowitz, David, 174
House Un-American Activities

Committee (HUAC) hearings, 96
"How Kaddish Happened" (Ginsberg), 104, 115
Howe, Irving, 41, 90
Howl. *see Howl and Other Poems* (Ginsberg)
Howl and Other Poems (Ginsberg), 1, 2, 3, 4
   analysis of, 58–60
   analysis of Part 1, 62–64, 65–66
   analysis of Part II, 67, 75
   analysis of Part III, 78
   Annotated, 51
   criticisms of, 35, 83
   effect of on youths, 61
   gay rights movement and, 97–98
   historicization and, 96
   influence of, 42, 90–91
   notions of solidarity in, 84
   poetic imagination in, 100
   political references, 87
   reviews of, 35
"Howl' Revisited: The Poet as Jew", 56
Howl: The Movie, 4
Huckleberry Finn (Ginsberg), 36
Hughes, Langston, 97
   "Montage of a Dream Deferred", 91
"Hum Bom!" (Ginsberg), 220–221
Humphrey, Hubert, 96
Hussein, Saddam, 143, 214, 216, 218

I Celebrate Myself (Morgan), 258
"I saw the best minds of my generation", 58
If I Had a Hammer... (Isserman), 4, 40, 69, 90
"Ignu" (Ginsberg), 122–123, 243
   analysis of, 122–123
"Improvisation in Beijing" (Ginsberg), 205
In Making Trouble: Essays on Gay History, Politics, and the University (D'Emilio), 254
In Retrospect (McNamara), 136
"Incantation by Laughter" (Khlebnikov), 221
industrialization, and effect on life, 98–99
inhibiting authority, 68
institutional discrimination, 85
Internal Security Act, 38
international modernism, 42–43
internationalism, celebration of, 90
Internet, 93
interpersonal solidarity, 79
Iranian hostage-takers, Ginsberg's view of, 198
Iraq War, 86, 141
   casualties of, 215
   poetry against, 120
   Washington Post-ABC poll and, 215
Isserman, Maurice, 70
   America Divided, 4
   If I Had a Hammer, 4, 40, 69, 90
   progressive tendencies, discussions of, 40–41

Jameson, Frederic, 261
"Jawah and Allah Battle" (Ginsberg), 187
   analysis of, 187–189
"JAWEH AND ALLAH SENT ME HERE!" (Ginsberg), 187–189
jazz. *see also* bebop jazz
   influence of, 66–67
Jehlen, Myra, 15, 18, 157, 170, 270
Jerusalem, New, 88
Jim Crow laws, 39

Index

Johnson, Lyndon, 135, 138–139, 149
"Junk Mail" (Ginsberg), analysis of, 189–190
"Just Say Yes Calypso", analysis of, 213, 217–218

Kabbalah, 117
Kaddish and Other Poems (Ginsberg), 101, 124, 127
 analysis of, 103-119, 133
 comparison with *Howl*, 105–106
 drug poems in, 129
 and Naomi Ginsberg, 103–119
 political references in, 101, 119
Kaiser, Charles, *The Gay Metropolis: 1940-1996*, 97, 254
Katz, Eliot
 apprenticeship with Ginsberg, 20, 173, 193
 meeting with Ginsberg, 172–174, 193
Kazin, Michael, *America Divided*, 4
Kellner, Douglass, *The Postmodern Turn*, 12, 155
Kenyon Review, 36
Kerouac, Jack, 46, 47, 100, 247
 influence of, 3
 On the Road, 2, 262
 The Town and the City, 47
Kerouac Festival, 259
Khlebnikov poem, the, 220
Khomeini, Ayatollah, 217
King, Martin Luther Jr., 41
Korean War, 37
Krassner, Paul
 Best Minds, 3
 The Realist, 2

Language Poetry school, 144

Language poetry theory, 269
Language poets, 12
Leary, Timothy, 128
left-leaning governments, overthrow of, 37
Lennon, John, 1, 141
Lentricchia, Frank, 45, 80
"Lester Leaps In", 55
Levertov, Denise, 92, 280
Life Magazine, 4
literary devices
 alliteration, 56
 machine-in-the-landscape, 98
literary modernism, criticism of, 14–15
Liverpool College of Art, 1
"London" (Blake), 180
 analysis of, 178
Long Shot literary journal, 172
Lord Montgomery, 39
"Los" (Blake), 180
LSD, 128–129, 132
Lukacs, Georg, 14

machine-in-the-landscape, 98
Madam Nhu, 135
"Magic Psalm" (Ginsberg), 129, 130
Malina, Judith, 64
"Marriage of Heaven and Hell" (Blake), 88
Marvell, Andrew, 48
Marx, Karl, 41, 89
 The Communist Manifesto, 95
 Economic and Philosophic Manuscripts of 1844, 41
Marx, Leo, 98
Matt, Daniel, 117
Mayakovsky, Vladimir, "An Extraordinary Adventure which Befell Vladimir Mayakovky in a Summer Cottage", 125
McCarthy, Joe, 38, 96
McCarthyite paranoia, 38

McCartney, Paul, 222
McDonald, Dwight, 69–70, 142
McGann, Jerome, 12
McLuhan, Marshall,
   Understanding Media, 142
McNamara, Robert, 135–136, 176, 213
   In Retrospect, 136–138
Me Decade, the, 175
media, mainstream
   and 1960s radicals, 174, 195
   and the Gulf War, 215
   and war, 143, 215–216
meditation, as a poetic tool, 203
Merwin, W. S., 207
Middle East peace, and Ginsberg, 187
Middle East, traditions in, 188
Middlesex Interfaith Partners with the Homeless, 221
Miles, Barry, 47, 224, 254
militarism, forms of, 73–74
"Millionaires" (Ginsberg), 200
Mills, C. Wright, 70, 90, 142
   influence on Ginsberg, 70
   and the New Left, 70
   The Power Elite, 70
   socio-political views of, 70–72
   White Collar, 70
Milosz, Czeslaw, 101, 157
Minh, Ho Chi, 136, 138–139
Mobe, the, 168
modernism, international, 42–43
Moloch, 68, 78, 89, 96, 153, 177, 178
   and Ginsberg, 72, 73–76
   and Urizen, 69
montage, use of, 144
"Montage of a Dream Deferred" (Hughes), 91
Montgomery bus boycott, 39
Moore, Michael, 143
Morgan, Bill, *I Celebrate Myself,* 258
Morgan, Michael, 215

Mottram, Eric, 224
Mourner's Kaddish, traditional, 114
Muste, A. J., 41, 64
Myles, Eileen, 6, 243
mythification, technique of, 72–74, 96

Nagasaki, 39
Naked Angels (Tytell), 47
Naked Lunch, 262
Naone, Dana, 207
Naropa Institute, 3
Nation, Carry, 161
National Committee for a Sane Nuclear Policy (SANE), 41
Nearing, Scott, 46
Neruda, Pablo, "Canto General", 91
New Criticism in America, 43
New Critics, 43
"New Democracy Wish List" (Ginsberg), 227, 234
New Jersey Anti-Apartheid Mobilization Coalition, 173
New Jerusalem, 88
New Left, 2, 3, 41, 65, 230, 238
"New Stanzas or *Amazing Grace*" (Ginsberg), 221–222
New York Times Book Review, 86
Newberry, Mike, 110
Nhu, Madam, 135
Nixon, Richard, 140
"No Credit", 53
"Not Dead Yet" (Ginsberg), 226
Nowik, Nan, 246
"NSA Dope Calypso" (Ginsberg), 213
nuclear power, 210
nuclear power plant accident, 178, 183, 210
nuclear technology, fear of, 39
nuclear weapons, 176–178
   anti-nuclear statement, 40

Index

use of, 39–40
"Nurses Song" (Blake), 168
Nuyorican Poets Café, 173, 273, 274

Obama, Barack, administration of, 73
Occupy Wall Street movement, 141, 235
Occupy Wall Street Poetry Collective, 275
Ochs, Phil, 141
"On the Conduct of the World Seeking Beauty Against Government" (Ginsberg), 225
On the Road (Kerouac), 2, 47, 262
"Operation Ranch Hand", 148
Orlovsky, Peter, 146
Ostriker, Alicia, 56–57, 58, 93, 265
    Complete Poems, Blake's, 172

Pach, Chester, 148
pacifism, American, 41
paragraphic prose poetry, 55
Parks, Rosa, 39
participatory democracy, 3, 82, 234, 238
Partisan Review, 70
Paterson's Communist Party, 46, 58
Peace Eye Bookstore, 2
Peck, Jim, 41
Pentagon Papers, 139
People's History of the United States (Zinn), 171
Perloff, Marjorie, 56
Perse, St. John, 55
"Pierre", 54
"Please Master" (Ginsberg), 244
"Plutonian Ode" (Ginsberg), 210
    analysis of, 176–183

plutonium, 177–179, 180–181
"Poem in the Form of a Snake That Bites Its Tail" (Ginsberg), 226
"POEM Rocket" (Ginsberg), 121–122
    analysis of, 121–122
Poems for the Nation, 223
poet, as prophet, 56–57, 58, 66, 88, 99
poetic techniques
    alliteration, 56
    assonance, 56
    demythologization, 25–26
    empirical detail, 21–22
    and Ginsberg, 19–34
    historicization, 25–26
    humor, 27
    modernism, 22–24
    mythification, 24–25
    personalization, 26–27
    surrealism, 22–24
poet-prophet. see poet, as prophet
poetry
    anti-war, 170–171
    Ginsberg's, influence on, 2
    political influences in, 18–19, 91–92
    prophetic tradition in, 57
poetry movements, 262–277
poet's role, 18
police, the, and the Chicago demonstrations, 168–170
political poems, 199–200
    and Ginsberg, 183–199
    humor in, 218
    legacies of, 230–234
politics, in Eastern Europe, 212–213
Port Huron Statement, the, 2, 3, 63–64, 73, 230
    goal of, 64
postmodern theorists, and poets, 11–12
Pound, Ezra, 45, 58

solidarity and, 79–80
Proletarian Literature in the United States, 52
proletarian poets, Allen Ginsberg and, 54

Quinn, Richard, 66

racism, 39
Ransom, John Crowe, *Criticism, Inc.*, 43
rational authority, 68
Rauvolf, Joseph, 212–213
Reagan, Ronald, 214
Rebel: A Personal History of the 1960s (Hayden), 3
Reconstructing the Beats (Skerl), 269
Redstockings, 2
Reich, Wilhelm, 74, 88
  The Function of the Orgasm, 74
  influence of on Ginsberg, 74
  The Mass Psychology of Fascism, 74
  theory of character analysis, 59
Reichian psychotherapy, 59
"Rejoice in the Lamb" (Smart), 54
Revelation, biblical, 87
Rexroth, Kenneth, 35–36
Reznikoff, Charles, 157
Ribicoff, Abraham, 170
Rich, Adrienne, 19, 157, 213, 245, 280
Rinpoche, Chogym Trungpa, 207
Rockland, 76–79, 81
Rosenberg, Ethel, 38
Rosenberg, Julius, 38
Rosenthal, Bob, 98, 210, 223
Rosenthal, M. L., 35
Ross, Bob, 4
Rubin, Jerry, 141, 174, 253
Ruggerio, Greg, 233

Rukeyser, Muriel, 157
  "Book of the Dead", 91
  "The Book of the Dead", 145–147
Rules for Radicals (Alinsky), 93, 159
Russell, Bertrand, 40
Russell-Einstein Manifesto, 40
Rustin, Bayard, 41, 64

'Sad-Eyed Lady Of The Lowlands', 164
Safer, Morley, 149
Sanders, Ed, 2
  A History in Verse, 170
SANE, 41
Sartre, 41
Schachtman, Max, 40
Schechter, Danny, 143, 215
school of Donne, 36, 37
schools, segregated, 39
Schumacher, Michael, 45, 78, 128, 250
Schweik, Susan, "Writing War Poetry Like a Woman", 142
SDS, 2, 3, 41, 63, 76, 82, 173
  and U.S. Cold War ideology, 90
Seaborg, Glenn, 178–179
Selected Poems (Ginsberg), 200
September 11, 2001, 120
"September on Jessore Road", 183
  analysis of, 183–184
"September on Jessore Road" (Ginsberg), 186, 200
Shapiro, Harvey, 36
Sheehan, Neal, 134
Shelley, Percy Bysshe, 116
  "Adonais", 117, 119
Shively, Charles, criticism of Ginsberg, 242
Shot, Danny, 55, 172
Siegal, Lee, 86
Silberman, Steve, 132
Silliman, Ron, 13

Index

Sinclair, John, 259
Six Gallery, 4
Skerl, Jennie, *Reconstructing the Beats*, 269
SLID, 41
Smart, Christopher, 54
  "Rejoice in the Lamb"
Smith, Dinitia, 271, 272
Snowden, Edward, 85
social madness, 144
social realism, 14
social revolution, Beat Generation and, 3
solidarity, vision of, 260–261
Solomon, Carl, 51, 60, 76, 78–79
  freeing of, 81, 87
  and "*Howl*", 100
Solomon, Norman, *War Made Easy: How Presidents and Pundits Keep Spinning Us to Death*, 147
"Song of Myself" (Whitman), 36, 39, 56-57, 74, 97, 131, 177
Soon to Be a Major Motion Picture (Hoffman), 2
South Africa, 173
Soviet Communist Party, 95
Spanish Civil War, 126
Spender, Stephen, *The God That Failed*, 11
sphere-differentiation philosophy, 16
Spring and All (Williams), 91, 98
St. Mark's Poetry Project, 203
Steinbeck, John, *Grapes of Wrath*, 98
Stimpson, Catherine, 242, 245
Stone, I. F., 38, 149
  feelings about nuclear warfare, 39–40
Stonewall (Duberman), 255
Stonewall uprising, the, 255
Streitmatter, Rodger, *Unspeakable: The Rise of the Gay and Lesbian Press in America*, 255
Student League for Industrial Democracy (SLID), 41
Students for a Democratic Society (SDS), 2, 3, 41, 63, 76, 82, 173
"Sunflower Sutra" (Ginsberg), 98, 98–99, 191–192

Testimony: Crises of Witnessing in Literature, Psychoanalysis, and History (Felman), 104
Tet offensive, 148
The Autobiography of Abbie Hoffman (Hoffman), 2
"The Ballad of the Skeletons" (Ginsberg), 222
The Beatles, 1, 2
"The Book of the Dead" (Rukeyser), 145–147
"The Bridge" (Crane), 108
"The China Syndrome", 182
The Communist Manifesto (Marx & Engels), 95
"The End" (Ginsberg), 129
The Function of the Orgasm (Reich), 74
The Gay Metropolis: 1940-1996 (Kaiser), 97, 254
The God That Failed (Spender), 11
"The Green Automobile", 51
"The Lion for Real" (Ginsberg), 127
  analysis of, 127
"The Love Song of J. Alfred Prufrock" (Eliot), 75
The Mass Psychology of Fascism (Reich), 74
The Masses, 44
"The Mental Traveller" (Blake), 76
The Nation, 222
The New Masses, 44, 52
The New York Post, 4

The Other America (Harrington), 40–41
The PEN Freedom to Write Committee, 223
The Politics of Modernism (Williams), 42
The Postmodern Turn (Best & Kellner), 12, 155
The Power Elite (Mills), 70
The Realist (Krassner), 2
The Sacred Wood (Eliot), 43
The Town and the City (Kerouac), 47
"The Wasteland" (Eliot), 1, 75, 82
theory of character analysis, 59
Thompson, E. P., 88, 178
"Thoughts Sitting Breathing II" (Ginsberg), 203
Three Mile Island nuclear power plant accident, 183
Till, Emmett, 39
"To Aunt Rose" (Ginsberg), 126, 127
"To Jacob Rabinowitz" (Ginsberg), 244
Trachtenberg, Alan, 39
Trigilio, Tony, 68, 99
   Allen Ginsberg's Buddhist Poetics, 144
Trilling, Lionel, 35
"Trilogy" (H.D.), 142
Tytell, John, 62
   Naked Angels, 47

Understanding Media (McLuhan), 142
University of Michigan, 4
Unspeakable: The Rise of the Gay and Lesbian Press in America (Streitmatter), 255
Urizen, and Moloch, 69
U.S. Cold War ideology, 90
   and SDS, 90
U.S. Communist Party, 40, 102
   and imprisonment, 96

"Velocity of Money" (Ginsberg), 226
"Verses Written for Student Anti-Draft Registration Rally" (Ginsberg), analysis of, 193–194
Vietnam War, 133-141, 213
   anti-war protests and, 139–140
   anti-war protests and Ginsberg, 140–141, 163
   casualties of, 135, 137–138, 149
   historical background, 136
   media coverage and, 135, 147–149, 188
   reason s for U.S. failures in, 138
   statistics on, 135
Vonnegut, Kurt, 279

Waldman, Anne, 6, 243, 278, 295
Walker, Margaret, 53
"War Is Over" demonstration, 160, 252
War Made Easy: How Presidents and Pundits Keep Spinning Us to Death (Solomon), 147
war poetry and women, 142–143
War Registers League, 223
Washington Post-ABC poll and, and the Iraq War, 215
watch lists, federal, 38
weapons-of-mass-destruction, 216
Weinberger, Eliot, 269
What Is Found There (Rich), 196, 245
What's the Matter with Kansas (Frank), 83
"When Lilacs Last in the Dooryard Bloom'd" (Whitman), 117

Index

"When the Mode of the Music Changes, the Walls of the City Shake", 54
whistleblowers, 85
White Collar (Mills), 70
White Shroud: Poems 1980-1985 (Ginsberg), 199
Whitman, Walt, 39, 52, 56, 57, 154
    "Song of Myself", 56, 57, 74, 97, 131, 177
    "When Lilacs Last in the Dooryard Bloom'd", 117
"Who Be Kind To" (Ginsberg), 150, 250–251
"Why I Meditate" (Ginsberg), analysis of, 201–203
"Why Johnny Can't Dissent" (Frank), 83
"Wichita Vortex Sutra" (Ginsberg), 141, 142–143, 145, 149–150, 150, 216
    analysis of, 149–163, 188
Williams, Raymond, 42–43
    The Politics of Modernism, 42
Williams, William Carlos, 22, 44, 49, 157
    "Spring and All", 91, 98
Wilner, Hal, 163
Winners and Losers (Emerson), 137
"Witchita Vortex Sutra" (Ginsberg), 192
WMD: Weapons of Mass Deception, 143
Wojcik, Jean, 57
women poets, 266–267
    Ginsberg's influence on, 245
"World Karma" (Ginsberg), 218–219, 226
World Trade Center, 120, 214, 260
World Trade Organization, demonstrations against, 78
Worldwide Web of Poets, Activists, and Alternative News Reporters, 174
Wright, Richard, 53
"Writing War Poetry Like a Woman" (Schweik), 142

Yeats, John, 166
Yevtushenko, Yevgeny, 258
"Yiddishe Kopf" (Ginsberg), 205–206
Yippies, 2, 168
"You Don't Know It" (Ginsberg), 211
Young, Lester, 56

Zach, Natan, 187
Zinn, Howard, 39, 136, 138–139
    A People's History of the United States, 93, 171
    and the Vietnam war, 37, 138–139
Zuccotti Park, 236
Zukovsky, Louis, 36

Author Bio

Eliot Katz is the author of seven books of poetry, including *Unlocking the Exits* (1999) and *Love, War, Fire, Wind: Looking Out from North America's Skull* (2009). His first full-length poetry book, *Space and Other Poems for Love, Laughs, and Social Transformation* was published in 1990, with introductions by Allen Ginsberg and Amiri Baraka, and a front cover drawing by Leon Golub. Katz is also the author of two prose e-books, *Three Radical Poets: Tributes to Allen Ginsberg, Gregory Corso, and Adrienne Rich* (2013) and *The Moonlight of Home and Other Stories of Truth and Fiction* (2013). He was a coeditor, with Allen Ginsberg and Andy Clausen, of *Poems for the Nation* (2000), a collection of contemporary political poems that Ginsberg was compiling in the 18 months before his death in 1997. A cofounder, with Danny Shot, and former coeditor of *Long Shot* literary journal, he guest-edited *Long Shot's* final issue, a "Beat Bush issue" released in Spring 2004.

Katz's poems are included in the anthologies: *Poetry After 9/11: An Anthology of New York Poets*; *Blood to Remember: American Poets on the Holocaust, 2nd ed.*; *The World the 60s Made: Politics and Culture in Recent America*; *Aloud: Voices from the Nuyorican Poets Cafe*; *Blue Stones and Salt Hay: An Anthology of Contemporary New Jersey Poets*; *Identity Lessons: Contemporary Writing About Learning to Be American*; *Bum Rush the Page: A Def Poetry Jam*; *Confronting Capitalism: Dispatches from a Global Movement*; and *In Defense of Mumia*. His essay, "Radical Eyes: Political Poetics and 'Howl'," is included in the prose collection, *The Poem That Changed America: "Howl" Fifty Years Later.* Of his piece in that collection, *the San Francisco*

Chronicle's reviewer, Allan Jalon, wrote that Katz's essay "gives the book its intellectual core." Katz is also coeditor of a bilingual poetry anthology published in France in 1997, entitled *Changing America: Contemporary U.S. Poems of Protest, 1980-1995.*

A one-time student (Naropa Institute, 1980) and a longtime friend of Allen Ginsberg's, Ginsberg called Katz "another classic New Jersey bard." Currently living in Hoboken, New Jersey, Katz has worked for many years as an activist for a wide range of peace and social-justice causes, including a decade spent as an advocate for Central New Jersey homeless families, during which he helped create several housing and food programs that remain ongoing. A webpage featuring selections of Katz's poetry, essays, and interviews about poetry and politics can be found at www.poetspath.com/exhibits/eliotkatz.

Photo by Vivian Demuth

www.ingramcontent.com/pod-product-compliance
Lightning Source LLC
Chambersburg PA
CBHW071153300426
44113CB00009B/1188